JUNIOR COLLEGE DISTRICT
of St. Louis - St. Louis County
LIBRARY
7508 Forsyth Blvd.
St. Louis, Missouri 63105

 PRINTED IN U.S.A.

MEDIEVAL ENGLAND

MEDIEVAL ENGLAND

A NEW EDITION
REWRITTEN AND REVISED

EDITED BY

AUSTIN LANE POOLE
D.Litt., F.B.A.

VOLUME II

OXFORD
AT THE CLARENDON PRESS
1958

Oxford University Press, Amen House, London E.C.4

GLASGOW NEW YORK TORONTO MELBOURNE WELLINGTON
BOMBAY CALCUTTA MADRAS KARACHI KUALA LUMPUR
CAPE TOWN IBADAN NAIROBI ACCRA

© *Oxford University Press 1958*

PRINTED IN GREAT BRITAIN

CONTENTS

VOLUME II

LIST OF ILLUSTRATIONS

VOLUME II

PLATES

TEXT-FIGURES

VOLUME II

XII. RELIGIOUS LIFE AND ORGANIZATION

1. *The Old English Church*

THIS short survey of the development and institutions of the Church in medieval England will for reasons of practical convenience begin only with the tenth century. By that time, indeed, more than six centuries had passed since the first introduction of Christianity to Britain, and more than four since a more fully organized ecclesiastical system had come from Rome to southern England with Augustine, and the flowering of that new life had been so widespread and luxuriant, both before and after its fusion with Celtic Christianity, that the first and greatest of English church historians, Bede the Venerable, had been able to make it the theme of a work which was treated at once and is still recognized as a classic. The memory of that age of monastic sanctity and missionary zeal was never lost, and the Church of the late Old English period inherited numerous customs and characteristics from the past, but the wholesale destruction of the monuments of that age, and the still more widespread breakdown of organized religious life owing to the invasion and occupation by the Danes of almost half the inhabited area of England, together with the confusion caused elsewhere by their raids and those of the Northmen, reduced the ecclesiastical life of England to what may be called its lowest possible terms: a Church with few bishops, no great buildings, no kind of organized education, no religious houses, and no centres of administration. Though the desolation may seem even greater than it was owing to the absence of material or literary memorials, there can be no doubt as to its gravity. The Church in England was reduced to little more than the performance by an ill-educated, ill-found clergy of the essential liturgical and sacramental services in the village churches and halls of the landowners.

Yet the situation of the Church, distressful as it was, and rendered more forlorn by the lack of any effective central authority or focus of culture in the western Church as a whole, must not be reckoned in terms of modern experience. The Danes, though often destructive, were not Mongols; they were akin to the peoples they invaded and willing to receive what they had to give, and there was not in the world of that day any rival religion or system of thought hostile to Christianity. Only peace and recovery were needed, and the fact that this recovery, at least in its early stages, came entirely from within the country and was the work of kings such as Alfred, Athelstan, and Edgar, and of bishops acting in close alliance with them, helps to account for the characteristic features of the Old English Church in the tenth and early eleventh centuries.

The Old English Church, then, was so much the product of its age and country that unless these are closely regarded every kind of inaccurate or anachronistic judgement is possible. Perhaps it is well to begin by recalling some of its negative characteristics. It had no doctrinal or institutional peculiarities. Its bishops held and desired to hold the doctrine and obser⁄vance of the Catholic Church as they had been handed down by Augustine and Theodore and Wilfrid and Bede. The Church itself had none of the peculiarities which racial habits and long isolation had introduced into the Celtic Church. Nor did the network of feudal dependencies exist which made of the higher ecclesiastics of France, and still more of Germany, a class of territorial magnates preoccupied with their own affairs and with their relations to Rome or to the Empire.

Yet this freedom from feudal ties did not make of the English Church a purely religious association. It was in fact more closely interwoven with the secular framework of the country than the Church of any other land; but this intermingling took its rise neither from theory nor from an act of power, but from the circumstance that Englishmen of every degree had had to achieve national liberty and to organize their social life in close co-operation, each contributing all he had. As a result, it was almost impossible to say where the boundary between the functions of Church and State lay. The bishops were appointed by the king, usually with the advice and during a meeting of the Witenagemot, of which the existing bishops and (in later days) abbots were influential members. The king, for his part, owed his position largely to the approval of the same body, and was crowned with a ceremony that recalled both the God-given monarchy of Israel and the hallowing of a bishop. The Witan, composed of elements both lay and clerical, counselled or de-cided all the affairs of the country, both temporal and spiritual, even fulfilling many of the functions of the synod which, so frequent in the days of Theodore, had now lapsed altogether. On a lower level, the bishop in the hundred court judged cases both lay and ecclesiastical. Bishops were often used for diplo-matic missions, and had often (as had abbots) wide adminis-trative powers as the lords of immunities or districts withdrawn from the immediate control of the king and his deputies. When monasteries came into being it was at a royal meeting, probably a reinforced Witan, that the code of their observance was ap-proved; the king appointed abbots and the monks and nuns regarded themselves as bedesmen and bedeswomen of the royal family.

Yet this interpenetration of Church and State, temporal and spiritual, which is at first glance so similar to the Erastian Church of later ages, reflected no positive desire to form a national church, still less to withdraw in any way from the see of Peter. Reverence and devotion to Rome had been charac-teristic of the Church in England since the days of Augustine. Pilgrims from England to the tombs of the Apostles were so numerous that they had given their name to a district in the City; the archbishops of Canterbury went to Rome for the pallium when this became a customary discipline (the first recorded visit was in 927), and since the days of Alfred, or perhaps of Offa, England alone of the countries of Europe had sent an annual free-will personal tribute of Peter-pence. It was an axiom that agreement with Rome was the final touchstone of any doctrine or principle of action. The whole state of things, indeed, which was based on no code or explicit set of ideas, but rested on a mutual understanding and sense of obligation, had in it, we may perhaps think, something of that sense of the practical and love of a working compromise that others have noted as typical of the Anglo-Saxon genius. Nevertheless, it was something essentially temporary, and could suit only an age when neither men in England nor popes in Rome felt any need to define precise rights or to make urgent demands.

If the relations between the secular and ecclesiastical author-ity were ill defined, the internal economy of the Old English Church was equally loose and transitional. The number of bishops had always been small, little more than one-half of that designed by Gregory the Great, and the invasions had reduced their number still further and had dislocated their activities. The East Anglian see of Elmham and the Mercian see of Leicester had been engulfed, and all England north and east of Watling Street had been without bishops save for the isolated and poverty-stricken see of York and the quasi-Celtic bishop-ric of Lindisfarne. The nine old sees that remained had been increased when peace returned by the revival of Elmham and Lichfield, but the void between Humber and Thames had never been filled, thus giving a vast territory to the diocese of Lincoln when the see was transferred thither from Dorchester after the Conquest. In the west, Anglo-Saxon colonization had been followed up at a long interval by the creation of three sees roughly corresponding to the shire divisions at Wells (Somerset), Sherborne (Dorset), and Crediton (Devon); for a short time a Cornish see existed at St. Germans. The lack of any local administrative personnel as well as of any central organization, together with the circumstance that the churches from which the bishops took their titles were in no sense centres of diocesan life, while the bishops met together constantly as counsellors of the king—all this considerably weakened the link between the bishop and his diocese and the internal co-hesion of the diocese itself, and what may be called a general blurring of outline was further increased by the long-standing

amalgamation of York and Worcester, by the shifting conditions west of Wiltshire, and by the occasional holding of two
sees by a single bishop. An energetic bishop in a small diocese,
such as Wulfstan in the now independent Worcester and Giso
at Wells, could leave his mark, but evidence of such local and
personal government is scanty.

The lack of organization and the fusion of lay and clerical in
the higher spheres had their counterpart on a lower level. It is
often said, and with truth, that the rural parishes of England
were in great part delimited and village churches in existence
before the Conquest on the sites where their successors still
stand, but the modern term 'parish' has canonical and administrative implications unknown to pre-Conquest England. Save
for a few districts, such as Kent and Northumbria north of the
Wear, where the principal churches were minsters founded by
bishops or by groups of missionary priests, save also for a few
surviving semi-canonical establishments, the churches of England were proprietary churches (*eigenkirchen*): that is to say, they
had been founded by landowners and other individuals or
groups of individuals who 'owned' them. Churches were in
truth extremely numerous in Anglo-Saxon England, though
the total population of the country was probably less than one-
and-a-half millions. They were equally numerous both in
country and town: Suffolk, for example, contained over 420,
and the town of Norwich, with a population of 6,500, had
20 churches and 43 chapels. Their owners came from all
the free classes: many of the richest belonged to the king, the
principal magnates, and bishops; a large number, from the
tenth century onwards, to the monasteries; of the remainder
many belonged to small landowners and (especially in towns
and in the Danelaw) to groups of two or more freemen. It
was not uncommon for six, eight, or even twelve men to
own a church, while a fraction of a church might by inheritance
come to be shared by half a dozen heirs. The ownership of
a church conferred advantages both spiritual and material.
The owner had the right to appoint the priest, from whom
he very frequently demanded a substantial entrance fee; he

had the first claims upon his services and prayers, some of which would be regulated on appointment; he also enjoyed the relatively small tax which the priest paid for his land. The church, therefore, as a potential source of material and spiritual wealth, could be sold, bequeathed, or given away, and the patronage at the disposal of those who owned several churches was of considerable advantage to kings or ambitious magnates. If the owner was a bishop he had episcopal rights over his church even if it lay outside his diocese; if the owner was a monastery its churches shared any immunity the abbey enjoyed; and churches of these kinds usually formed the nucleus of the fairly numerous enclaves or 'peculiars' belonging to the bishop of another diocese, or exempt from any diocesan control. Nevertheless, substantial as were the advantages of ownership, the proprietors of churches in England before 1066 had not engrossed the revenues so completely as had their neighbours over the Channel. Tithes and oblations still went to the priest, though it is possible that monasteries owning churches had begun to appropriate some of their tithe.

It was a consequence of this system of private ownership that the priest had few of the canonical rights or social duties of a 'parson' of Chaucer's time. He was in a sense only a servant in things spiritual of the lord, and there are instances in Domesday of services similar to those of sergeants being demanded of priests. In most rural districts he was drawn from among the people of the village; he was poorly educated and, though the ancient discipline of celibacy had never been abandoned in principle, and had been reasserted by the monastic bishops, a domestic union recognized as marriage was common, if not universal, though the bishops were always, save for occasional scandalous individuals, celibate. Nevertheless, the lower clergy of England were in some respects in better case than their neighbours in Normandy and elsewhere before 1066. They were generally drawn from the class of freemen and ranked as ceorls; their endowment of land was twice that of the ordinary villager, thus putting them near to the small landholder, and they were not liable to the exacting and sometimes menial tasks demanded of the Norman country clergy, who were often of servile origin. In addition, they often enjoyed what may be called sub-ownership of the church, which was heritable by a clerical son, and it is noteworthy that the hereditary churches were often both the most wealthy and the most worthily filled. Moreover, in consequence both of private ownership and of loose organization, the country priest was almost entirely un- molested by the bishop. Synods and visitations were rare, if not non-existent; the bishops (save for some notable excep- tions) rarely perambulated their dioceses, and almost the only regular contact was the annual visit to the cathedral for holy oils, which no doubt was itself sometimes neglected. All this made up a state of things which could only be regarded as tolerable in an epoch and region where all were in tacit agree- ment, and where the claims of mature institutions, of definite codes, and of professionally educated men were non-existent.

This formless, unlearned, and largely rudimentary church received a great accession of spiritual and intellectual strength from the monasteries which were established in such numbers in the second half of the tenth century. Besides giving the in- dividual scope for a more intense and ordered religious life, the monasteries were from the start integrated into the life of the nation. They gave education to some, at least, of the children who afterwards passed to clerical or lay life; they wrote and translated works for the secular clergy and the laity; they per- formed the liturgy at some of the more important cathedral churches, and above all they gave a steady succession of their ablest inmates to rule the church as bishops. Though exact figures are unobtainable, it is known that every diocese in the century before the Conquest was filled at least once by a monk, and in some, such as Canterbury and Winchester, the suc- cession was all but unbroken.

If the new Danish invasions and the dynastic changes of the early eleventh century broke such of the harmony of aim— the *concordia ordinum*—as remained from the days of Dunstan, the Old English Church under the last king of English line began to feel the stirring of the new forces of the great religious revival that was awakening Italy and France. New types of bishop appeared: a Norman monk or two, half a dozen royal clerks from Flanders or Lorraine; the canonical movement began to have its effect, both in Harold's foundation of Waltham and in the re-establishment by archbishops of York of communal collegiate bodies at Ripon, Southwell, and Beverley. More significant still, English bishops attended the synods and councils which the reformed papacy was holding, and papal legates visited England.

2. The Anglo-Norman Church

(a) Lanfranc's reforms

Nevertheless, the general picture of the English Church remained unaltered, and it was that of a *Landeskirche*, the Church of a region, penetrating and penetrated by the national and secular life at every level, with little organization and no sense of corporate action. How far it was positively debased or degenerate has long been debated; the most probable judgement would seem to be that, granted the framework of a particular age and region, it was not intolerably corrupt and decadent, though far-reaching institutional reform was certainly needed before it could take its place in any articulated and developed ecclesiastical society. Had there been no political revolution it is probable that new ideas and methods would have gradually filtered in from the Gregorian reform. As it was, the English Church was certainly reformed to some purpose, but not directly from Rome.

The Norman Conquest marks the beginning of a new epoch in English church life, as it does in every department of English life save the cultivation of the land. It is indeed the only moment between the coming of Augustine and the fall of Wolsey when something like a revolution occurred. The effect of the Conquest was threefold: the transference of direction and control from Englishmen to Normans; the reorganizing by William I and Lanfranc of the whole fabric of the Church; and the infiltration of new ideas and movements from the Continent now that the Channel was no longer a moat. The first is in a sense accidental; the last was a long-term result which continued for more than a century; the direct reorganization must be considered first.

The large tract of north-western France invaded and settled by the Northmen in the early part of the tenth century had for some time remained pagan, but towards the end of that century it had developed a religious life of remarkable fecundity, radiating chiefly from the newly founded monasteries but affecting all ranks, particularly that of the feudal baronage, in a virile but in so many ways lawless and uncivilized society. Duke William the Bastard had early appeared as a patron and protector of the monasteries, and as conqueror of England he set the reform and wellbeing of the island Church in the forefront of his programme, choosing for this purpose as archbishop of Canterbury the celebrated Lombard lawyer and theologian Lanfranc, then abbot of his new foundation at Caen. Both William, who had grown to power in his remote self-contained duchy, and Lanfranc, now a man of sixty years, who had known only the Italy of the days before the reform, were in a sense twenty or thirty years behind the swiftly moving times, in which a rejuvenated papacy was rapidly assuming effective leadership and exploiting all its latent powers of action and supervision and coercion. William, like the emperors Otto the Great and Henry II, considered it his task, and his alone, to control and reform the Church within his dominions; Lanfranc, for his part, with the compilers of the earlier, pre-Gregorian canonical collections, saw in the regional metropolitan the natural centre of authority and activity for the English Church; the unorganized Anglo-Saxon Church, in which bishops and abbots depended willingly upon the king, offered no kind of opposition either in theory or in practice. Both William and Lanfranc looked to Rome for approval and help, especially in the first years of change, and both were in close relationship with Alexander II; it need not be said that both regarded the pope as the supreme fount of doctrine and authority. When, however, the papacy under Gregory VII made increasing use of legates *a latere* and of legatine councils, while at the same time the issue of lay control of elections and benefices was being brought to a crisis, both king and primate relaxed their contact with Rome and discouraged papal advances. They were aided in their policy by the existence of an anti-pope, while Gregory, with his hands full and recognizing the essential zeal of William and Lanfranc, made no attempt to precipitate a quarrel. As a result of all these circumstances, added to the existing insularity of the Church in England, the Conqueror was able to preserve his conquest as an administrative unit and enjoy, in close association with Lanfranc, complete freedom in its reorganization.

Before Lanfranc had taken the reins, however, the king had effected a change which, though it provoked very little contemporary comment, and had probably no motive but the immediately practical, was in fact decisive in the history of the medieval English Church and has had repercussions down to the present day. He gathered up all the existing bishoprics and abbeys into the tightly woven net of the newly established feudalism, and, by imposing on all the bishops and most of the abbots the obligation of knight service and feudal incidents, gave the Church a secular status and linked it firmly to the Crown in an economic and legal dependence which was none the less real for being in origin based on no high theory of state. It would indeed have been well-nigh impossible for the loosely knit and politically involved Old English Church to have attained under any circumstances to the position of a 'free Church' in a feudal world. The action of William I was none the less a decisive moment which settled the character of the relations of Church to Crown for centuries.

While the hedge between the Conqueror and the pope had not yet grown, and before the implications of feudalism had been felt, the king and Lanfranc, aided by papal support and papal legates, ordered and regularized the hierarchy. Four sees were moved, as the canons directed, from decaying villages to towns which had a future; the bishops of Dorchester, Ramsbury, Elmham, and Selsey took the new titles of Lincoln,

Salisbury, Thetford (later Norwich), and Chichester; a little later two others made a somewhat different move, which did not extinguish the ancient cathedral but added Bath and Coventry to the titles of Wells and Lichfield. When all personal irregularities had been adjusted the number of diocesan bishops was fifteen, and the dioceses thus established remained unchanged till 1540 save for the creation under Henry I of the two small sees of Ely and Carlisle, the latter in territory never effectively controlled by William I. With similar papal approval and questionable documentary support Lanfranc succeeded in winning, if the expression may be allowed, the first round in the long contest between Canterbury and York, and obtained from his opponent the canonical oath of obedience. This was only part of a very ambitious programme, closely linked with the designs of William I in the secular sphere, which aimed at making the British Isles into a single ecclesiastical area, a kind of patriarchate of Canterbury. Wales was easily and permanently included; York was encouraged to claim metropolitan rights over southern Scotland, and English-educated monks were consecrated in England for more than one Irish see, while from one of them, the archbishop of Dublin, Lanfranc had no difficulty in obtaining an oath of obedience. This grandiose scheme of Lanfranc's died with him; besides its intrinsic impracticability, it was outmoded by papal policy and by the new canon law, which did not recognize metropolitans with vast provinces; but while the primate lived his energy and prestige made him the arbiter wherever Norman arms or English influence made themselves felt.

Lanfranc's pontificate was distinguished by a series of important national councils held (with some intervals) annually. In these he made a number of important reforms, including a decree in which he reaffirmed the traditional obligation of celibacy upon all ordinands. Priests already married were not to be disturbed, but future transgressors were to forfeit their benefice or their married status. It was a compromise: but, if effective, this legislation would have produced a celibate clergy in little more than a generation. As it was, the result was not universally apparent. Clerical marriage, at least in some districts, continued to be regarded as respectable, or at least as tolerable, but the application of canon law in the early twelfth century gradually reduced both the numbers and the prestige of priests who remained in a state of what was now officially re⁄garded as concubinage.

The Conqueror's original policy in England was to take over existing rights and institutions with as little change as possible, and to secure the support of all in positions of im⁄portance. The bishops and abbots therefore continued to at⁄tend his court and council as they had attended the Witan, and the feudal bond which made the vassal a councillor of his lord ensured the continuance of this duty. The Great Council, in⁄deed, tended to become an assembly of greater feudal magnates, summons to which had its basis in the tenurial bond, and though later kings succeeded in extending the summons to ecclesiastics outside the feudal circle in order to broaden their resources of taxation, the tenurial obligation was alone ad⁄mitted by the courts of law, and became the legal criterion for a summons to Parliament. In this respect, therefore, as in so much else, the action of the Conqueror was ultimately responsible for the inclusion of the bishops and abbots of the original mon⁄asteries in the parliamentary body, thus perpetuating the inter⁄penetration of Church and State that had begun in the Old English Church, and was to have its influence upon, and to endure long after, the religious changes of the sixteenth century.

Lanfranc was a lawyer by training, and there is evidence that as archbishop he devoted much time to the editing and dif⁄fusion of the canons of the Church; but here again he was a pre⁄Gregorian, emphasizing the powers of bishop and metro⁄politan, but omitting the strongly papal canons of the pseudo⁄Isidore, and ignoring the recent papal pronouncements on the unlawfulness of all lay control of parsons and benefices. In fact, the Conqueror, like the Confessor, appointed bishops and abbots, and on occasion removed the latter, but it is certain that Lanfranc's advice was regularly taken, and it was Lanfranc who deposed those guilty of canonical offences; no difference of opinion ever arose between the two, and the quarrel of papacy and empire had as yet no echo in England. One great innovation, however, of permanent significance, was made by the king, almost certainly at the demand of his primate, and perhaps as an enforcement of a conciliar decree of 1076. In the last century, at least, of the Old English Church the bishops, sitting with lay magnates in the hundred court, had given judgement on canonical as well as on secular causes. In 1080 or thereabouts, by a general writ to his sheriffs, the king estab-lished separate episcopal courts in each diocese with full powers, and guaranteed the support of the secular arm in bringing those accused to justice. The aim of this decision was to leave the decision in spiritual cases to those holding spiritual authority and acquainted with the canon law; it was not directed towards the protection of clerical offenders as such; it was an elementary and necessary unravelling of a tangled skein; but it was to have weighty consequences.

Along with this major reform went a number of smaller ad-ministrative changes, all tending to bring England into line with continental practice, which was in most cases the ancient traditional discipline of the Church. Foremost among these was the establishment of a disciplined body of clergy at the cathedral church of each diocese. Save at the existing monastic cathedrals of Winchester, Worcester, and Canterbury there was little that could be called organization of worship or administration. Gradually the Norman bishops introduced a system of prebends and officials such as already functioned at Rouen, Bayeux, and elsewhere. The cathedral chapter so formed, with duties of performing the liturgy and overseeing the revenues attached to the cathedral, gradually acquired a standard form with a rota of attendance under the 'quadri-lateral' of officials—dean, precentor, chancellor, and treasurer— and a norm of liturgical observance, taking its name from the cathedral where Osmund, one of the Conqueror's bishops, had been an influential reformer, was gradually adopted all over England and became the Sarum rite. A body thus came into being which soon found itself invested with the right of electing the bishop and administering the see during a vacancy; it gradually developed that traditional jealousy of episcopal interference which gave birth to some of the most bitterly contested litigation of the middle ages and ended in the paradoxical situation which made of the cathedral close a territory exempt from the bishop's jurisdiction and of the chapter a body unamenable to episcopal visitation, leaving the bishop without control of the fabric of his cathedral and deprived of his palace in the city as a place of permanent residence. As has been noted, however, a very important group of cathedrals was already staffed by monks. Lanfranc, though a monk himself, seems at first to have regarded this as one more undesirable insular custom, unfitting for monks and hampering the bishop. He was, nevertheless, a man of his age sufficiently to regard the monastic order and its ideal as the panacea for all the ills of the time, and not only accepted the existing state of things but integrated it firmly at Canterbury and countenanced its extension elsewhere. Before the end of the century Durham, Norwich, and Rochester were flourishing cathedral monasteries (followed a little later by Ely), while at Bath and Coventry, where bishops had attempted to invade monastic territory, a monastic chapter acquired similar rights.

(b) The cathedral and the parish

In addition to the cathedral officials, the administrative machinery of the diocese gradually took shape. Whatever may have been the case in earlier ages, it would seem that in 1066 an archdeacon existed, if at all, only in the diocese of Canterbury. With the introduction of ecclesiastical courts the office became essential, and in a short time (before the end of the eleventh century at latest) one or more, as circumstances demanded, are found in every diocese. Rural deans followed in the first half of the twelfth century, and towards its end the bishop's Official, who held his courts. With the organization thus growing and the path indicated by the archbishop, the diocesan synod was introduced, probably in the early decades of the twelfth century.

But though the Conquest brought reform and regularity in

so many ways, it hardened rather than loosened the private
ownership of churches, which was more comprehensive in
Normandy than in pre-Conquest England, and had been
given an institutional and half-legal status by being taken up
and knit into the feudal system. It was, indeed, the conception
of ownership and supreme dominion over churches that made
the imposition of feudal service and burdens upon the bishoprics and abbeys an easy and natural step for the Conqueror.
The Normans, moreover, were in the habit of engrossing the
tithes and often also the oblations of their churches, and the
practice was adopted in England by lay and monastic owners
alike. Consequently, the value of the small church to its priest
declined, and with it his status in the community, which became nearer to that of the villein, while on the other hand the
church became more valuable as a pecuniary asset to its new
owner, who gained from tithe more than he had lost by his
greater scrupulosity, stimulated by the reforming legislation,
over receiving money as an entrance fee from his priests. Feeling
against lay ownership of tithe, however, increased, and received ecclesiastical sanction, and it became common for lay
owners to farm out their churches to a clerk, or to bestow their
assets in tithe, with or without the church itself, upon religious
houses. These latter came to have more and more churches in
their possession, from which they drew more of their income
than before. In the early decades after the Conquest, some
churches were given to the monks and more to the regular
canons, in the hope of assuring a more regular and decorous performance of the services, but in practice the religious rarely un-
dertook the cure of souls. Instead, they carried out their duties
by means either of a clerical 'farmer' or of a priest-pensioner;
they had thus in fact gone nine-tenths of the way towards impropriation. As is familiar to all, the lay control of churches
great and small was a principal object of attack for the Gregorian reformers, and the revived canon law, which was their
principal weapon, knew nothing of it. After their success in
the investiture contest they hoped also to abolish lay ownership
of advowson even in the lower churches. In this they failed, and

advowson remained in lay hands, though Alexander III reduced it to the bare right of presenting a candidate to the bishop
for approval. They failed also, in the case of those churches
that had clerical or monastic owners, to vindicate for the actual
incumbent the whole of the church's income, and the *status quo*
was legalized by the admission of impropriation as a canonical
process. Thus came into being the vicarage system; together
with lay patronage, it was a lineal if enfeebled descendant of the
proprietary church. Relatively uncommon as a canonical act,
though not as a practice, in the twelfth century, it became very
frequent in the thirteenth, when a number of energetic diocesan
bishops were at great pains to regulate the details by a formal instrument ensuring a fair income for the vicar and apportioning
responsibility for repairs, the chancel and its furnishings re-
maining the share of the impropriating body. With the growth
of legal machinery, impropriation could no longer be achieved
by the mere will of the owner; some catastrophe or unusual
burden was alleged by the monastery. In the sequel, and in the
long run, the process was no doubt injurious to religion, and
helped to depress the status of the lower clergy; on the other
hand, a fixed income and the certainty of a relatively suitable
priest might well be an improvement over less regular conditions, while when a church was bestowed upon a monastery
with the understanding that it would be impropriated, a regularized vicarage might be preferable to an absentee or pluralist
rector. Seen by the historian, however, like so much else in
medieval practice, it will appear not so much as an abuse as a
survival, in a slightly changed form, of what had gone before.
Vicarages were a consequence on the one hand of the steadily
appreciating, and perhaps even originally excessive, endowments of the church on the one hand, and of the proprietary
church and the lay enjoyment of tithe on the other.

(c) The 'freedom of the Church'

When Lanfranc died in 1089, after less than twenty years in
a strange land that he had found in a turmoil, the Church in
England had passed through a revolution. This revolution,

in part a result of the Conquest and in part the effect of the
so-called Gregorian reform, would have occurred piecemeal
whoever might have been at Canterbury, but in fact it was controlled and given a force and a direction by Lanfranc. With
the possible exception of Theodore of Tarsus he did more to
mould the shape of the Church in England than any church-
man between Augustine and Cranmer. Yet from another point
of view the Church of the Conqueror was *sui generis*. Though
no conflict of Church and State had arisen in the realms of the
duke of Normandy and king of England, the Conqueror did
in fact delimit the action of the papacy with precision. Though
England was in full communion with Rome there was in practice a ring-fence around it. William I maintained, in the oft-
cited words of Eadmer, that he decided (when the occasion
arose) who was legitimate pope; no papal letters were to be
received without his permission; no prelate was to leave the
country without the same permission; and no bishop was to
excommunicate a tenant-in-chief unless the king allowed it.
The change from the days of Edward the Confessor is at once
apparent. William I, while claiming to do no more than assert
the rights which he had inherited from the Old English
monarchy, was in fact meeting a changing world with new
methods. In the flux of years, as in all other changing things,
one cannot step twice into the same stream.

With the passing of William and his primate the time of
peace passed also. The harmonious and fruitful alliance between king and archbishop, resting on no firm principles,
ceased. The unscrupulous and unstatesmanlike Rufus showed
the danger of dependence on the monarch at the very moment
that high Gregorian ideas were extending their sway over the
Church, and circumstances combined to introduce England
to the problem, inescapable in a self-conscious society, yet in
practice unsusceptible of final solution, of the relations between
Church and State, and for the first time, when Rufus died, the
undertaking was asked of and granted by the new king, that
the Church in England should be free.

For almost eighty years this problem was to lie near the surface of English ecclesiastical life. A compromise in the king's favour, though verbally safeguarding canonical demands, under the moderate Henry I gave place to what was almost a parody of Gregorian theory during the anarchy of Stephen when his brother, Henry of Winchester, used his position as papal legate and his assertion of canonical theory to cover every kind of violence and intrigue. The attempt of Henry II to re-adjust the balance led to endless frustration and ultimately to tragedy, partly because in human affairs the past can never be restored without doing violence to the present, partly because the issue, soluble only by good sense and good will, was con-fused beyond remedy by error and passion in different measure on either side. The result was once more a compromise, this time in favour of the Church, and the compromise of the late twelfth century was never completely and permanently dis-turbed till the reign of Henry VIII, though the course of events gradually turned the balance more and more in favour of the king. In the sphere of administrative practice the Church had established two rights: the right of free election by cathedral chapters or monastic communities to bishoprics and feudal abbeys; and the right of all clerks to trial before an ecclesiastical court. But beyond this the whole character of English ecclesi-astical organization and thought had been changed by the gradual infiltration, which soon became saturation, of the 'Gregorian' conception of the pope as the effective ruler and legislator and judge of the whole Church—a conception which developed insensibly into that of the pope as universal Ordi-nary. This conception, whatever resistances and evasions oc-curred in practice, was victorious in the twelfth century. It carried with it the right of the pope to issue privileges, to com-mand under sanction of excommunication and interdict, to send his legates to act with plenary power, to summon to judge-ment or to receive appeals at every stage of the case, as also to give answers on all questions of discipline which became *ipso facto* law applicable to similar cases throughout the Church. England in the last decades of the twelfth century had its share —had, indeed, more than its share—both in developing the

new discipline of canon law and in soliciting new papal pronouncements. Henceforward the canon law, as approved by
popes and interpreted by the great canonists, was the ruling
code in the English ecclesiastical courts.

3. *The Religious Orders and Institutions*

Hitherto the Church has been considered in its organization
and administration, with only passing references to the monks
and other religious orders who filled so large a space in the
medieval canvas. Here again the story is one of great growth
and steady elaboration. England, indeed, even before the days
of Bede, had filled a notable page in monastic history, and had
subsequently taken a large part in giving the monastic life to
Germany. But long before the reign of Alfred organized monastic life had ceased to exist within the bounds of what is now
England. The revival of the tenth century is always associated
with the names of Dunstan and his two colleagues in the habit
and in the episcopate, Ethelwold and Oswald; it is also associated with the name of King Edgar, and the combination of
Church and State is once more characteristic of the land and
the age.

Before the death of the last survivor of the three bishops there
were more than thirty large houses of monks and seven nunneries in England, and by 1066 their numbers had risen to
forty and twelve. All these monasteries followed the Rule of
St. Benedict; they were entirely English in origin and spirit,
though they drew many of their customs and observances from
Cluniac and Lotharingian sources. They, and all the monasteries of the body known throughout the middle ages as the
'black' monks, and in more recent times as Benedictines, followed the way of life expressed in the Rule of St. Benedict with
the traditional modifications that four centuries of European
history had introduced. They were all fairly large and fairly
well endowed communities of men devoted to a common life
of liturgical service, meditative reading, and such work as the
copying, adorning, and binding of service and other books, to-

gether with the lesser arts and crafts; their days were spent in choir and cloister, with a common dormitory and refectory. The monasteries also housed a small population of children of all ages from infancy to adolescence, placed there for education by their parents. Many of these, who had been solemnly 'offered to God', passed into the ranks of the monks; children of the cloister were, indeed, in the tenth and eleventh centuries the main source of recruitment. All these black-monk houses were self-contained, self-governing units owing allegiance to no external prelate or community, save for the post-Conquest Cluniacs. In the Old English Church which, as has been remarked, was rudimentary in its institutions, the monasteries of necessity formed the only spiritual and intellectual focus for ability and fervour, and they were a reservoir upon which all drew heavily. They were the source of all the religious and historical literature of the age, and of most of the religious art; they gave the country a majority of its bishops for more than a century. They had therefore a valuable and essential function in society apart from their purely spiritual *raison d'être*, and with their extensive estates, their jurisdictional immunities, and their treasures they came to form an important element in the economic and administrative life of the country. Besides the monasteries there were in pre-Conquest England a few secular colleges in which a small number of clerks or canons, often only seven in number, lived together, or at least lived as neighbours, in the service of an important or royal church. Eminent among these were the chapters of the three 'sub-cathedrals' of the archdiocese of York, at Ripon, Beverley, and Southwell, but there were others up and down the country, as at Chester and Crediton, and at a group of royal free chapels in the north-western midlands. Shortly before the Conquest a notable foundation was made by Harold at Waltham. These were not in origin religious houses, for they followed no Rule and took no vow of poverty and obedience, and though a few, with Waltham, converted themselves into houses of Austin canons, the majority, with the innate conservatism of ecclesiastical institutions, continued throughout the middle ages under their

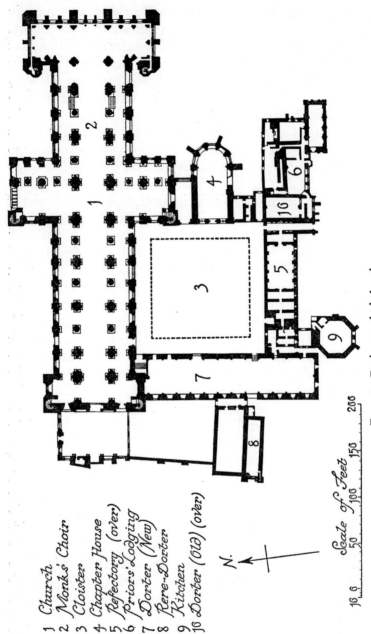

1 Church
2 Monks' Choir
3 Cloister
4 Chapter House
5 Refectory (over)
6 Priors Lodging
7 Dorter (New)
8 Rere-Dorter
9 Kitchen
10 Dorter (Old) (over)

N.

Scale of Feet

50   100   150   200

FIG. 98. Durham cathedral and monastery

PLATE 74

Durham Cathedral and Monastery

PLATE 75

Kirkstall Abbey

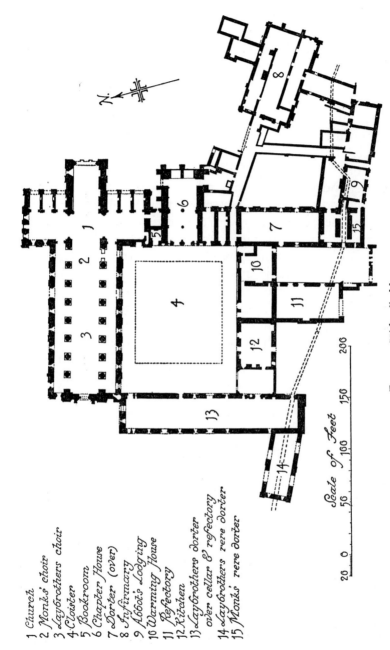

N.

1 Church
2 Monks' choir
3 Laybrothers' choir
4 Cloister
5 Bookroom
6 Chapter House
7 Dorter (over)
8 Infirmary
9 Abbot's Lodging
10 Warming House
11 Refectory
12 Kitchen
13 Laybrothers' dorter
   over cellar & refectory
14 Laybrothers' rere dorter
15 Monks' rere dorter

Scale of Feet

20 0   50   100   150   200

Fig. 99. Kirkstall abbey

original form, leaving few monuments behind them but the magnificent fabric of their churches.

Immediately after the Conquest there began a great monastic invasion which continued almost without pause for a century and a half. In some respects it resembled the waves of invasion that poured into the Roman Empire; successive orders, like successive tribes and nations, crossed the frontiers as it were impelled by those behind who had come from a greater distance. The first to arrive were the Norman monks from the Conqueror's duchy, many of them men who combined the native energy and power to command of their race with the zeal of a new and fervent religious movement. Some of them were picked men, chosen to govern the existing monasteries; others came to colonize the new foundations such as Chester (Bec) and Battle (Marmoutier), or to reinforce existing communities and their daughter-houses, as at Canterbury, Rochester, and Colchester, or to man the small priories and cells which sprang up all over the great Norman fiefs, where lesser lords, unable to found an abbey, hoped to set up a small community in their castle or near their hall, or where conscience-stricken owners of churches wished to substitute edifying celibate ministrants for the boorish married priests whom they found. In all this Lanfranc, the 'father of monks', gave wise direction and counsel, and it would be impossible to exaggerate the regenerating power of the great Norman abbots and priors of the first and second generation, but the English abbeys lost none of their autonomy: the Norman influence was the work of individuals within the houses, not of authority without. The Norman monks were soon followed by others. Foremost among these were the Cluniacs, who had already covered all the rest of western Christendom with their network of dependencies. They were planted in strength at Lewes by William de Warenne, and branched rapidly out into a family that depended immediately or mediately upon the great Burgundian mother-house. Though numerous, the Cluniac houses were almost all small and uninfluential. They were never caught up into the life of the country by feudal dependence on the king, and only at Lewes, Thetford, Much Wenlock, and one or two other priories could they have presented the spectacle of a strictly ordered community following a rich liturgical life that was Cluny's 'message' to the tenth and eleventh centuries.

Following the monks came the regular canons, the Austin or 'black' canons as they were called, having as their code the short Rule of St. Augustine and importing the customs of some great church in northern France or Flanders, and propagating their observance all over England. Notable among them were the houses deriving from the celebrated centre of St. Victor at Paris. They too were introduced by the new landowners in small groups to leaven the mass of the country clergy, though in fact they did little or no apostolic work, but served their churches with the liturgical offices of a semi-monastic life. Like the black monks, the black canons were isolated, autonomous communities.

All these, however, were but spies to the battalions that were to come. Chief among the new orders were the Cistercians or 'white' monks, professedly an austere and militant reform, who aimed at following the Rule of St. Benedict to the last dot (*ad apicem litterae*). Their earliest plantations were at Waverley in Surrey and Rievaulx in Yorkshire; thenceforward they spread with phenomenal rapidity over England and, later, over Wales, asking only waste land in remote and uncultivated districts. The Cistercians restored agricultural work to honour for monks, but the tasks of clearing forests, draining marshes, over-seeing flocks and crops in wild and desolate places, were be-yond the powers of unaided choir monks; the Cistercians, by recruiting cottars and small freeholders as lay brethren, opened the religious life to classes hitherto excluded from it, and created a labour force of great economic potentiality that for a century did much to further the contemporary extension of the limits of cultivation and to add to the bulk of the profitable wool clip of the land.

In the wake of the Cistercians came the Premonstratensian or 'white' canons, who had originated as an apostolic preaching institute but had felt the pull of St. Bernard and the Cistercians, and had become a semi-monastic order, with houses in remote districts like the Cistercians, and with flocks like theirs in Yorkshire and Lincolnshire.

Hitherto there had been little scope for women. The relatively few nunneries were old, selective, and often aristocratic Benedictine houses, almost all in Wessex or near London. A few had been added after the Conquest, but the real need was not met till a new order came into being that was in origin and always remained (save for a single temporary exception) English in personnel, though its codes and observances were all drawn from the Continent. This was the order of Sempringham, founded in a village of south Lincolnshire for women of the district by Gilbert, a small landholder of Norman blood turned priest. The group of devout women directed by himself rapidly increased; Gilbert, who had a genius for organization as well as for spiritual direction, added lay sisters to the nuns, who followed the Rule of St. Benedict; later, lay brothers were added on the Cistercian model and with the Cistercian Uses to exploit the nuns' property, and finally an institute of canons, following the Rule of St. Augustine, was created to supply spiritual direction and serve the nuns as chaplains. Last of all, Gilbert unwillingly consented to join his own order as Master. He had drawn up a long and complicated set of constitutions, with elaborate provision against abuses in the 'double' establishments of nuns and canons, where the two families lived each round its own cloister, separated by the church of the nuns, in which a medial wall divided the halves of the choir reserved to the nuns and canons. The Gilbertine nuns long remained numerous and fervent, but they were in effect a Lincolnshire order, with a fringe of houses in south Yorkshire and in the north-east midlands, and a rare outpost elsewhere.

A 'double' order of another type, the aristocratic family of Fontevrault, had a few nunneries in England, the largest being at Amesbury, but spread no farther. Vocations of women, however, increased; during the twelfth century both the Cistercians and the Premonstratensians were compelled, against their original wishes, to allow communities of women to follow their customs and statutes and be guided by resident chaplains of their order. At the same time numerous houses of Augustinian canonesses were coming into being and continued to multiply throughout the thirteenth century. All these nunneries, it may be noted, were of a single basic type, following the traditional liturgical life, though with a certain freedom, in the absence of a strict 'enclosure', unknown to their counterparts in the modern world. There was as yet nothing of the austere, penitential way of life later associated with the Poor Clares and Carmelites, and the middle ages in England knew nothing of the innumerable 'active' orders devoted to teaching, nursing, and charitable works of all kinds that have grown up in such profusion since the fifteenth century.

Finally, two orders of men, following a severe and quasi-eremitical way of life, appeared in England at this time. The one was the order of Grandmont, a monastic institute with elaborate constitutions of an almost fiercely logical severity; its houses in England were few, remote, and small. The other was the more celebrated and long-lived order of the Chartreuse, which at this epoch of its history was made up of two separate communities—the monks, who lived in small houses surrounding a large cloister, and the lay brothers, who lived in a group of buildings half a mile or so away. The Carthusians were, and have remained, a strictly enclosed hermit group. They were long in multiplying from their two earliest houses in Somerset and never became numerous, but from first to last they were something of a spiritual *élite*.

Three other classes of religious family must be mentioned to complete the picture of the late twelfth century. There were, first of all, a few colleges of secular priests living together. This, as has been seen, was an ancient form of organization akin to the groups of clergy at a cathedral, and existed here and there at the Conquest. Its aims were realized and extended by the regular canons, who had a great vogue from the beginning of the twelfth century, but a few of the collegiate groups survived. Some of them were relatively well endowed, with no obligation save that of Masses and prayers for the founder and other specified persons, and as the prebends were often in the gift of the king or of a bishop they soon became desirable sinecures for royal or episcopal clerical employees, who often performed their statutory duties through paid substitutes or vicars. The colleges of Hackington near Canterbury and of Lambeth, planned by the Archbishops Baldwin and Hubert Walter, which led to the *cause célèbre* between the archbishop and the monks of Canterbury, were to be of this type. Though exter/ nally similar, they were in character quite different from the academic and residential colleges that later became so nu/ merous.

The second class was that of the military orders of the Temple and of St. John of Jerusalem. These, a direct consequence of the Crusades, were perhaps the most characteristic, or at least the most singular, manifestations of the piety of an epoch. By combining the monastic and the military ideals they united in uneasy equilibrium two ways of life the most diverse, each of which appealed powerfully to the society of its day, and, like the Cistercian lay brothers at the other end of the social scale, they threw open the religious life to a new class of society, that of the knights and men/at/arms. The Templars were founded for purely military service, the Hospitallers for the protection, re/ ception, and healing of pilgrims, but the resemblances between the two were more important than the differences. Both had, in the twelfth century, an effective part to play in the life of Outremer, but both soon became possessed of innumerable small properties throughout Europe, and established posts for recruitment as well as for the exploitation of their estates and the collection of their revenues. Save for the London Temple and the priory of St. John at Clerkenwell the preceptories and com/ manderies scattered over England were small and religiously insignificant.

The third class was that of the hospitals. History shows that the organized care of the sick in buildings erected for that pur/ pose only develops in countries where large agglomerations of population exist, as in the Byzantine empire and Persia. There is scarcely a trace of such establishments in England before the Conquest, save perhaps in a few urban monasteries. In the twelfth century, however, the growth of towns, and the development of travel and commerce, together with the appearance of new diseases such as leprosy, true and supposed, and the existence of a large class of potential benefactors, led to the multiplication of hospitals, many of which combined the functions of hospice, clinic, and almshouse. Their organization was assisted and in some ways conditioned by the experience gained in the east and by the needs of returned pilgrims and crusaders. These hospitals gave scope for the promiscuous services of many charitable persons who had found no scope in the monasteries and nunneries of the age; they were staffed almost invariably by a quasi-religious body, and founders always made provision for the spiritual needs of the inmates; many were served by a group of brethren or sisters or both, who followed a regular life, often based upon the Rule of St. Augustine, making it difficult for historians, as it was for contemporaries, to distinguish between a religious house and a hospital. Though medically primitive and entirely without influence on the development of surgery or clinical practice, the hospitals are impressive in the aggregate if only by their numbers, and their services in the relief and consolation of the sick and aged must not be left out of the reckoning when the religious balance sheet of the age is being drawn up.

By the end of the twelfth century the spiritual forces released by the revival of the previous age and by the birth of the new monastic and canonical orders were approaching exhaustion. The monks and canons had become possessed of a large fraction of the land and potential wealth of the country; their houses were ubiquitous, more than six hundred in number, and their numbers formed a notable percentage of the free population. It might have seemed that the age of regression was approaching. The scene was transformed, however, by the arrival, at the end of the first quarter of the new century, of the recently founded Friars Preachers and Friars Minor or, as they later came to be called, the Dominicans, the 'black' friars, and the Franciscans, the 'grey' friars. Their story has often been told and need not be repeated; it is enough to note that their primary work lay among classes of society hitherto neglected, the new and rapidly increasing urban populations which in the thirteenth century and later formed a section of the people far more homogeneous in its interests and needs than were the later industrial and mercantile cities with their aristocracy of wealth and their residue of paupers, and with their sharp distinction between employers and employed. In the towns the friars lived, and from them they drew a majority of their recruits, though the call to a new form of the religious life, as yet in its first enthusiasm, and, a little later, the dazzling attractions of a brilliant academic career, drew many from the higher ranks. Preachers and Minors were followed by Carmelites and Austin Hermits and lesser 'splinter' groups such as the Friars of the Sack. They were soon established in every sizeable town in England and Wales, preaching, confessing, and visiting, but their work in the Church was given an unpredictable impulse and direction by their success and appeal at the newly organized universities, where they captured on arrival some of the outstanding masters and their most brilliant pupils, and then became themselves preponderant in the schools. This again is a twice-told tale, but even in the briefest survey the reader must be reminded that for nearly two hundred years the theological life of England (and therefore of the universities of Oxford and Cambridge) was directed and dominated by the friars. The monks had ceased to be the leaders of religious thought, and though many of the bishops were university masters, it is significant that the only two thirteenth-century prelates who have a place in the history of European thought are the two mendicant archbishops, Kilwardby and Pecham.

4. The Thirteenth Century: administration and jurisdiction

The twelfth century was for the medieval world the luxuriant season of May and June, in which ideas and institutions of all kinds sprang suddenly from the new blade to the full ear, often before the guardians of the field could thin the crop or weed the soil. The thirteenth century by contrast was the time of selection and harvest, and the turn of the century between the two ages gained a real significance from its coincidence with the pontifi- cate of Innocent III and the celebration of the Fourth Lateran Council, from the formal foundation of the universities, and from the rise of the orders of friars. The papacy, indeed, as a result of the vagaries of King John, had under Innocent III acquired a great, if accidental and in some ways excessive, interest in English affairs. This passed, and the reaction under Edward I more than recovered the ground for the monarchy. The real significance of the century lies not in the realm of eccle- siastical politics but in that of organization, administration, and consolidation. The bishops of England, from the days of Stephen Langton to those of Robert Winchelsey, were for the most part men trained in the schools; they were also, if consi- dered as a body, men of practical ability and upright character which often approximated and sometimes attained to the high level of sanctity. It was, therefore, a century of diocesan bishops who, instructed in the canon law, and fortified by the ancient powers of correction reaffirmed by the Council and by the new precision of sacramental legislation, worked methodically throughout England at the task of establishing an educated, respectable, and economically independent priesthood and of providing preachers and confessors for the increasing popula- tion, both in the country and in the new urban centres. The new tasks and the trained minds demanded tools and agents, and the thirteenth century saw the bishop's household and the diocesan courts take final shape, while the appearance of official registers and archives of every kind reflect and perpetuate the new methods of administration. They deserve consideration in somewhat greater detail.

Before the Conquest diocesan administrative machinery, where it existed at all, was simple and primitive. The bishop must always have had a few priests and other clerks who made arrangements for him and assisted him in the ordinations, con- secrations, and confirmations that he performed, and besides the collection of charters that were his warrant for his see's properties there must always have been at least an embryonic chancery and archive which the trained king's clerks appointed to bishoprics such as Leofric of Exeter and Giso of Wells immediately before the Conquest may have considerably developed. Ordinarily, however, both household and chancery must have been humble in scale. As for the judicial work, this was accomplished, as has been seen, in the hundred court along with secular business, and what record there was would have been kept by the court's clerk. The Conquest brought the elements of a secretariat and the institution of the episcopal court, but for long all business was discharged by the bishop in person or by the clerks of his household acting for him. Although by the middle of the twelfth century the archive and secretariat had developed, the clear view of an archbishop in action that we derive from the letters and biographies of St. Thomas show us an administration still largely personal and unformalized. The clerks of Theobald and Thomas, who counted in their number Vacarius, John of Salisbury, Herbert of Bosham, and future bishops and curialists, were as distinguished and able as any that served a prelate in any age of the Church, but their activities were largely individual and direct; they were men of ability, young or mature, who had chosen or had been chosen by the archbishop, and they looked forward to a career of similar distinction. Though the *familia* of Canterbury was in some ways exceptional since the monastic chapter performed many of the duties of the see's regular officials, what we know of Chichester and York at the same date shows the same personal attachment of a group of clerks to the bishop. The great change came in the decades on either side of the Lateran Council: the development of canon law; wider administrative duties; the appearance of a large class of professional lawyers and secretaries; the disappearance of the independent literary man, half-scholar, half-churchman, of the type of John of Salisbury and Peter of Blois—all this brought about a revolution comparable to the change from the handwritten ledgers, letter-books, and personal accounting of the family businesses of the early nineteenth century to the apparatus of stenography, file-cabinets, stencils, microfilms, and mechanical calculators deployed by an army of trained accountants and statisticians in the work of helping or hindering the efficient conduct of a great combine or National Board.

Episcopal lists and registers survive from the middle decades of the thirteenth century, isolated and summary at first, but soon ubiquitous and full, covering all the activities of the bishop in his diocese, and we soon begin to see the whole group of officials in action. These varied considerably from diocese to diocese and from age to age in number, function, and title, but speaking generally the administration had finally crystallized by the second half of the fourteenth century, when the custom of appointing as bishops government officials who continued to occupy posts in the king's service became normal, implying a quasi-permanent absence of the bishop from his diocese and the consequent devolution of important duties on subordinates. The group surrounding the bishop when in his diocese, and acting as his council and executive, were still known as his clerks, but they were in fact a group of officials with defined spheres of action in which they were all but Ordinaries[1] themselves. Besides the bishop's Registrar, a notary public, the most important of the group were the Official and the Vicar General. The former was the bishop's permanent delegate and *alter ego* in judicial affairs; he had full powers in the consistory court, and there was no appeal from him to the bishop, though the latter reserved his right to judge in person, anywhere in the diocese, special cases at will. The Vicar General was the bishop's delegate with full powers in all jurisdictional and administrative functions. Originally appointed for the occasion when the bishop was leaving his diocese for a considerable time, he was in later centuries, when bishops were often absentees, appointed in permanence to take over whenever the bishop was away. He never, in the mid-medieval period, formed an essential figure in every diocese as he does in modern

[1] An Ordinary, in canonical terminology, is a prelate with full jurisdiction, i.e. having the right to issue and enforce commands and to judge causes and allot penalties.

canon law, acting alongside of the bishop as an alternative as well as a substitute. Later, there was a tendency to combine the offices of Vicar General and Official in a single holder who was usually the Chancellor; this last, originally holding a secretarial post, had developed in dignity without a corresponding in- crease in duties of importance. There were, however, certain actions, such as ordinations, consecrations, and blessings, which required episcopal orders and which in consequence neither of the bishop's customary delegates could perform. For these suffragan bishops were employed, who were neither (as with some Anglican dignitaries holding the title) charged with the administration of a district nor (as in modern Roman Catholic practice) dignified or office-holding members of the diocesan clergy, but temporary assistants, usually Dominican, Franciscan, or Carmelite friars, and later also Austin canons, who had been furnished by the pope with titular or inaccess- ible Irish sees. They were usually maintained by the gift of a benefice in the diocese, and took no part in its conduct.

While the bishop's duties as Ordinary and consecrator were thus performed or shared by a group of delegates, other tasks were permanently executed by subordinates. The chief of these was the archdeacon. This functionary was of ancient institu- tion as the bishop's principal assistant in a primitive urban diocese, and he existed before the Conquest at Canterbury, if nowhere else. Originally a single official in a see-city, the arch- deacon remained sole in small dioceses; in larger sees there might be as many as five (York) or eight (Lincoln). The arch- deacon's powers were merely visitatorial and penal; he was a standing example of the medieval axiom that a court is a pecu- niary asset (*magnum emolumentum justitia*). His two functions were those of parochial visitation and the imposition of fines for moral and ecclesiastical offences, and it soon became customary for him to receive a fee instead of visiting and to collect fines out of court by deputy, he thus became a target for satirists and the most cordially disliked official of the diocese. Beneath the archdeacon were the rural deans, who are first seen in being in the early twelfth century. They were members of the clergy who had within their restricted area of competence powers similar to that of the archdeacon, whose office they in fact filled in certain small territories such as the isolated deaneries in Essex and Sussex depending upon Canterbury; they also executed small tasks for the bishop by mandate.

While the bishop's direct control was thus lessened functionally by the multiplication of officials it was restricted in area by local and personal exemptions of every kind. Hitherto the diocese has been spoken of as though it were (as it is with inconsiderable exceptions in modern Anglican practice) a plain area in which the bishop could exercise all his normal jurisdiction. Actually, the medieval diocese was a honeycomb of local and personal exemptions of every kind, some of them dating from early Saxon times, others attaching to persons who were members of this or that order or institution, and still others that had resulted from the persevering obstruction of individuals or corporations. The simplest to reckon with were those of the religious orders. Originally, the monastery had been not only within the diocese in the ancient Church but had had in the bishop the guarantee of its wellbeing. The vast majority of the houses of black monks and black canons were still in this position, and in the days after the Lateran Council were visited officially by the diocesan, who also confirmed their elections. A certain number, however, never very large, had obtained a privileged position. Some of these had royal immunities of immemorial antiquity guaranteeing them against interference from the bishop; such immunities were granted by kings to their foundations before the Conquest—Bury St. Edmunds is an example, Westminster another—of what were in fact royal *eigenkirchen*, and the Conqueror followed the example at Battle. Others had commended themselves to the Apostolic see and obtained the right of depending upon it without the intermediary power of a bishop (*nullo mediante*), and most of the anciently immune abbeys hastened to obtain such privileges as a 'hedge' or counterinsurance. In most of these cases an area, great or small, outside the abbey was included in the immunity. At Westminster it was only the church of St. Margaret; at

Battle only the *leuga* or small district round the abbey; but at Evesham and St. Albans it included a group of churches with their parishes, and occasionally a group of the abbey's churches (as at Glastonbury) was exempt while the abbey itself was not. This class of exemption, besides being small, became fixed as the result of a series of suits in the twelfth century; it was en-tirely local and private in character. On the other hand, certain orders were totally exempt. The Cistercians had begun by asserting their dependence upon the diocesan, but as they asserted with equal force the inviolability of all their statutes and uses, and complete freedom of election, the bishop was in fact debarred from all effective jurisdiction, and in time the whole order became officially exempt. Cistercian example carried the Premonstratensians along the same path, and the mendicant orders were dependent directly upon the papacy from the beginning. The bishop could, indeed, in the case of the monks and canons prohibit the first entry into his diocese, but with the friars this was in practice impossible, and though for a time the bishops retained the power of prohibiting the friars from hearing confessions and preaching in the diocese, this also was curtailed in favour of the mendicants by the papal privileges, and an equilibrium, fair to both parties but guaran-teeing adequate facilities to the friars, was only established in 1300 by the celebrated bull *Super cathedram* of Boniface VIII, which remained substantially effective till the Council of Trent.

But the exemptions of the regulars, though extensive and applying also to the precincts, had at least some elements of order about them and were chiefly personal in their effects. Far more galling to the bishop were the numerous enclaves in his diocese that withdrew numerous parishes and their clergy and some of his own churches and functionaries from his jurisdiction. There were, in the first place, the churches of other diocesan bishops. These, relics of the old system of proprietary churches and ill-defined diocesan boundaries, were churches owned by a bishop situated within the diocese of another. Known in England by the name of 'peculiars' these had always depended for all purposes upon their owner; thus Canterbury had scattered peculiars in Sussex, Middlesex (Harrow), and Essex; York had (among others) the enclave of Hexham in the diocese of Durham. The detailed map of medieval England shows innumerable islands of this kind, even more ubiquitous than the isolated fragments of counties that appear on older maps of England which themselves (as in the case of the islands of Worcestershire in Warwickshire and Gloucestershire) were often the scattered parishes of a bishopric. Next, there were the areas which in the course of time had won partial or total exemption such as the archdeaconry of Richmond in Yorkshire or the royal free chapels of Staffordshire. Finally, there were the capitular bodies, and in particular the chapters of the secular cathedrals, who enjoyed exemption, which they communicated to the churches owned by them in the diocese. Instances could be multiplied of results verging on the ridiculous; one such was at Chichester, where the city and close in which the bishop's palace stood were the peculiar of the dean and chapter; he had only to cross a street to find himself in a detached fragment of the diocese of Canterbury; while the parishes west of his park were in the jurisdiction of the canons of Bosham, a royal free chapel immediately subject to the bishop of Exeter.[1]

5. The Papal Government: taxes, provisors, and pluralism

For 150 years after the Conquest the concentration of Church government in the hands of the papacy had steadily increased, despite such moments of tension and controversy as the investiture contest, the struggle of Alexander III with anti-popes and Barbarossa, and the Becket upheaval. During that period the popes with scarcely an exception had acted as leaders and supporters of a great religious revival and had upheld the interests of the Church at large. Freedom of election to bishoprics and abbacies had been asserted and in large part won; protection

---

[1] A. Hamilton Thompson, *The English Clergy*, p. 75.

had been given to the goods and privileges of churches and monasteries; a coherent body of law had been established; a higher justice had been made available; and the papacy had been a living source of counsel and encouragement. In all this the papacy, by and large, had acted as a head working in solidarity with its members and for their good, and despite very real abuses and justified complaints the pope was, and was felt to be, a support and a guide from whom individual churches received more than they lost. The costs of litigation and protection, if sometimes excessive, were at least borne by those concerned, and such quarrels as arose were between the secular power and the Church or between bishops and regulars, not between the papacy and its subjects.

The climax of this development, so far as England was concerned, came in the pontificate of Innocent III (1199–1216), from whom, in the reign of John, both the king and his opponents solicited aid which the pope did his best to give, and to whom John in desperation commended his realm as to a feudal overlord. That episode was at once the climax and the watershed in the history of the political relations of the papacy with England. Thenceforward, at first slowly but afterwards more rapidly, the solidarity of interest between the Curia and various parts of the Church began to loosen. The papacy, wielding unquestioned authority, advanced with apparent success claims to complete and immediate jurisdiction over every branch and member of the Church, but often gave the impression of irresponsible and autocratic action. The Curia began to exploit the rest of the Church for its own profit, and the papal court, swollen out of all recognition since the days of Gregory VII or even of Innocent III, began to be regarded and to act as a bureaucracy whose interests might well conflict with those of the Church as a whole. Two administrative developments which attained maturity in the thirteenth century were at once causes and symptoms of this new state of things: papal taxation, and papal interference with the customary processes of appointment to prelacies and benefices.

Before the end of the twelfth century the papal Curia had

lived, sometimes with considerable difficulty, upon the revenues of the patrimonies of St. Peter together with the normal
charges and gifts taken from litigants and petitioners and the
relatively small annual census levied upon monasteries and
fiefs that had sought papal protection, and from the free-will
offerings of individuals and countries (such as the ancient
Peter's pence of England, imitated later in Scandinavia and
Poland), and occasional solicited aids from abbeys and prelates. Towards the end of the twelfth century the papacy, in
imitation of secular rulers, levied a tax for the Crusade of one-
fortieth on clerical incomes. This was often repeated in the following century and finally replaced by a similar tax 'for the
needs of the Church'. Taxes implied tax-collectors: at first
bishops and abbots were employed, but gradually the papal
camera developed a service of collectors, usually foreigners and
armed with full spiritual powers of coercion. A bureaucracy
tends always to proliferate and to be wasteful; taxes are always
considered excessive; and medieval men, unused to an elaborate machinery of government, did not realize that an efficient
central government, either domestic or foreign, had to be supported by its beneficiaries; in England in particular all taxation
was resented as something essentially extortionate.

Besides the direct tax on clerical incomes a number of other
resources were tapped. Archbishops and exempt abbots, who
needed confirmation at Rome for their election, had for long
given substantial presents in the Curia; these were gradually
(c. 1275) made obligatory at a high fixed tariff which (as in all
similar cases) by no means excluded subsidiary gratuities; later
these irregular sums were turned by actuarial calculation into an
annual tax. A little later than this (1306), under Clement V an
old tax was given a new direction, owing partly to its connexion with papal provisions. This was the annates, a part of
the first year's revenues of a benefice hitherto sometimes paid to
chapters or prelates and now diverted to the pope and made universal. Similar to this was another tax, levied during vacancy on
all benefices falling vacant in the Curia (i.e. by the death of the
occupant while in or near the papal court); yet another was the

spolia, a death duty on the property of bishops and clerics dying in the Curia. Although the total sums involved were small if compared with the burden of taxation in the late Roman and Byzantine empires or the modern world, their impact was considerable, coinciding as it did with stringent royal demands, and beyond the actual financial sacrifice there was a not unjustified fear of what might come next from a papacy that advanced with relentless logic from tax to tax, progressing steadily in financial efficiency, and using for its purposes the spiritual sanctions of excommunication and suspension. Feelings of grievance were aggravated in the fourteenth century by the knowledge that wealth was passing out of England into hands that were now regarded as bound in sympathy with the national foe. To judge, however, by contemporary comments, protest came in its most forcible form not so much from the clergy as from the king and his officials, who felt that others were profiting from the taxes. In the sequel, what with subsidies voted for the king by the command of the pope and a handsome 'rake-off' on the papal taxes themselves, the government derived more profit from papal taxation than did the Curia, but the economic pressure here, as among the centralized orders, was one of the principal psychological forces that broke down the existing conception of a united Latin Christendom.

Concurrently with the development of papal taxation, and in part arising from the same causes, was the practice of papal intervention in the bestowal of benefices known as papal provision. This affected in different ways two different classes: the so-called major benefices or bishoprics; and the minor benefices ranging from official dignities such as deaneries, provostships, and treasurerships to rectories, canonries, prebends, and small offices. As regards bishoprics, direct papal appointment as a general practice was slow in coming. It had, indeed, been maintained from ancient times by the Apostolic See that as diocesan bishops were ecclesiastical brethren of the pope and owed allegiance to none save the Prince of the Apostles, a pope could on occasion appoint or depose a bishop. Nevertheless, one of the principal aims of the Gregorian reform had been to assert the free canonical election of a bishop by his chapter as against the claims of secular rulers, and free election continued to be the demand of the English bishops in the days of John, and was supported by Innocent III. For this reason the applica⁄ tion to bishoprics of the centralizing tendencies of the thirteenth century was late in coming, and was in a sense the result rather than the cause of papal provision to smaller benefices.

There, the ancient discipline had never changed. All minor benefices, from the days of the primitive Church, had been directly controlled by the diocesan, just as appointments in Rome fell to the pope as bishop of the city. When, therefore, lay control was being excluded, the bishop took his canonical place once more. The régime of the proprietary church, how⁄ ever, had shaken the whole fabric of tradition, and from the middle of the twelfth century onwards the papacy had begun first to solicit, then to demand, and ultimately to enforce the bestowal of a certain number of benefices throughout Europe for its protégés. Whatever the ultimate cause or causes of this change may have been—inevitable or logical development, the natural tendency of lawyers to extend claims and precedents, or mere political advantage—one of the most common uses to which this procedure was put was to provide or augment the income of the officials, high and low, of the Curia. Beginning with comparatively rare requests, the demands of the popes of the late twelfth century increased in frequency and urgency till by the middle of the following century the freedom of bishops in filling their churches and chapters was becoming notably curtailed. Paradoxically enough, the rights of lay patrons were consistently respected, though there was some friction in England between the courts Christian and the royal courts, both of which claimed the right of decision as to the fact of lay patronage.

An important canonical step was taken by Clement IV in 1265: while asserting the pope's right over all benefices he proclaimed his exclusive control over all those vacated by their holders while in the precincts of the Curia. John XXII extended this reservation to cover every kind of cession—by death, resignation, deprivation, or translation—and every kind of cleric and benefice, and widened the precincts of the Curia to a two-days' journey in any direction. As those who ended their days in or near the Curia were, almost by definition, richly beneficed, this gave the pope considerable freedom. Finally, the reservation was applied to all benefices vacated by a bishop appointed by the pope. In addition to direct confer-ments, expectations to benefices were also bestowed in great numbers, and the situation was further complicated by the fact that all that the papal grant conferred was the right to claim a benefice, which might be disputed in the papal courts or elsewhere.

During the first century of papal provisions, before the great decretals of reservation had been issued, most of the appoint-ments went to curial dignitaries and officials—to foreigners, that is, or at least to absentees—and it was towards the end of this epoch, when the Church in England was being simul-taneously exploited in the interests of the Savoyard connexions of Henry III, that the opposition was most vocal. The succes-sive waves of reservation, while greatly increasing the number of provisors, also widened the scope of the papal bounty, and gave hopes to both careerists and poor clerks in every country, while the legislation against pluralism, to be mentioned shortly, spread the supply still more widely. As the royal and lay pa-tronage was left untouched, the king and barons had no per-sonal grievance and so did not press their opposition; indeed, the king himself used the system widely by entering the market as petitioner for his protégés and officials. To strike the balance of loss and gain to religion is a task which, even if possible, would lie far outside the scope of these pages, but it is worth while noting that from the end of the fourteenth century on-wards considerable use was made by Oxford and Cambridge of the papal largesse of preferment to university clerks who might well otherwise have been left unbeneficed.

As has been already noted, the fortunes of major benefices followed a different rhythm. Free canonical election, fought for under Henry I, Stephen, and Henry II, was demanded and secured by Langton in Magna Carta, and for several decades was respected by both pope and king. Disputes, however, factious and genuine, abounded at election time, and if taken to Rome the smallest irregularity in carrying out the somewhat stringent canonical precautions gave the pope the right to quash the election and appoint; there was also opportunity when a bishop was translated or died in the Curia or (like Kilwardby) was recalled to be cardinal. Nevertheless, the canonical forms of election, often influenced by the king, were still honoured, though papal reservation of individual cases continued. Finally, in 1363, Urban V reserved to himself all episcopal sees however vacated. Consequently, from 1349 until the Reformation, with the insignificant exception of a few months in 1416–17, every appointment to a bishopric in England and Wales was made by papal provision, though this was normally preceded by a canonical election by the chapter acting on what was in effect a royal mandate. Three methods of appointment were thus, so to say, concurrent or conflated, and while all agree that the canonical electors had little to say in the choice, historians have not been in complete agreement as to the relative shares of the two major parties in the result. Undoubtedly political considerations kept the pope from appointing any clerk outside a narrow class of those distinguished either by high birth or close connexion with the king's circle of officials, and hence some kind of royal favour was a paramount consideration; on the other hand, the need for papal confirmation was probably one of the causes that kept the English episcopate respectable, and there were several cases where, of two eligible government officials, the king proposed one and the pope provided the other. Moreover, the papal right to translate, and to fill the see thus left vacant of his own initiative, was not in dispute and was in fact untouched by English legislation, though here again the frequent translations of the fifteenth century were often moves in the political game. Speaking broadly, it may be said that episcopal appointment was achieved by a collusive process in which the king usually got the man he asked for, and always one he could accept, while the pope in return was left unhindered in his other spheres of provision and dispensation. The system was not ideal; but it is hard to see that, given the mental and spiritual climate of Rome and England in the fifteenth century, any other method would have greatly altered the character of the episcopate. There were no distinguished apostolic priests, no saints or theologians among the monks and friars who could have dominated the religious scene and ousted the civil servants.

The great and unpredictable advance in centralization, re-flected in taxes and provision, had serious repercussions upon English sentiment. The extent and precise character of anti-papal feeling in the country will probably always remain a debatable and debated question, though it would add greatly to the clarity of discussions if care were taken to distinguish between a recognition of the paramount spiritual authority of the papacy which, despite the views of conciliarists, was never questioned in practice, save by Wyclif and the Lollards, be-fore the sixteenth century, and the acceptance of new and questionable administrative principles and practices which, though deriving from spiritual claims, were neither essential nor irreversible consequences of them. Somewhat paradoxically, it was while papal claims were still moderate, and while the monarch, the long-lived Henry III, was most complaisant, that the spirituality of the realm, symbolized by Grosseteste and Matthew Paris, were most vocal in their protests. When, in the age of the two first Edwards, the king and the magnates, apprehensive of a loss of rights and wealth, revived in a more modern form the theories of patronage and regalian rights— echoes of the proprietary régime, which had national and anti-clerical undertones—the bishops and regulars were less en-thusiastic and the measures taken against the papal prerogative did not have their official approval. The king, with the sup-port of Parliament, secured legislation in 1307 and again in 1351 (Statute of Provisors) against the implementing of re-scripts of provision, and in the Statute of Praemunire (1353,

1365, 1393) outlaw and confiscation were made possible penalties for those who secured papal privileges against the royal rights or appealed to papal courts in matters where the royal courts claimed jurisdiction. This last statute, however, though it was to have a redoubtable future, was severely limited in its original aim and was rarely invoked in practice. At the moment of its third enactment the opposition in some quarters to papal government had become much more theo-logical and drastic, but the promoters of these views were re-garded as heretical and the enemies of government in Church and State alike.

Another feature of medieval church life, not wholly un-connected with the proprietary church on the one hand and with papal centralization on the other, was pluralism, or the simultaneous occupation of more than one lucrative benefice or dignity. Never wholly unknown in a well-endowed church in any age, the evidence of Domesday and the familiar case of Stigand show that it was present in a mild degree before the Conquest, but the relatively modest endowments of the Church at that date, and the almost total absence of any lucra-tive office or prebend save that of a cure of souls, prevented it from becoming a common abuse. The rich endowments following upon the redistribution of land at the Conquest, the enduring piety of the age, and the great increase in the wealth of the country, together with a host of other causes—the growth of a large clerical staff at court and in the law courts and bishops' households, the new learning and its expenses, the multiplication of clerks with a consequent plethora of potential vicars and *locum tenentes*—all this led to a rapid in-crease in pluralism and an ever-sharper division between the clerical proletariat and the highly born or highly gifted careerist. As early as the middle of the twelfth century Thomas Becket, while archdeacon of Canterbury, amassed a rich and miscel-laneous bundle of benefices and posts. It had been an axiom of ancient discipline that a priest was the priest of a single flock under the bishop, and the Lateran Council of 1179, followed by its successor of 1215, reiterated the familiar principle that only one benefice with cure of souls was allowable, though the fathers of 1215 realistically added that some form of dispensation must be made available for highborn clerics and men of letters. With or without such dispensations, the distinguished clerks of the thirteenth century made their age the golden age of pluralism, and John Mansel, the servant of Henry III, with four important dignities, eight or nine rectories, and half a dozen prebends, and the familiar Bogo de Clare, with twentyfour parish churches and a dozen benefices besides, were only *primi inter pares*.

Meanwhile the papacy was making determined and on the whole effective attempts to remedy with its right hand the evil which it was doing something to foster with its left. The two energetic legates Otto and Ottobuon, whose reforming decrees in 1237 and 1268 remained classic for almost three centuries, made stringent regulations against holding more than one benefice which Archbishop Pecham in 1281 did his best to implement, and Boniface VIII made a dispensation necessary for holding even a sinecure along with a cure of souls. It was still possible, however, to obtain a 'blanket' dispensation covering all types of benefice up to a specified total value. It was left to John XXII in 1317 to promulgate an epochmaking decree with his bull *Execrabilis*, which laid it down that not even by dispensation could a clerk hold more than one benefice with a cure of souls and one without, all others save these two being resigned. Urban V did no more than emphasize this when he ordered returns to be made of each diocese so that pluralists might be deprived of all save the canonical two benefices, but it is to this action that we owe our knowledge of the English pluralists of the day, including the egregious William of Wykeham. He certainly had a long list, but one far less scandalous than Bogo's, for the superfluous benefices were all without cure of souls. With Clement's decree the worst was over in England. Pluralists were not unknown, but they were, so to say, an economic rather than a spiritual scandal, and were not a major cause of weakness in the early Tudor Church.

6. The Fourteenth Century: parishes, parliament, and convocation

We have already glanced at the origins of the vicarage system, which in its beginnings and for some two centuries was largely an adjustment of monastic demands. Though responsible for a majority of appropriations, however, the re- ligious houses were not the only interested parties. Bishops appropriated their own proprietary churches to the episcopal *mensa* or to a secular chapter, and from the fourteenth century onwards lay owners of advowsons, desirous of founding col- leges or chantries, made over their rights to their foundation on the understanding that these would subsequently petition for the impropriation that was unlawful for laymen. Though bishops often delayed or obstructed, there was never any movement towards a complete *non possumus*, partly because the conception of a church as a pecuniary asset died hard, partly because the petitioners could usually, at somewhat greater expense, secure a papal privilege. After 1366, indeed, when Urban V ostensibly laid a moratorium on impropria- tion throughout the Church, a papal permission was neces- sary in every case. This did not of itself act as a brake, but the rate of appropriations fell in the fourteenth century and re- mained low for the rest of the middle ages, partly, no doubt, because the monasteries had reached an equilibrium where further impropriations, by lessening the patronage in the hands of the house, would have been on the balance an economic disadvantage. Occasionally, however, we find an abbey in the fifteenth century obtaining a privilege to farm out a number of churches, even without the consent of the bishop. But by that time a very high proportion of the parish churches of England —one in four in some dioceses, one in five or six in others— had been appropriated.

The system as a whole has been severely judged by modern historians, as it had been long ago by medieval moralists and reformers. In the abstract it has little to commend it, and in the long run it probably had considerable influence in lowering the economic condition of the clergy, and consequently the quality of their spiritual services. On the other hand, it is not a question that admits of a single, clear-cut answer. It could scarcely have arisen but for the fact that the Church, owing to indiscriminate gifts, to the appreciation of property, to the rise of population, and to the wider exploitation of the land, had become very wealthy. The Church, indeed, from *c.* 1160 on-wards, was too wealthy, while the relation of tithe to the needs of the rural clergy was quite arbitrary. The rich benefices, which *ex hypothesi* were the natural objects of impropriation, had been the first, before impropriation, to fall into the hands of pluralists, absentee rectors, and (later) of provisors. To sub-stitute one abuse for another, however, is not necessarily an advantage, and appropriation no doubt played its part in widening still further the gap between the small class of bene-ficed clerks and the vast clerical proletariat.

The 'church' that has been the subject of the preceding paragraphs is the church of a recognized group of persons and of a delimited district—a 'parish church'. It has been already remarked that the parish churches of medieval England were almost all in existence before 1100; this was stated in negative form towards the end of his life by the scholar of our genera-tion most competent to give such a judgement:[1] 'It would be difficult', he wrote, 'to point with any certainty to a decree which created a new parish.' Granted that before 1250 a bishop's act of this kind might well have disappeared, the judgement is striking when we remember that between the Conquest and the Black Death the population of England more than doubled itself, and that the area under exploitation increased to a striking, if incalculable, extent. Besides the in-nate conservatism, however, which preserved so many pre-Conquest boundaries through the centuries, the economic difficulties in the way of creating a new parish would have been great, and the collision with the vested rights of patron and incumbent considerable. Overhead reforms of this kind were not made easily, save by a ruthless act of power, till the

[1] A. Hamilton Thompson.

nineteenth century. Nevertheless, the need was imperative for more churches, as cottages grew to hamlets, and hamlets to villages five or ten miles from their parish church up a York/shire dale or in the Surrey heathland, or sundered by a river unfordable after heavy rain. It was met chiefly by two processes, working towards the same result in different ways: the one was the enlargement of the lord's chapel in an upland manor, which never became a parish church but developed into a quasi/parish church with a rector admitting dependence upon the mother church; the other was the construction of a parish chapel (the modern chapel/of/ease) with a resident curate ap/pointed by the rector or vicar and directly dependent upon the parish church. Such chapels might originally have had no right of burial (for the burial fee was a noteworthy part of the incumbent's income) and might acknowledge an obligation to visit the parish church on certain annual occasions when oblations were customary. These chapels were as frequently established in growing cities as in remote moorlands; it has been noted that one of the claimants to be 'the most noble parish church in England', St. Mary Redcliffe at Bristol, was in fact during the medieval centuries a 'chapel' to Bedminster.

But if the number of benefices with a rector or canonically established vicar was, if not small, at least finite, the number of priests, even excluding the regulars, was legion. The rector or vicar of a large parish had under him the vicars or 'rectors' of chapelries, as well as at least one 'parish priest', who took something of the place of the modern curate, and probably a deacon to boot. In addition there would be a hospital or two and a chantry and possibly a nunnery, all of which would need priests; it will be remembered how the early editors of Chaucer strove hard to eliminate the 'prestes thre' that the prioress took on pilgrimage with her. In a town or city of fair size, with colleges, guilds, and almshouses added, the clerical numbers would be multiplied out of all proportion (to our eyes) to the population. Some of these, from the vicar downwards, would be substituting for absentees; few could expect to rise far in the economic scale. How did these men come to be or/

dained? What training, intellectual and spiritual, did they have? These are questions which the modern reader inevitably asks, but they touch one of the most obscure points of medieval life, and a satisfactory answer has yet to be given. It has at one and the same time to explain the numerous rectors who could not repeat the *Pater* in Latin and the author of *Piers Plowman* who, though probably only a singing-clerk, had a knowledge of spirituality and of moral problems that would have left many a bishop as astonished as it leaves the reader of today. That the system could produce parish clergy of the type of Chaucer's parson, as well as ruffians, is perhaps not remarkable, for men's capabilities of feeling and of action, enlarged by Christian faith, are not bound by the limitations of educational or administrative systems.

We have seen that the bishops and abbots, who had taken a principal part in the deliberations of the Witan, took an equally important place in the Great Council of the Conqueror, which almost immediately became a feudal gathering of important vassals under their king and lord. This Council remained a function of government for two centuries, changing somewhat in composition; attendance, at least for the abbots, became a burden rather than a privilege, but the obligation of answering the royal summons remained. In the political disturbances of the mid-thirteenth century, when the Council was changing by slow degrees to Parliament, all parties threw their net wide in order to obtain the greatest possible measure of consent to their proceedings, and many abbots and priors, not holding in chief and in many cases holding in free alms, were summoned, and attended. Edward I used this broad-based Parliament for taxation, and swept in a still larger number of ecclesiastics. While the bishops, who necessarily took an important place in public life, and now began to take on themselves a heavy burden of administration, accepted attendance as part of their profession, for most of the religious it was an unprofitable waste of time and money, and they gradually succeeded in ignoring or escaping the call save a nucleus of about twenty, almost all abbots of pre-Conquest houses; and during the reign of Edward

III the principle was established in the courts that ancient and unbroken summons, and that alone, implied the right and duty of attending Parliament. Henceforward this group of regulars, together with bishops almost equal in number and far more important in influence, formed a majority, and at times a considerable majority, in the House of Lords.

Meanwhile, another assembly, known as Convocation, composed of clergy alone and meeting in two provincial gather/ ings, had become formalized. The provincial council was one of the organs of ancient church discipline revived and en/ couraged by the Gregorian reformers, and their celebration was again enjoined by the Fourth Lateran Council. They were held at irregular intervals under archbishops and papal legates during the twelfth and thirteenth centuries. When Edward I began to summon his great gatherings for fiscal purposes, he ordered the bishops to summon similar gatherings of lesser pre/ lates, together with representatives of chapters and the lower clergy. These met simultaneously with Parliament, and an endeavour was made by the king to secure the assent of all to/ gether to taxation. The clergy resisted the demand, as being against the privileges of their order and papal command, but they agreed to deliberate in their own assembly. The practice therefore grew up of summoning a provincial council or con/ vocation (the terms were long interchangeable) to meet either on the same day as, or shortly after, the meeting of Parliament. Ordinarily the two convocations did little but vote, after dis/ cussion and appropriate protest, taxation for the king, but they retained the powers, which they used chiefly in meetings un/ connected with Parliament, of legislation for spiritual persons and affairs. As the courts throughout the middle ages recognized canon law as the code of the Courts Christian and the spiri/ tuality, convocation and Parliament functioned side by side without difficulty, save in the border territory which both com/ mon lawyers and canonists claimed as their own.

It has often been noted that this successful insistence of the clergy in retaining the right to tax themselves was a chief factor in preventing the growth of a third house of Parliament corre/

sponding to the clerical estate in France. An additional factor, sometimes overlooked, may be found in the Old English inter-penetration of Church and State in the persons of the magnates of each, which was continued in the Great Council. This created a solidarity among the lords spiritual and temporal which was not disturbed by the additional ecclesiastics tem-porarily added by the two first Edwards; these, unlike the burgesses and knights of the shire, had no representative impor-tance. It would have required a planned reorganization, wholly out of harmony with the methods of the monarchy or the spirit of the times, to disengage the essential elements from Parlia-ment and convocation and unite them in a single assembly of their own. Convocation therefore remained an essential if lethargic witness and guarantee of the independence of the Church, and its abdication of sovereignty was rightly seen by both More and Cromwell as the end of a chapter.

In the earlier decades of the fourteenth century the number of religious houses in England and Wales, and of religious men and women within them, reached a total which was never sur-passed. The losses in numbers from the Black Death were slowly repaired, but only in part, and although there were a few new foundations—notably a handful of Charterhouses and the Bridgettine Syon Abbey—these were more than offset by the disappearance of a few houses, and the suppression of many of the alien priories. At almost the same time, in the later de-cades of the same century, the administrative organization and the parish and guild life of the medieval Church attained its fullest expansion. The Great Pestilence of 1348–9 has often in the past been regarded as a catastrophe to religion, but in fact the feature that was most characteristic and, as the event proved, most pregnant with consequence in the last medieval centuries—a hierarchy recruited almost exclusively from gov-ernment circles and largely absentee—had nothing to do with the plague, while the most significant of the new appearances—the birth of Lollardy and the flowering of college foundations—were symptoms of energy rather than of decay. It was an accident, if a striking one, that the last medieval archbishop of

Canterbury to rise to that eminence from a combination of personal holiness of life with theological eminence—the profound
Thomas Bradwardine, who sowed much seed that was long in
coming to harvest—should have died of the pestilence a few
weeks after his consecration. The mid-fourteenth century is a
dividing line, not by reason of the plague but because all over
western Europe currents of thought were beginning to flow
that would stream far beyond the dates that have been chosen
to mark the end of the middle ages. Yet it is also true that in
England, at least, and in the English Church, time seemed to
stand still in the fifteenth century in some such way as, in late
August or early September, the course of nature seems to
slacken and windless days pass without apparent change over
the rich countryside till the inevitable storms of autumn come.
Such a comparison is no more than a fancy, but it is at the
beginning of the epoch of formalized government, unspiritual
but not visibly decaying, undisturbed (after Lollardy had been
driven underground) by opposition from without or reform
from within, that we may end this brief survey.

7. The Spiritual Achievement

Much of this short survey has been concerned with the institutional framework of religion. What, we may ask, was the
spiritual life for which alone all this outward show existed, or
should have existed, and which alone gave to it any religious
value and real significance? The historian cannot be God's spy;
the Spirit bloweth where He listeth, we know not why nor
whence. Nevertheless we can say that certain epochs have been
notable for the external manifestation of spiritual power, and
others for its absence. The period of awakening and reform
from 1000 to 1250 was undoubtedly one of remarkable spiritual
renewal and achievement; thenceforward, for more than two
centuries, the August sunshine waned to December.

Speaking very loosely, we may call the century and a half
from 1070 to 1216 the monastic period of English spirituality;
the period, that is, when the monastic ideals and virtues not

only drew multitudes to the cloister but were also the exemplar and inspiration of all others who aspired to a life of holiness among the clergy and layfolk. During this period, and especially perhaps among the ranks of the new Anglo-Norman ruling classes, England could show many examples of sanctity, even if the list is strictly drawn to include only those sainted by papal or popular judgement. Among the men of English blood we have Edward the Confessor, Wulfstan the monk-bishop of Worcester, Godric the hermit of Finchale, Ailred, abbot of Rievaulx, and Waltheof, abbot of Melrose. Of native Anglo-Normans there are Gilbert of Sempringham, Thomas of Canterbury, and Robert of Newminster, and among those of foreign birth who lived and worked in England there are Anselm of Canterbury, Osmund of Salisbury, Gundulf of Rochester, William, first abbot of Rievaulx, and Hugh of Lincoln. To these might easily be added a dozen of acknowledged holiness of life such as Lanzo, prior of Lewes, and Robert of Bethune, bishop of Hereford. Taken as a group, it is a notable list for a country of perhaps a million and a half inhabitants. One comment may be made: no woman saint is among the number, though St. Margaret of Scotland might fairly be included. Neither in this age nor in any other of the later middle ages did England give birth to a Hildegarde, a Clare, or a Catherine.

The thirteenth century was the century of friars and bishops —the former preaching a way of simplicity and poverty, more individual and in a sense more evangelical than what had gone before; the latter presenting the Christian life and virtues as they had been analysed and defined in the schools. Among the early friars there were many examples of sanctity, though from the nature of things only a domestic fame was won. Among the bishops there were several of unusual holiness of life, and it is noteworthy that the only Englishmen of the period to become canonized saints were diocesan bishops, none of whom was a monk or friar. Edmund of Canterbury, Richard of Chichester, and Thomas of Hereford attained the altars of the universal Church; the cause of the great Robert of Lincoln was repeatedly taken to Rome, and that of his successor half a century later, John Dalderby, went there too; these failed, but popular veneration made of their tombs a place of pilgrimage as it did also of the tombs of William of Wells, Roger of London, and Walter of Worcester. The shift of popular sentiment was not misplaced nor accidental, for it was in this century that a race of great bishops laid the foundations of the parish life of England that was to be a notable religious and social force in the following age.

The fourteenth century saw neither monk nor friar nor bishop canonized. The one canonized saint was, significantly enough, the obscure prior of a house of the Austin canons at Bridlington, and his rival in popular devotion was Richard Rolle, the hermit of Hampole. Each in his way was connected with what is the most remarkable external manifestation of English religion at this time, the growth of an attraction to the contemplative life and to a mystical approach to the problems of theology and conduct. This phase of sentiment is seen in the spread of the Charterhouses when other orders had ceased to multiply, and in the deeply introspective outlook of the poets of the age, such as William Langland and the author of *The Pearl*, and above all in the group of writers, of whom Rolle was one and the Austin canon Walter Hilton another, known as the English mystics. In the fourteenth century the monastic spirituality, the theology of the schools, the preaching of the friars, and the reforming labours of the bishops bore fruit in the lives of a multitude of men and women up and down England. Both Hilton and Rolle wrote for layfolk, who were served also by a number of new collections of prayers and devotions. Nor must we forget that new earnestness of thought of which Lollardy is an indication, the first recognizable appearance of that urgent, untutored, racy, fiercely independent, half-sour religious zeal that was to become, under many changing names, such a powerful and characteristic force in English history. But if we set aside the mystics and the zealots, we can find no clearer evidence of the penetration of every aspect of religion into the consciousness of the people of the time than in the works of the two great poets of the age. Chaucer, for all his satire and coarseness, is at every point the unquestioning believer, at home with the devotion of his time and admiring simple piety wherever he sees it. Langland, with a far deeper and more melancholy vision, ponders the mysteries of providence and grace, of the active and contemplative lives, that had exercised Bradwardine and Wyclif and the writer of *The Cloud of Unknowing*, but sees in charity, divine and human, the essence of all religion and the answer to all problems. He and Chaucer are very different in mind and character, yet to both the traditional faith is the foundation of their world, which is the world neither of the Cistercian cloister nor of the conventicle, but of the medieval church, a net holding all manner of fishes.

WORKS FOR REFERENCE

There is no recent or authoritative history of the Church in England, and for many topics and personalities the relevant sections in Stubbs's *Constitutional History* are still of value. Chapters in such volumes as have appeared of the *Oxford History of England* summarize the findings of recent scholarship and briefer (but still valuable)accounts are given in the 'Pelican' books dealing with medieval English history. For the early period (*c.* 500–1189) vols. i and ii of *English Historical Documents*, ed. D. Whitelock and D. C. Douglas (London, 1952, 1955) are of importance. The following books and articles may be mentioned as useful on particular aspects of Church history:

The Old English Church

BOEHMER, H. 'Das Eigenkirchenwesen in England', in *Festgabe für F. Liebermann* (Halle, 1921).

DARLINGTON, R. R. 'Ecclesiastical Reform in the Late Old English Period', in *Eng. Hist. Review*, li (1936).

The Conquest and After

BOEHMER, H. *Kirche und Staat in England und in der Normandie* (Leipzig, 1899).

BROOKE, C. N. L. 'Clerical Marriage in England, 1050–1200', in *Cambridge Hist. Jnl.* xii, p. 1.

BROOKE, Z. N. *The English Church and the Papacy* (Cambridge, 1931).

The Thirteenth Century

DOUIE, D. L. *Archbishop Pecham* (Oxford, 1952).

GIBBS, M., and LANG, J. *Bishops and Reform 1215–1272* (Oxford, 1934).

MOORMAN, J. R. H. *Church Life in England in the Thirteenth Century* (Cambridge, 1945).

POWICKE, F. M. *Stephen Langton* (Oxford, 1927).

The Fourteenth Century

PANTIN, W. A. *The English Church in the Fourteenth Century* (Cambridge, 1955).

PERROY, E. *L'Angleterre et le Grand Schisme d'Occident* (Paris, 1933).

WOOD-LEGH, K. L. *Church Life in England under Edward III* (Cambridge, 1934).

Papal Provision and Taxation

BARRACLOUGH, G. *Papal Provisions* (Oxford, 1935).

DEELEY, A. 'Papal Provision and Royal Rights of Patronage', in *Eng. Hist. Review*, xliii (1928).

LUNT, W. E. *Papal Revenues in the Middle Ages* (New York, 1924); *Financial Relations of the Papacy with England to 1327* (Cambridge, Mass., 1939).

THOMPSON, A. HAMILTON. 'Pluralism in the Medieval Church', in *Associated Architectural Societies' Reports and Papers*, xxxiii, pp. 35–73.

WAUGH, W. T. 'The Great Statute of Praemunire', in *Eng. Hist. Rev.* xxxvii (1922). .

The Religious Orders

COLVIN, H. M. *The White Canons in England* (Oxford, 1951).

DICKINSON, J. C. *The Origins of the Austin Canons* (London, 1950).

GRAHAM, R. *St. Gilbert of Sempringham and the Gilbertines* (London, 1902); *English Ecclesiastical Studies* (London, 1929).

GWYNN, A. *The English Austin Friars* (Oxford, 1940).

HINNEBUSCH, W. A. *The Early English Friars Preachers* (Rome, 1952).

KNOWLES, M. D. *The Monastic Order in England* (Cambridge, 1940); *The Religious Orders in England*, vols. i and ii (Cambridge, 1948, 1955); (with R. N. HADCOCK) *Medieval Religious Houses* (London, 1953).

LITTLE, A. G. *Studies in English Franciscan History* (Manchester, 1917).

Preaching

OWST, G. *Preaching in Medieval England* (Cambridge, 1926).

Administration

CHURCHILL, I. *Canterbury Administration* (London, 1933).

THOMPSON, A. HAMILTON. *The English Clergy and their Organization in the later Middle Ages* (Oxford, 1947).

Devotional Life

Article *Angleterre* in *Dictionnaire de Spiritualité*, ed. M. Viller (Paris, 1932); chapters in *Cambridge Medieval History* and *History of English Literature*; Pantin, W. A., op. cit.

Map

Ordnance Survey *Map of Monastic Britain*; this shows dioceses (with all 'peculiars' and exempt territories) as well as all religious houses, hospitals, and colleges.

XIII. ECCLESIASTICAL ARCHITECTURE

THE first great age of English architecture begins with the last years of the eleventh century and, compared with the building then begun, the architecture of the Anglo-Saxon age seems rather tentative and unformed. This is not to decry its interest. England is fortunate compared with other countries in northern Europe in the possession of surviving buildings of the early Dark Ages and though only one, Brixworth, is of monumental scale, it is enough to give us an idea of the quality and character of the important buildings of whose existence we know only from literary sources. Brixworth church dates from the last quarter of the seventh century (Fig. 100 and Pl. 76). It consists of a nave of four bays, with arches turned in Roman brick opening to what are believed to have been a series of rectangular cells which may have been linked together to form a kind of aisle, but was almost certainly conceived not as one continuous passage but as separate compartments opening off the nave. To the east there was a square unaisled presbytery, originally separated from the nave by an arcade of three arches, and beyond it again a narrower apsidal chancel. The east wall of the presbytery is pierced by a single arch leading to the chancel, flanked by two small windows, and at a later date pierced also by two openings leading down to a passage round a crypt beneath the apse. At the west there was a porch, flanked by chambers to the north and south, though these were subsequently pulled down, as were the chapels flanking the nave. The nave and presbytery are some 30 feet wide in the clear and even in its truncated state, with the arches of the nave walled up, the interior remains, with the eighth-century sculptured friezes at Breedon in Leicestershire, to show that the first heroic age of English church art produced buildings of a scale and quality not altogether unworthy of its achievements in painting and sculpture.

In the tenth century Brixworth church underwent serious modifications. It is probably at this time that the five lateral compartments of the nave were pulled down, and certainly the western porch was raised into a tower. It seems likely that the new floors added above the porch, together with a gallery at the west end of the nave, formed some sort of state pew for a local

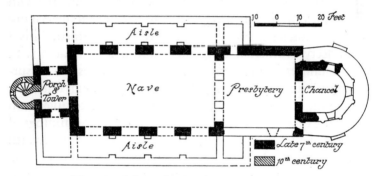

FIG. 100. Brixworth Church. Pre-conquest church

dignitary. There are analogies to this arrangement of the west end both in England and in churches of the Carolingian age on the Continent.

The great outburst of building which began about 1090 owes almost everything, but not quite everything, to the Norman Conquest. This is true both of the general social and economic conditions, which made building on such a scale possible, and of the architectural ideas and techniques with which the builders embodied the energy, ambition, and practical organizing ability that the Normans brought to religion as to every other aspect of life. The old name for the style then developed was Norman, though we now call it Anglo-Norman Romanesque, to indicate the truth that it forms part of a great artistic movement which is shared by all western European countries, and that in England its character differs in many ways from the architecture of Normandy itself. The old name had more than a mere chronological significance, but the

architecture of Normandy at the time of the Conquest was not
an isolated phenomenon, and of recent years it has been increasingly realized that it had a greater variety and drew from
a wider range of sources in central and north-eastern France
than the accidents of survival among major buildings might at
first lead one to suppose. Moreover, the Norman conquerors
were not all Normans and the Conquest quickened relations between England and all northern France and the Low
Countries. The latter seem to have been the most important
source of continental ideas affecting the architecture of the later
Anglo-Saxon period and remained influential after the Conquest. The attention of students, and not only English students,
has been concentrated on Normandy itself and later on the area
round Paris, while the great importance of north-eastern France
and the Low Countries in the history of English architecture
of the twelfth and early thirteenth centuries has been neglected.
This is natural enough, as far more important early buildings
have survived in Normandy and the Paris district, but this
accident has caused a great gap in our knowledge.

The most important surviving examples of architecture of
the late eleventh century in England are the crypt and transepts
of Winchester, the crypt and choir aisles of Gloucester, the
crypt at Worcester (Pl. 77 a), the centre part of the west front at
Lincoln, and the tower, transepts, and part of the nave at St.
Albans. The last ten years of the century show the beginnings
of the great churches at Ely and Norwich, and, most important
of all in quality and achievement, at Durham and Tewkesbury. In addition, we have evidence from excavation and
the study of surviving fragments above ground to fill out the
picture very considerably.

The first characteristic of most of these buildings is their
grandiose scale. This was made possible by the share of the
spoils of the Conquest that eventually came to the Church,
and was occasioned by the appetite for material splendour
in worship which characterized the reforming period in the
Church associated with the name of Cluny.

The influence of Cluny was already strong in Normandy,

and though only four new monasteries actually under the
authority of the great institution itself were founded in England
before 1100, this is no measure of the importance of its example, or even of its direct influence. The reforming movement
was, above all, Roman in spirit, using the word in the sense of
historic sentiment as well as more narrowly, and one of the ideas
for which the Roman name stood was magnanimity as expressed in the scale and ordered splendour of buildings. This
was not altogether a new thing in England in the late eleventh
century; the monastic reform movement of the tenth century
associated with St. Dunstan and St. Ethelwold shared this
feeling and expressed it in buildings of more than considerable
size, though they were far surpassed by those that succeeded
and replaced them. In this connexion the changes made at St.
Augustine's abbey at Canterbury in the tenth and eleventh
centuries as shown by excavation, are particularly interesting
(Fig. 101). The earlier St. Augustine's consisted of a series of
three churches set axially and dating from the earliest years of
Christianity in Saxon England and of great traditional sanctity
as associated with the saint himself. In order, from east to west,
these churches were St. Pancras, St. Mary's, and SS. Peter and
Paul, in the last of which St. Augustine and his early successors
and the Christian kings of Kent were buried. To the west of the
church of SS. Peter and Paul an outer narthex and a further
western porch (making ultimately three in all) were added by
St. Dunstan, thus greatly increasing the splendour of the
ceremonial approaches to the church itself. The capitals from
this western extension show the consciously Roman sentiment
of the builders, being quite clearly an attempt to imitate the
antique Corinthian order. Later, in the time of Edward the
Confessor, the two churches of St. Mary and SS. Peter and
Paul were linked by a new building, an aisled rotunda, circular
inside and octagonal without. To make room for this building
the apse of SS. Peter and Paul was pulled down. After the
Conquest all this was swept away and a single unified building took the place of the two westernmost churches with their
tenth- and eleventh-century additions. Only St. Pancras was

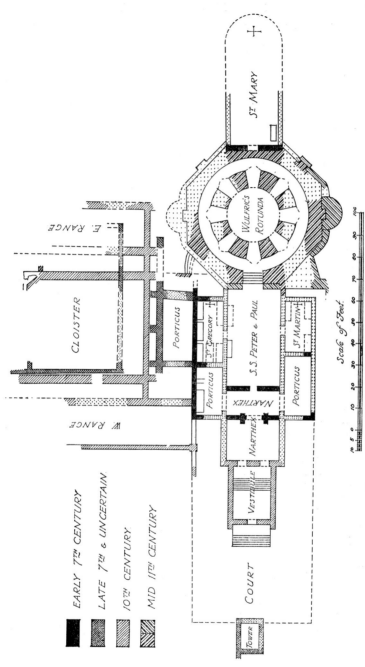

E. RANGE

CLOISTER

W. RANGE

PORTICUS

ST GREGORY

PORTICUS

S.S. PETER & PAUL

NARTHEX

NARTHEX

ST MARTIN

PORTICUS

WULFRIC'S ROTUNDA

ST MARY

✝

VESTIBULE

COURT

TOWER

EARLY 7TH CENTURY

LATE 7TH & UNCERTAIN.

10TH CENTURY

MID 11TH CENTURY

Scale of Feet.

10 5 0   10   20   30   40   50   60   70   80   90   100

FIG. 101. St. Augustine's, Canterbury. Pre-conquest churches

left, a detached building to the east of the enlarged church. A rather similar process seems to have gone on at Glastonbury, where again a very early monastic establishment consisted of a number of small churches laid out axially, which were eventu/ ally linked to form a continuous series of buildings, and lastly, though much later than St. Augustine's, superseded by a great unified scheme. At Glastonbury the legendary sanctity of the early wooden church at the west of the group was so great as to prevent its ever being absorbed completely in any reorganiza/ tion of the building, and even after the complete reconstruction in the late twelfth century it retained its separate identity. These examples, where excavation has shown the actual process of change from the early system of a group of small churches to the single unified building of impressive scale, are perhaps the most telling, but the evidence of Sherborne shows that the tenth century could on occasion produce new buildings of impres/ sive size, for the width of the central vessel of the nave at Sher/ borne, as built at the end of the tenth century, seems to have been the same as that of its Gothic successor which still exists, and the crossing space beneath the central lantern tower was prob/ ably actually reduced in size in the modifications made by Bishop Roger of Sarum in the 1120's. At Winchester, too, the evidence of the size of the great organ, which is recorded as needing seventy men to blow it, implies a building of con/ siderable proportions.

All this evidence from pre/Conquest England only shows that the desire for the single great church of impressive scale was not a new importation from Normandy in the late eleventh century, but unquestionably it was greatly promoted by the wholesale importation of churchmen from the Continent which then took place. The desire was common to all Europe, and it was greater resources, both wealth and technical re/ sources, and perhaps a sense of quickened missionary zeal on the part of the new/comers, which gave to the new outburst of building in England its specially monumental character.

The dimension in which the new churches took on their great increase in size was more particularly length. The new

PLATE 76

Brixworth Parish Church: interior from the west

PLATE 77

a. Worcester Cathedral: crypt

b. Tewkesbury Abbey: nave

Anglo-Norman churches were longer, both east of the crossing and especially west of it in their naves, not only than their Saxon predecessors but than most of the contemporary churches on the Continent, and the greater English churches retained this characteristic throughout the Gothic period. No really satis-factory explanation of this has ever been put forward, and it was as marked at Lincoln, Ely, and Peterborough, where the west end is elaborated in a manner that derives from the practice of late Carolingian times, as it is in the churches which finished simply in a gabled front or two western towers in the later French fashion, so that the additional bays added to the English churches can hardly have been a substitute for these western elaborations. The first example that we know of was the Con-fessor's church at Westminster, which seems to have had a nave of twelve bays arranged in pairs after the manner of the existing cathedral at Durham, deriving probably from Jumièges in Normandy, where, however, there are only eight bays.

The existing buildings of this period, including the great crypts, show two main types of plan. All of them, with the exception of Old Sarum, were cross plans with a central lantern tower at the intersection of the limbs of the cross, the difference between the types being in the treatment of the eastern limb. This was ended either in a series of apses corresponding to the main vessel and the two aisles, or by returning the aisle round the curved end of the central vessel and providing chapels set radially as at Gloucester or tangentially to the curve as at Nor-wich. There were generally apsidal chapels projecting from the eastern side of the transept, and at St. Albans, and its daughter house at Binham in Norfolk, there are two of these to each transept, the inner ones next to the aisles having greater projec-tion than those to north and south of them, the whole eastern part of the church forming a group of seven apsidal-ended spaces set *en échelon*. At St. Albans, the early Lincoln, Old Sarum, and elsewhere the aisles were separated from the main vessel by solid walls. These two systems were both to be found in Normandy in the mid-eleventh century, the three-apsed one being the more common, though such influential buildings in the abbey of Jumièges and the cathedral at Rouen had the aisle returned round the central apse. This latter plan seems to be especially associated with the central regions of France and, indeed, the first example known in England, Battle abbey, near Hastings, begun in 1070/1 and finished within the lifetime of the Conqueror, was colonized by monks from Tours, who are recorded to have personally supervised the building. It is remarkable that there seems to be no sign of any regional distribution of these two types of plan, and at Canterbury the two great contemporary monasteries, Lanfranc's Christchurch and the new St. Augustine's, provide examples of each.

Structurally the most important characteristic of these buildings is their immense massiveness as compared with earlier churches. This is especially marked in England, possibly for economic reasons. The extraordinary outburst of building may well have made for a shortage of skilled labour and so tended to increase the dependence on rubble as against wrought stone. Walls and piers were built of a core of rubble faced with cut stone, and the unribbed vaults of the great crypts are also made in a sort of concrete technique of small stone and mortar brought to a tidy finish with a mortar rendering. Very considerable skill and a realization of the flexibility of this method of vault building appear quite early in these crypts, which, being generally of the apse and ambulatory form, gave rise to complicated shapes in the compartments of their vaults, notably at Winchester and Worcester.

The two great buildings which were begun in the last years of the eleventh century, Tewkesbury abbey and Durham cathedral, though they are both highly individual works, may be taken to represent two aspects of the architecture of the twelfth century. At Tewkesbury the monks were put in possession of their new quarters in 1101, and this means presumably that at least a large part of the eastern end of the church must have been usable by that date. It was, as we know now, built with an eastern limb designed internally in four storeys, consisting of a giant order of cylindrical piers surmounted by arches embracing both the opening into the aisle and above it the opening into the tribune. Above the giant order was a triforium with small double-arched openings, and above that a clerestory. The vestiges of this arrangement can only be deduced by minute examination of the existing choir of the church, which was drastically altered in the fourteenth century, and by a comparison with the remains of the early arrangement in the transept. In the nave the giant order of cylindrical piers and arches was maintained but the tribune was omitted and the great arches of the arcade left open to their full height, the resultant system being three-storeyed rather than four (Pl. 77 b). This highly original arrangement may have derived ultimately from central France, but it had no future in that country though it was certainly imitated in a number of important buildings erected in England and Scotland during the twelfth and early thirteenth centuries. They include Romsey abbey, the cathedral at Oxford, Jedburgh abbey in Scotland, the great church at Glastonbury abbey, and, latest of all, the cathedral at Waterford in Ireland. At Glastonbury and Waterford the scheme is translated into Gothic with pointed arches, and at Romsey the influences of other regions than the Severn basin have profoundly modified the scheme. At Tewkesbury the early pre-Romanesque tradition is clearly perceptible in the broad expanses of plain wall surface which play so large a part in the total effect. The same use of plain wall surfaces is recognizable in other eleventh-century buildings, notably the transept at Winchester, and may be taken as a continuation of an architectural tradition which dates back to Carolingian times and to the Carolingian-type buildings erected in England before the Conquest. It was perceptible also in the treatment of the west end of Lincoln cathedral, which dates from about the same time as the work at Tewkesbury. Tewkesbury has been mentioned first by reason of these old-fashioned traits in what is otherwise a highly original design.

Durham, which has indeed many interesting qualities of treatment which derive from this late Carolingian tradition, is a building which in two important ways anticipates the later development of medieval architecture. There can be no ques-

tion that Durham is one of the most precocious and one of the
most completely assured designs of the early middle ages. It was
designed from the beginning in the 1090's to be covered with
stone vaults, not only in its aisles but also in its main span, and
these vaults were no longer of the concrete groined type such as
are found in the great eleventh-century churches of Germany,
or in the crypt of the other eleventh-century buildings in England, but were from the beginning ribbed vaults, anticipating
by several years the development of such vaults in the Paris area,
where the great steps in the development of the ribbed vault
which led to the early Gothic structural system were to be accomplished (Fig. 102). In addition to this structural precocity,
the design of Durham is also precocious in that it abandons the
simple exploitation of plain wall surfaces in favour of a system
whereby the main parts of the structure are outlined by complicated mouldings, so that the structural forms of the building
are clearly differentiated one from another. This new development is clear enough in the eastern parts of the church which
were first undertaken, but is carried much farther and with increased richness of moulding in the western parts. In addition
to this use of mouldings to define, by clearly-marked lines, the
fundamental structural divisions of the building, Durham also
shows a tendency to break up any broad, plain stone surfaces
with a purely decorative system of linear patterns. The church
is built on a scheme of double bays, consisting of complex
rectangular piers alternating with cylindrical ones (Pl. 78). The
plain surfaces of the cylinders are enriched with a variety of incised lines, spirals, zigzags, or lozenges, or in some places with
shallow ribs in relief, and the aisle walls below the windows,
even in the earlier parts of the church, are adorned with inter-
secting arcading so as to present an interesting continuous linear
pattern. The newly invented ribs of the great vaults suggest
equally a desire to carry this linear definition of the parts of the
building not only over the wall spaces but over the vaults also,
and thereby give a consistent linear quality to the whole interior of the building. It has been suggested that the whole of
developed medieval architecture took its character from the

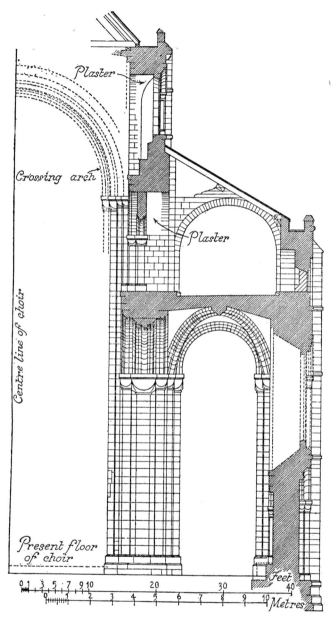

Plaster

Crossing arch

Plaster

Centre line of choir

Present floor
of choir

Feet

Metres

FIG. 102　Durham. Halfcross-section of Chair. North side

desire of the builders to express in line the component parts of the design. If this theory is tenable, Durham stands at the beginning of a development which in France led to some of the greatest achievements of European architecture. But the greatest examples in France are all characterized by a strong sense of direction in the linear embellishments of the building, which are almost always governed by the essential structural system which they adorn. At Durham this is true also, but the purely pattern-making treatment of the plain surfaces without any structural reference is also marked, and this last characteristic was exploited in England and gave its character to the whole development of the medieval architecture in this country down to the end of the thirteenth century and beyond, and distinguishes it from the art of northern France with which in other respects it was so closely allied. The sources of the Durham design can be traced to a variety of places. It is remarkable that throughout the building the cushion capital employed was one which was in common use in Germany and the Low Countries, but hardly known in Normandy at the time that the building of Durham was undertaken. Equally the cushioned capital was familiar in late Saxon architecture, the close connexion of which with the Empire has already been mentioned. This plan, including the system of alternate piers and double bays, can be associated with buildings known in Normandy such as Jumièges, but Jumièges itself is a Norman building with strong affinities outside the province of Normandy and comparable with the work of regions to the east and north. The outstanding quality of Durham, however, apart from the structural ingenuity and daring of its builders, resides in the masterly quality of the synthesis that they have made from what appear to be diverse sources. We are very apt to attribute to one man works of the middle ages which were probably due to the collaboration of several persons. Durham is one of the few buildings and certainly the earliest whose individuality makes this unhistorical approach excusable.

A number of other great monastic buildings were initiated in the last years of the eleventh and first part of the twelfth cen-

PLATE 78

Durham Cathedral: nave

PLATE 79

a. Fountains Abbey, Yorkshire: north
aisle of nave

b. Roche Abbey, Yorkshire: transepts from the north-west

tury, notably Ely, Norwich and, a little later, Peterborough, all in the eastern part of England. In point of scale they are even grander than the great church at Durham, but otherwise they show little of the structural enterprise of that building. In them, however, the tendency noticed at Durham, which was to be of such immense importance to the future of English architecture, was carried even farther in a variety of ways. This tendency was to create an over-all impression of linear pattern by breaking up the main structural forms such as piers with subordinate shafts, pilasters, and mouldings so that the areas of plain surface are reduced to a minimum. This is a progressive tendency and can be traced as between the earlier and later parts of all three churches, and as between Ely, Norwich, and Peterborough, in that order, which is the order of their beginnings. Much dis-cussion has been occasioned by the custom in these designs of dividing each bay from the next with a long, attached, half-round shaft which rises from the ground-level to the top of the clerestory. Writers have speculated as to whether these imply an original intention to vault the main span of the church, which was subsequently abandoned through timidity in favour of a wooden ceiling rather than a stone roof. This seems an unlikely explanation, and whatever the origin of these half-round shafts between the bays it seems likely that they were continued in use because by the sharp division between each bay the linear pattern of the succeeding bays was accentuated. That the pur-pose of this device was probably a matter of taste is made more likely by the fact that in all of these three great churches, and more markedly in the later than in the earlier parts, extra vertical members in the form of half-columns or breaks in the plan of the compound piers are introduced without any struc-tural justification, apparently because the builders liked the look of them, and this habit of design continues far beyond the early Romanesque that we are discussing well into the de-veloped Gothic of the thirteenth century. It is as though the structural relevance of the pattern devised by the master of Durham had few imitators in this country, where the increasing technical mastery of stone-cutting and the great variety of new mouldings which were introduced into architecture in the first third of the twelfth century were exploited largely to increase the effect of all over linear surface pattern. This taste for linear pattern spread over broad surfaces is extremely marked in certain build-ings of the mid-twelfth century, notably in the additions made to the upper parts of the earlier west front at Lincoln and in the treatment of the broad gable-ends of the transepts at the great church at Southwell. It is extremely difficult to determine any regional distribution of these habits of design, except that we can say that the nave of Gloucester cathedral seems to be a ver-sion of the Tewkesbury nave design, but carried out with a use of the new variety of mouldings to emphasize its various parts, and that the most completely developed examples of the taste for breaking up the main masses of the building, notably the great piers of the interior, by minute subdivisions seems more common in the east of England than in the west. Such interiors as that of Southwell nave, which show an awareness of the new taste for enriched mouldings, seem, however, to have deliberately rejected the vertical division into bays and to have held fast to the tradition of the unbroken wall surface which at Tewkesbury and elsewhere seems to be a survival of an earlier architectural tradition.

One structural device of great importance to the future of English medieval architecture was certainly imported from Normandy, most likely from the Caen area, and appears in the transept of Winchester in the late eleventh century. This is a method of giving strength to the clerestory wall by making the upper walls of the building specially thick. So much so that in many cases the wall above the main piers exceeds the thickness of the piers themselves and over-sails on to the haunches of the vaults of the side aisles. The middle storeys of the bays are occupied at tribune level by arches and at clerestory level by an arcaded gallery, thus leaving the thickened wall as a sort of en-larged pier between each bay. This device makes it unneces-sary to provide a special abutment in between each bay on the exterior of the building and in some cases the whole line of the clerestory wall was treated externally with a pattern of blind arcading into which the open arches of the windows were fitted. The arcaded galleries on the internal face of the clerestory wall were linked from bay to bay by low vaulted tunnels through the intervening masses of masonry. It seems that this system once imported from Normandy appealed to the desire for decoration which characterized the architecture of the twelfth century and was exploited with enthusiasm by English builders, who continued the system well into the thirteenth century. One of the latest and most developed examples is the late thirteenth-century eastern extension of Lincoln cathedral, where the clerestory consists of two planes of tracery, one in the outer face of the wall glazed, the other on the inner face open. This system of thick double walls to the clerestory, with arcaded galleries on the inside, seems to have been abandoned com-paratively early in Normandy in favour of the elaborated but-tress system which was being developed in the Paris area, and its survival and increased use in England is the more remarkable.

In the second quarter of the twelfth century the Cistercian order founded its first House in England. The order was par-ticularly successful in this country and a series of great houses grew up, notably in the north, and almost equally in Wales and on the Welsh borders. The first Cistercian buildings, especi-ally the two Cistercian abbeys, Rievaulx and Fountains, show that the new order imported its architectural ideas almost wholesale from Burgundy, the region of France where the order took its rise. At Rievaulx we know the form of the early nave from excavations, and at Fountains the nave has, in the main, survived (Pl. 79 a). The Rievaulx nave was of extreme architectural severity and very close indeed to such early Bur-gundian Cistercian churches as Fontenay. Two character-istics in particular recall Burgundy, the use of pointed barrel vaults set transversely to the direction of the church, and the consequent employment of the pointed arch for the main arcades. At Rievaulx the pointed barrel vaults appear to have been constructed as continuations of the soffits of the arcade arches. At Fountains both these devices are found in a slightly more sophisticated form and there are signs that the Burgundian traits are being modified by the influence of the native Anglo-Romanesque, chiefly by the introduction of mouldings of Anglo-Norman character. The church at Fountains also, while clearly related to that of the great French Cistercian churches, shows one important departure undoubtedly deriving from the later Anglo-Norman practice, that is, the church was given a very distinct crossing-space at the intersection of the four main limbs of the church. Such a crossing clearly implies a tower, and this is the more remarkable as towers were one of the architectural features expressly forbidden by the regulations of the order. The naves of Rievaulx and Fountains belong presumably to the 1130's or possibly early 1140's. In the Cistercian churches of the 1150's and 60's, such as Kirkstall in the north and Buildwas in Shropshire, the Anglo-Norman traits are far more marked, and not only in the mouldings but also in the introduction of the ribbed vault, which is used together with the pointed barrel form.

The prestige of the Cistercian order in the north, particularly during the lifetime and immediately after the death of St. Ailred of Rievaulx, had a great influence which was not confined to the Houses of the order alone, and in 1170 a new architectural phase makes its appearance at Roche abbey, a Cistercian house in south Yorkshire (Pl. 79 b). This represents a second importation of French ideas, this time not Burgundian Romanesque but north French Gothic. The new fashion set at Roche soon spread to other buildings, such as the Canon's church at Ripon and the great new Cistercian house at Byland, and from there spread throughout northern England and Scotland, as much in the buildings of the Augustinian canons as in those of the Cistercians themselves. This architectural movement in the north was characterized by a quality of elegance and sophisticated Puritanism which may possibly be associated with the personality of St. Ailred and his followers, but it is interesting to note that even at Ripon, which was begun within a very few years of Roche, the design, though clearly deriving from the Cistercian building, shows a tendency to greater elaboration, especially in the direction of linear pattern-making, and this tendency continues and grows throughout the later twelfth and early thirteenth centuries. The example of Ripon is a peculiarly marked one, as Archbishop Roger of York, who began the rebuilding of the church, had only a few years earlier carried out works at his own metropolitan church in York in a most sumptuous and ornamental Anglo-Norman Romanesque manner. Equally, though the restrained elegance of the Cistercian fashion ultimately prevailed in this region, it was not unchallenged, and the evidences of the remains of sculpture from St. Mary's abbey at York show all and more than all of that richness of representational decoration against which St. Bernard and St. Ailred had both inveighed.

In planning, the early and middle years of the twelfth century show a very important development which was to influence the whole character of English church architecture in subsequent centuries. This was the gradual abandonment of the apsidal-ended plan, whether the three-apsed or the apse and ambulatory plan, in favour of a rectangular treatment of the eastern parts of the church. There are three main variations of this: the simple rectangular presbytery projecting one or two bays beyond the aisle ends; the treatment whereby both aisles and the main vessel are carried out and finished off square to the east in a great flat eastern façade; and a third system in which the aisles are returned at right angles round the east end of the main vessel, forming an ambulatory, sometimes double the width of the aisles themselves, so as to accommodate chapels on the eastern side. No completely satisfactory explanation of this development away from the apsidal treatment has yet been found. At Chertsey, at Southwell, and in the reconstruction of the cathedral of Old Sarum in the 1120's, rectangular eastern arrangements were adopted before any question of Cisterican influence could arise, but it seems unquestionable that the influence of the early Cistercian church, which implies a rectangular treatment of the presbytery, often even simpler than any of the types already described (the aisles of Cistercian churches were often not carried farther east than the transepts), greatly reinforced the tendency to abandon the earlier apsidal treatment in favour of the new square-ended forms. By the end of the twelfth century the rectangular fashion of planning had triumphed almost completely. The effect of this development in planning was widespread and continued throughout the middle ages, and gave to English church-building some of its most remarkable opportunities in the great eastern façades which have no parallel in continental Gothic.

Contemporary with the building of the Cistercian church at Roche the monks of Christchurch, Canterbury, were compelled to rebuild the eastern parts of their church as a result of a disastrous fire in 1174. This is one of the most remarkable enterprises of the twelfth century, not only in scale and splendour but because we have a very full and business-like account of the circumstances in which the work was undertaken and carried on, written by a man who took part in the organization of the building work. A mason from northern France was imported to carry out the rebuilding, which was conditioned to some extent by the desire of the monastic body to retain as much as possible of the pre-existing building. The plan consisted of a choir of five bays to the east of the great transept, an eastern transept and crossing, a presbytery of four bays, and then an eastern chapel of two bays and an apse, the aisle being returned round the apse in the French fashion. To the east of the returned aisle a circular chapel projects flanked by two staircase turrets. The outer walls of the western part of this great building, the size of a major church in itself, belong to the pre-fire building, and the plan, with its eastern transept and two chapels placed north and south one bay farther to the east, derives from that period. The whole of the internal effect of the main body and eastern transepts was, however, due to the new French mason and the English mason who succeeded him after he had been injured in an accident. It has even been said that the mason, William of Sens, imported at Canterbury the Parisian style as it had been developed at that time, and this is certainly true of such important features as the capitals of the great piers and the character of the vaulting, which is of the type known as sexpartite (i.e. with an extra transverse rib in each bay, meeting the diagonal ribs at the centre). But it is curious to note that the structural system as a whole appears to be a curious compromise between the Anglo-Norman thick-wall system and the newly developed buttress structure of northern France. However this may be, undoubtedly Canterbury was a major means of the introduction of up-to-date French ideas which had immense influence throughout the country. One characteristic of the Canterbury work was particularly influential; that was the use of special marble-like stone imported from Dorset for use in the subordinate shafts, so as to enhance the effect of the linear pattern made by these shafts by the contrast of their textures and colour with that of the main stone used in the building. This fashion of contrasting materials for the subordinate shafts and the main building material which formed their background had an immediate success and was imitated far and wide, first at Chichester and Rochester, then on an exaggerated scale at Lincoln, and from thence spread all over the country in the course of the thirteenth century. It is likely that the scheme came originally from the north-eastern part of France and the adjacent parts of the Low Countries where there was an abundant supply of black marble from Tournai, but the destruction of much of the important medieval building in those areas has rather obscured the question. The prestige of the great cathedral monastery at Canterbury, more particularly in the years following the martyrdom of St. Thomas Becket, ensured that its example should be known and imitated far and wide. The most ambitious of the early imitations was that begun by St. Hugh at Lincoln in 1192, when the rebuilding of the eastern parts of the great cathedral church was undertaken. In plan the eastern parts of Lincoln as begun at that time are very clearly derived from the new work at Canterbury, and the imitation extends to details of capitals, of the vaulting in parts of the church, and above all to the prodigal use of Purbeck marble for subordinate shafts. Two interesting and significant departures from the Canterbury model can, however, be observed at Lincoln. First, the number of subordinate shafts is increased, sometimes without any structural justification, and the effect of linear pattern-making is much more strongly marked than at Canterbury. Secondly, though the sexpartite system of vaulting is to be found in the eastern transepts and rather later in the great transepts themselves which followed the re-erection of the eastern limb of the church in the early years of the thirteenth century, the main vessel of the eastern limb was vaulted with an original system of ribbed vaults, the purpose of which seems to have been to provide a consistent pattern of ribs both for the normal bays of the choir itself and for the larger bay of the eastern crossing and thereby to avoid the interruption of the pattern of the vaulting, which is a marked feature of the Canterbury design, where the system changes from sexpartite to quadripartite at that point.

Work on the church at Lincoln seems to have been continued steadily throughout the greater part of the thirteenth century. The great transepts which were in building in the early years of the century, one of the most remarkable features of the church, are of exceptional breadth and aisled both east and west. Work on the nave continued during the 1220's and 1230's, and in the early 1240's, under the episcopate of the celebrated Grosseteste, the western parts of the church were reached and the central lantern tower was rebuilt. The character of the work remains remarkably consistent throughout in spite of important changes, notably in the character of the vaults and in the greater richness of the bay design, especially at the tribune level and in the clerestory (Pl. 80 a). At the west end of the church the remarkable late eleventh-century western block, which had already been enlarged and enriched in the mid-twelfth century, was profoundly modified by having its western face framed by a great screen wall which extended considerably farther to the north and south and rose to a level parapet line at the height of the twelfth-century gables. These alterations were in part made necessary by the greater height of the new thirteenth-century nave, but also offered a space for large chapels built flanking the west end of the church to the north and south outside the aisles. The nave vault shows

PLATE 80

a. Lincoln Cathedral: nave from the
south transept

b. Wells Cathedral: nave

PLATE 81

a. Peterborough Cathedral: the great west portico

b. Salisbury Cathedral: chapter house
interior

an interesting development from the experimental character of the vaults farther to the east. There is a longitudinal ridge rib to which five ribs spring from each side, and a short transverse ridge rib which stops at a point where it is met by two additional ribs. The effect of the transverse ridge ribs and the large boss at the central point of each bay is to place the main interest of the pattern in the middle of the bay rather than at the transverse rib dividing one bay from another. This tends to emphasize the continuity of the pattern of ribs in the length, as against the sexpartite system used in the transepts, where the division into bays is very clearly marked. Moreover, the multiplication of ribs, as compared with a continental church of the same age, extraordinarily reinforces the impression that the main preoccupation of the designers of these vaults was the continuity of linear surface pattern.

Almost exactly contemporary with Lincoln, the canons of Wells began the reconstruction of their church. The scale of the building was much less ambitious than Lincoln and the eastern limb, the transepts, and a considerable part of the nave seem to have been completed by about 1215 or shortly after (Pl. 80 b). As originally built, Wells had a square east end with the aisle returned round the east end of the main vessel to form an ambulatory with chapels opening off it to the east. That this was the original plan of the late twelfth-century church is fairly well established, though the whole of the eastern part of the church was profoundly modified in the early fourteenth century. During the 1220's and 1230's the nave of the church was continued westward and the whole work was completed by the celebrated west front, with its towers, which flanked the aisles of the nave to the north and south. The earlier Wells work is entirely different in character from the Canterbury-derived style of Lincoln. It is carried out consistently in one-coloured freestone and is distinguished for the high quality of its sculptural decoration, notably in the foliage capitals which in the transepts contain a large number of small genre figure subjects and grotesques. The plan of the piers, with their groups of triple attached shafts, and especially the treatment of the triforium openings, is very typical of a west country school of design which can be traced at Malmesbury from about 1150, at the neighbouring great church of Glastonbury, and at various other important buildings in the lower Severn basin and South Wales. Though the Wells work has so strong a regional character and seems to represent a different tradition from that of Canterbury and Lincoln, French influences are almost as marked in the design as at Canterbury itself. This is very clearly seen in the character of the clerestory treatment and of the vault. The clerestory has, indeed, a passage in normal Anglo-Norman tradition, but whereas at Lincoln everything is done to exploit this feature with elaborate arcading, everything is done at Wells to minimize its effect and almost to deceive the spectator into supposing that a French galleryless clerestory existed. The original form of the clerestory windows at Wells—rather broadly proportioned lancets —and the form of the middle storey of the eastern limb and parts of the transept, equally suggest French influence, but rather of the kind that is represented by Roche and may well also have come through some Cistercian building as an intermediary. The vault is also rather French in character, being a simple quadripartite ribbed treatment, very accomplished but, as compared with the many-ribbed vaults of Lincoln, curiously inconsistent with the elaborate linear treatment of the lower parts of the interior elevation. Wells before the fourteenth century had a bold and well-designed lantern tower over the crossing, a feature which is common to almost all the great churches of the twelfth and thirteenth centuries in England. The most celebrated features of Wells cathedral are the north porch of about 1215 and the great west front, which was being finished about 1240. The north porch, which is the main ceremonial entrance to the church, is the most sumptuous example of the later work of the west country school of masons mentioned above. The west front, however, with its elaborate detached shafts of special material, shows a complete breakaway from this regional style and implies the influence of either Lincoln or Canterbury. This most celebrated of English medieval façade designs is partly distinguished from the great façades built in northern France in the first half of the thirteenth century by the fact that it is not intended to embody a ceremonial en-trance to the church, which was provided by the north porch. The façade is therefore treated as a great screen of figure sculp-ture in tiers, and the three doorways, corresponding to the main vessel of the nave and the two aisles, are kept very small in re-lation to the total height of the façade; indeed, the aisle doors do not reach above the plinth mouldings and the central door only just above them. This device gives an extraordinarily enhanced sense of scale to the whole composition. Wells is fortunate as compared with other great thirteenth-century churches in that its façade has retained almost all its original figure sculpture, much of it of very high quality.

The other great church which has retained a façade of the early thirteenth century of importance comparable to Wells is the great monastic church at Peterborough. The Peterborough front is one of the most original compositions which survive to us from the middle ages (Pl. 81 a). The completion of this great Anglo-Norman church was begun in the last quarter of the twelfth century when work on the two western towers originally intended was discontinued; the nave was then carried west-ward two further bays and a western transept to the full height of the main vessel of the church was begun (Fig. 103). In the first years of the thirteenth century the work was continued on the western transept, and a great portico, equal in length and height and almost equal in width to the new transept, was built to the west of it. The portico is open to the west with three great arches, the two outside ones being wider than that in the centre. These arches rise the whole height of the portico and transept, some 73 feet. They are flanked by two slender towers and surmounted by three elaborate gables, having tall, spire-like pinnacles be-tween them. The original intention was that the composition should be completed with two substantial western towers rising behind the gables of the portico above the bays of the western transept, corresponding to the aisles of the nave. Only one of these towers was built and has now lost the wooden spire which was probably intended to finish it. This extremely original de-

sign appears to be in some ways a Gothic derivative of the west
front of Lincoln as then existing, that is, with the eleventh-

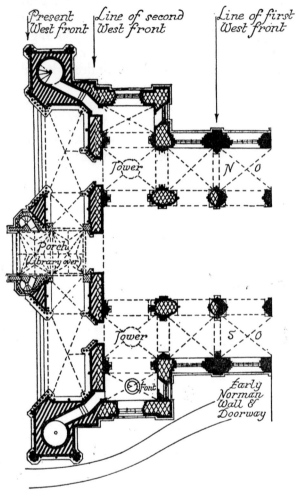

FIG. 103. Peterborough Cathedral: plan of Western Transepts and
Great Portico

century western building enriched and enlarged in the mid-
twelfth century. A certain amount of sculpture originally
adorned the slender flanking towers and the western face of the
wall dividing the portico from the transept and has survived in

the upper parts of the composition. Evidence of the original treatment with figure sculpture also still remains in the other parts. The Peterborough façade, the additions to the west front of Lincoln made in the 1240's, and, as it seems, the south façade of the great transept which was built at York minster in the middle years of the century, probably inspired by the Lincoln transepts, all share a manner of treating their decorative figure sculpture in relation to the architectural lines of the composition. The figures are placed on brackets against a flat, broad wall sur, face and are framed in a relatively delicate linear system of arcades. At Wells the sculpture is treated rather differently and the main figures are placed in tabernacle,like housings with gable tops. These give a far greater sense of design in depth than the more clearly linear treatment at Peterborough and Lincoln, and seem to point the way to the elaborate niche compositions of the late thirteenth and fourteenth centuries.

At its first setting,out the designers of the new church at Wells made provision for a chapter,house to the north of the choir; this was to be an octagonal building raised on an under, croft. Only the undercroft, however, was completed in the early part of the thirteenth century, and the chapter,house itself was not finally built until about a hundred years later (Pl. 82). In the meanwhile, however, an early thirteenth,century chap, ter,house of polygonal plan was built on a large scale at Lin, coln. This was placed to the north of the church and provided with a large and elaborate rectangular vestibule which rises to the full height of the chapter,house itself. The chapter,house at Lincoln is a decagon with pairs of lancets in each side. It is vaulted to a central column with an elaborate ribbed vault. It measures some 59 feet across. The fashion for polygonal chapter,houses seems to have been initiated in the early twelfth century by the work at Worcester, where, however, the build, ing is a rotunda vaulted to a central column, but the circular plan was soon translated into a polygon at Margam and a little later at Abbey Dore (two Cistercian houses) which were both examples with twelve sides. The most celebrated examples of the polygonal chapter,house are the great octagons at West, minster abbey, completed in the early 1250's, and at Salisbury, finished about fifteen years later (Pl. 81 *b*). This form of chapter-house seems to be a peculiarly English invention and became extremely popular, fine examples continuing to be built well on into the fourteenth century and beyond.

The second quarter of the thirteenth century was a period of very active building enterprise, and in the work then under-taken at such buildings as Salisbury, Beverley, Worcester, Southwell, and many others, the influence of the fashion for elaborate pattern-making, with boldly projecting and deeply cut mouldings, and detached shafts of special marble, which has been traced from Lincoln and Canterbury, spread to all parts of the country. The work of this period is characterized by an increasing richness of detail, and this is particularly marked in the eastern extension built at Ely, where work was in full swing in 1239. This increasing decorative elaboration begins to foreshadow the new developments which were profoundly to change the character of English church architecture in the second half of the century. One other factor of extreme impor-tance, however, must be reckoned as the chief instrument of that change. This is the new type of large traceried window first found at Binham priory in Norfolk, a daughter-house of St. Albans, where the window dates from about 1240. This type of window had been in use in France for more than twenty years, but the English builders had remained attached to their peculiar national form of tall, narrow lancet window, a type possibly originating with the Cistercians and possibly ulti-mately of Burgundian origin. Appropriately enough, the finest examples of the use of lancets are to be found in the north, in such compositions as the eastern façades of Whitby and Tyne-mouth and in many fine examples in Scotland and the Border country. Both in Scotland and in the north the vogue of the lancet continued almost to the end of the thirteenth century and delayed in those regions the adoption of the new French fashion which came in, naturally enough, through the influence of the court and in the London area. The great exemplar of the new fashion in windows was the new church built by

PLATE 82

Wells Cathedral: section through chapter house and choir

PLATE 83

a. Lincoln Cathedral: east front of Angel Choir

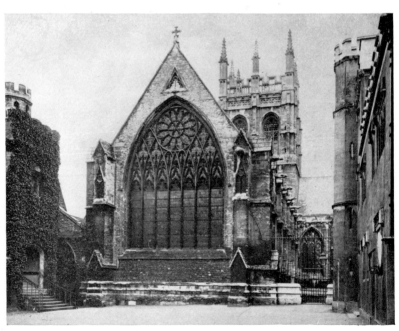

b. Merton College, Oxford: east window of chapel

Henry III at Westminster, when he took over the work in 1244 and carried out a complete reconstruction of the main parts of the church, together with a part of the cloister and a new chapter-house, completing the work, which included several bays of the nave, by 1269. Westminster abbey is in many ways an extremely French design; it is a return to the apse and ambulatory plan which had almost completely gone out of use in England since the mid-twelfth century, though at Westminster it is revived in the developed form of contemporary French churches. All the windows in the church are traceried on a geometrical system consisting of a pair of foiled lancet lower lights surmounted by a circular foiled figure above. The most remarkable Westminster windows were, however, in the chapter-house, which was an octagon in plan, and henceforward the octagonal form generally prevails as giving better opportunities for the new fashionable windows than would be afforded by a greater subdivision of the walls.

Beside the plan and the very tall, rather narrow proportions of the main vessel of Westminster, both French characteristics, and the introduction of the French type of traceried window, King Henry III's building was revolutionary also in its decorative treatment. It is traditional that he was attempting to rival St. Louis's splendid chapel in his palace at Paris, which was, however, begun a year after Westminster, though completed within three years. One of the outstanding qualities of the design of the Sainte Chapelle was the elaboration of its internal colouring, the whole surface of the stonework of the building being coloured or gilded. Equally at Westminster the decorative treatment of the interior is carried a stage farther than in any of the immediately preceding or contemporary English buildings. It is, moreover, different in character, the emphasis being rather on quality of texture and colour than on linear pattern. This is clearly seen if one considers the treatment of a single bay of the main vessel of the church. The piers of the arcade are entirely of Purbeck marble, a material valued for its colour and texture; the arches are very elaborately moulded even for English thirteenth-century work and the spandrels of the arcade are filled with an elaborate diaper pattern in low relief. The middle storey, which is a tribune—that is, a practical upper storey to the aisles, having its own windows—has elaborately moulded and enriched arches filled with a geometrical tracery pattern, and the spandrels of the tribune arches are again treated with diaper. It is only in the clerestory, which in the French fashion was almost entirely filled with a traceried window, that any plain, unenriched masonry is to be found, and the proportions of the church are such that these plain surfaces hardly tell from the viewpoint of the floor. How far the carved work of the middle storey and the diapers of the spandrels were coloured is questionable; certainly where figure sculpture was employed, as in the transept ends, these were treated in full colour, and it is reported that in some parts of the church diaper was painted with gold and red, though it seems unlikely that this is true of anywhere except the actual presbytery. The decorative treatment extended equally to the treatment of the aisle walls, which have elaborate blind arcadings with foliage or figure sculpture in the spandrels. Certain important features of the church, including the great ceremonial entrances to the north transept and the doors from the cloister through the chapter-house vestibule and the door within the chapter-house itself, were treated with figures and foliage sculpture arranged in a manner which clearly derives from the practice of manuscript illuminators. Indeed, the building as a whole gives the impression of being largely conceived in terms of painted decoration and special materials chosen for their texture. This characteristic continues in the English architecture of the rest of the thirteenth century and is one of the most important elements in the type of architecture which reached its full maturity in the first half of the fourteenth century. Westminster abbey, as the personal work of a splendour-loving king, is of course much the most extreme example of this new taste. It was, moreover, a building very celebrated in its time and so placed as to exercise the widest influence throughout the country—for example, from an early date Parliament and other great national assemblies were held in the new chapter-house. The continuation and development of the decorative tradition established at Westminster can be traced clearly enough. The French fashions introduced by the king's builders are somewhat more elusive. Certainly the French type of apse and ambulatory plan had little or no lasting effect in this country, but the tall, narrow proportions are liable to appear in works of the late thirteenth and early fourteenth centuries where there is some direct court influence; notable examples seem to be the lady chapel at Lichfield and the new choir at Gloucester, both buildings of the fourteenth century. Another French trait which is perpetuated is the continuance of the lines of the vaulting shafts right down to the lower parts of the internal elevations, even on occasion right down to the ground level, though these devices may be explained as a means of emphasizing the vertical lines of the building in lieu of the tall and narrow lancets which provided the strongest vertical lines in the designs of the earlier part of the century; when such lancets were superseded by the new broad-traceried windows some means had to be found to restore the vertical emphasis in the composition. A notable example of this seems to be the design of the nave at York minster, a work begun in the last years of the thirteenth century. Of direct imitations of Westminster—or rather of features of the Westminster design —the most outstanding examples are the new north transept at Hereford, built in the 1260's, and certain characteristics of the nave at Lichfield.

The two greatest building enterprises of the second half of the thirteenth century—for the nave of York was not begun until 1290—were the eastern extension of Lincoln cathedral, which was begun in 1256 and to which St. Hugh's body was translated in 1280, though work continued on the building until after 1300, and Exeter cathedral, which was begun from the east end about 1270 and continued on a very consistent scheme until the nave was completed about 1350, the west front being added in the last years of the century. The Lincoln work is largely a very enriched version of the eastern extension of Ely but with certain characteristics—notably the angels in the spandrels of the middle storey—which appear to be related to the Westminster treatment; it is, however, profoundly different from Ely in that the fashion for the great traceried window is exploited at Lincoln on a colossal scale. The great east window of the church (Pl.83 *a*), as occasioned by the continuance of the main vessel at full height to the extreme east end, is one of the largest ever constructed and is the first of the colossal traceried windows which give a special character to the buildings of the east and north of England in subsequent years. The Lincoln window is of eight lights, treated as a series of lancets sur-mounted by foiled circles, a geometrical method of composi-tion common in France, and at Lincoln possibly derived from Westminster, which was soon to be superseded by far more varied and ingenious systems of design. Above the main east window at Lincoln is a second window lighting the space above the vaults. This window, though still based on the lancet and foiled circle motif, has five lights and, this being an odd number, indicates one of the forces which tended to break up the perfect geometry of the early traceried patterns. Later thirteenth-century windows employed a greater variety of geometrical motifs, such as trefoils, small dagger-shaped openings, a pro-digal use of cusping to the lancet shapes themselves, and an astonishing variety of patterns composed of those elements, a favourite device being to incorporate one large circular figure within a surrounding network of trefoils, almost as if the motif of a small rose window were embodied in the traceried pattern. There are good examples of this at Merton College, Oxford, (Pl. 83 *b*), at the very end of the century, and rather earlier in the east window of the lady chapel at Exeter. These varied de-veloped geometrical traceries were never, in fact, entirely super-seded, but in the first years of the fourteenth century the use of the double-curve or ogee led to a new type of tracery with flow-ing lines and an even greater freedom of composition which seems to anticipate the flamboyant windows of the fifteenth century on the Continent. One early form of developed geo-metrical tracery met most frequently in the west of England has been called the reticulated, filling the upper part of the window with trefoil or quatrefoil figures of equal size, giving the effect of a network. Good early examples are to be found in the eastern parts of Wells, dating from just before 1300. The builders of the second half of the thirteenth and first half of the fourteenth centuries show an extraordinary fecundity of invention both in the geometrical tradition and in the freer-flowing patterns. The development of these large windows gave a new character to the whole of the architecture of this period, as the complicated linear patterns of these traceried designs were concentrated in the areas of the window heads and so tended towards a general conception of a design of contrasting areas enriched with linear pattern and plain areas of stonework to set them off. This is very noticeable in early fourteenth-century compositions such as the exterior of the choir of Selby abbey in Yorkshire. This seems to be a development of that change from the all-over linear pattern which characterizes the architecture of the first half of the thirteenth century and is anticipated by the attention given to surface textures in the design at Westminster. With the growth of this feeling for surface textures and the greater amount of light admitted to the buildings by the new large windows came a change in the mouldings and eventually also in the character of the carved decorations, such as capitals. The early thirteenth-century system of pronounced roll mouldings and deep-cut hollows—a device suitable for the linear treat-ment then in vogue—is superseded in the latter part of the century by broader mouldings with shallower hollows and less-pronounced projections, sometimes even broad mouldings of double curvature employing the new fashionable ogee curve. These later thirteenth- and fourteenth-century mouldings are subtler in effect than the earlier type and also more suited to show off the colour, and especially the gold, with which they were often enriched. The change in the nature of the foliage carving on capitals seems to follow a similar course. From West-minster onwards one finds examples of the extreme naturalism in foliage carving which appears rather earlier in France; but about the end of the century a new stylization sets in in which the surface of the leaves is given a rippling effect calculated to make the most of the gilding and colour with which they were

to be adorned. Good examples of this are to be found in the
early fourteenth century in the alterations to the east end of
Wells, notably in the capitals of the ambulatory piers. Some
of these changes are already to be observed in the earlier parts of
Exeter, notably the contrasting patterned areas of the window-
heads and the plain ashlar which surrounds them and in the
way the Purbeck marble is used in the piers, the attached shafts
of which are all much less boldly projecting than the earlier
Purbeck shafts of Lincoln and its early thirteenth-century contemporaries. As in the case of Westminster it seems clear that
the material is being used not for the contrast of its colour,
which would reinforce the linear pattern, but for the quality of
its surface texture.

Another development of the late thirteenth and early fourteenth centuries which seems to be connected with this change
of taste appears in the planning and general distribution of the
buildings. At Wells in the last years of the thirteenth century a
reconstruction of the whole east end of the church was undertaken; this was finally completed about 1335 (Fig. 104). The
original form of the east end of Wells was, as mentioned above,
that its aisle returned square round the east end of the presbytery. The new building included a lengthening of the presbytery, the addition of transeptal chapels projecting north and
south from the ends of the choir aisles, and the building of a lady
chapel projecting from the new ambulatory to the east. The
lady chapel, the first part of the new work to be undertaken, is
in the form of an elongated octagon, the east end of which in-
terpenetrates with the ambulatory as it returns across the end of
the new presbytery. The lady chapel is of considerably greater
internal height than the adjacent parts of the ambulatory and in
consequence this interpenetration produces a relation of internal spaces of extraordinary complexity, and it is managed
most ingeniously. It is clear that the new building is intended to
provide a great variety of vistas from different viewpoints and
represents a breakaway from the logical geometrical planning
of the earlier Gothic buildings. Also in the earlier fourteenth
century a new porch was added to the church of St. Mary

Redcliffe at Bristol, or rather, the existing early Gothic porch was enlarged by the addition of a domed hexagonal outer porch, again producing on a smaller scale an effect of variety and contrast of spaces as between the new building and

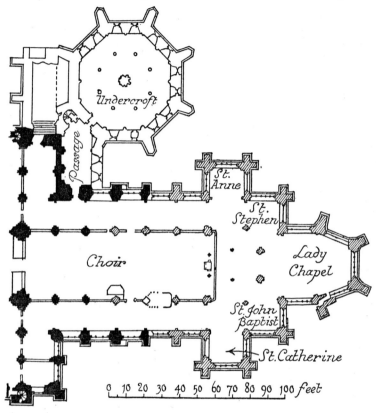

FIG. 104. Wells Cathedral: Plan of choir and eastern extension

the simple rectangular vaulted structure to which it was attached. Perhaps the most grandiose example of this fashion was undertaken at Ely cathedral as a result of the accident in 1322 when the central tower fell, destroying the older—i.e. western—part of the original eastern limb. In the rebuilding of the crossing and central tower an octagon some 70 feet across was devised by taking into the crossing space one bay of each of the main limbs of the church. This great octagonal central

space was covered in by a wooden roof surmounted by an open
lantern, one of the most remarkable feats of structural engineer-
ing in European architecture. The effect is to break up the
logical rectangular system of planning which had been inherited from the late eleventh century when the great church was
first undertaken. The construction of the octagon roof and
lantern is, with the roof of Westminster hall built some years
later, the best known and most spectacular of the great timber
constructions of that age. It is not, however, the first. In the last
decade of the thirteenth century a new chapter-house was
undertaken at York and this is 58 feet across, covered with a
wooden roof without internal support, ceiled in imitation of
vaulting. The York chapter-house has round seven of its sides
a series of canopied stalls, the canopies having bayed fronts,
part octagon in plan, so giving the effect of a rippling line
around the great building immediately below the window
level. This is a good and early example of the tendency to dissolve the logical structural lines of a building of which the
planning at Wells and Bristol are more complicated and
elaborate examples. The same tendency appears in the hand-
ling of the clerestories at Exeter and later, in the early fifteenth
century, at Winchester, where the traditional way of treating
the clerestory in two planes, an inner arcaded gallery and an
outer arcade containing the window, is abandoned in favour
of a gradual stepping-in from the inner wall to the plane of the
window so as again to produce a rippling effect down the
length of the church. This tendency to develop effects in depth
or in the thickness of the walls is to be seen in the exploitation of
niche forms as well as in the treatment of the jambs of windows.
One of the most remarkable of all these niche compositions is
to be found at the east end of Howden (Pl. 84), a composition
with a great eastern façade, comparable to, though not as large
as, that of Lincoln. In it the great east window is surrounded
by a pattern of elaborately decorative niches which not only
provide the contrast of areas of plain and enriched stone surface
but also of a play of light and shade between the outer surface
of the wall and the shadowed recesses of the niches. The most

remarkable examples of this new fashion are, however, to be found in the smaller objects, such as tomb canopies and church furniture, the sedilia at Bristol cathedral and the tomb of Edward II (Pl. 85) being amongst the most striking. The Bristol sedilia have a series of tall finials alternating with free-standing figures surmounting the canopies and, set well behind them, a row of niches which provides a shadowed background to the figures rather than an enclosing frame. The tomb canopy of Edward II at Gloucester is so contrived that the miniature buttresses are set at an angle to the tomb chest and attached to the inner canopies by a series of miniature flying buttresses. Owing to the angle at which the vertical buttresses are set these flyers are seen on a diagonal view and so lead the eye inwards towards the upper stages of the canopy and its pinnacles, a curious example of diagonal composition rather than the more normal series of parallel planes one behind another.

The generation that saw the development of these new archi-tectural tendencies is also that of the most remarkable spires and towers the middle ages have left to us. Outstanding among these are those of Salisbury and later those of Wells and Gloucester, and, latest of all, the great central tower of Canter-bury. At Salisbury the spire was raised on a thirteenth-century lantern tower which had presumably originally been sur-mounted by a wooden pyramidal roof. It is interesting to note that, both at Salisbury and at Wells, the increased height of the central feature of the church was apparently undertaken entirely for external appearance and that the original function of a central tower as a lantern over the crossing-space was abandoned and the lantern itself ceiled off internally with a vault. The most remarkable example of this process, however, was at Glou-cester, where the rebuilding of the eastern limb of the church included a vault at a much higher level than the original roof, and this vault was carried westwards, uninterrupted by the eastern arch of the crossing, to cover the entire space of the monastic choir which in the normal way occupied the crossing-space as well as part of the western limb (Pl. 86). A similar unification of the choir and presbytery space for a monastic church by the device of continuing the vault of the presbytery over the crossing was carried out at Sherborne in the fifteenth century. In general, however, the great churches at Canterbury, Lincoln, and Durham retained the internal lanterns over the crossing which they had inherited from Anglo-Norman tradition even when their central towers were rebuilt in the fourteenth and fifteenth centuries.

The alterations to the eastern parts of Gloucester are also celebrated as the earliest surviving example of a fashion in architecture which was to become widespread over the whole country in the course of the later fourteenth and fifteenth centuries and to a large extent to supersede the type of design which we have been discussing in connexion with Wells, Exeter, and Ely. This new fashion is now believed to have originated in London in the first years of the fourteenth century, where its most striking examples were the new chapter-house built in the 1320's at St. Paul's (Pl. 87a) and the splendid chapel made for the king's palace at Westminster, which was begun in the 1290's and only finally completed about 1360. The St. Paul's chapter-house and St. Stephen's chapel, Westminster, were the work of masons whose main employment seems to have been for the court and many of whose names are known to us. This court style is distinguished by an extraordinary refinement and elegance of mouldings and also for a continued taste for geometrical forms and a rather sparing use of the new ogee double-curved line so popular in other works of the time. It seems likely that this predilection for geometrical forms is a reflection of the close association of the court and London with the Continent, especially Paris, and many of the motifs of the court masons can be traced to French practice of the later thirteenth century. Two of these motifs call for special mention: first, the device of covering one set of structural forms by another set formed of openwork tracery. This is well known from the Continent. There are notable examples in the west front of Strasbourg. Amongst other examples it was adopted on the exterior of the king's new chapel, where the lines of the

PLATE 84

Howden Church, Yorkshire: east front of choir

PLATE 85

Gloucester Cathedral: tomb of King Edward II

mullions of the windows are carried down below the window-
sills on the exterior to interpenetrate the hoodmoulds of the
windows of the undercroft and so form a web of tracery lines
over the whole exterior of the building. Another motif, also as it
seems deriving from French practice, is to enclose an arch in a
rectangular moulded frame and to fill the spandrels so formed
with a pattern of cusped arch-headed panelling. This motif is
found in the lower parts of St. Paul's chapter-house design and
on a magnificent scale in the interior of St. Stephen's chapel,
as recorded by the nineteenth-century draughtsmen who saw
that building before the fire of 1834. These two motifs were
exploited on a grand scale in the new eastern limb of
Gloucester. A large part of the original eleventh-century structure at Gloucester was allowed to remain up to the top of the
tribune level. The original clerestory was removed and a new
clerestory with very tall windows built on top of the Romanesque masonry, the whole being covered with the vault already
mentioned, the vault shafts of which were carried down unbroken to the floor. The mullions of the clerestory windows
were also continued down across the face of the Romanesque
tribune and even below the arches of the Romanesque arcade.
They were linked at intervals by horizontal mouldings so as to
form a web of panelled tracery largely disguising the Romanesque structure behind them which, however, is in part visible
and lends a sort of piquancy to the contrast of the earlier structure with the new additions. The actual form of this tracery
screen seems largely derived from the second of the two motifs
we have mentioned at St. Stephen's. The outstanding quality
of the work at Gloucester is its extraordinary ingenuity. The
Romanesque church had been built with a three-sided apse and
ambulatory; the whole of this apse was removed in the course of
the new work, and the last bays of the central vessel were canted
outwards slightly to the north and south; the east end was then
filled with a colossal window composed of cusped tracery
panels, the effect of the canted bays being to disguise the angles
of the main structure with the east window so that in the longitudinal vista the whole east end of the church appears to be

formed of a great grille of stained glass—a striking example of the desire to get away from the logical and easily comprehended forms of the earlier architecture.

In addition to these developments in planning and tracery design, the late thirteenth and early fourteenth centuries saw equally remarkable developments in vaulting. A great series of vaults was perfected in the west country, notably at Bristol cathedral, Gloucester cathedral, and as part of the remodelling of the eastern parts of Tewkesbury. The Bristol vaults are the earliest and almost the most remarkable. The church, an Augustinian house, was built on the plan with the central vessel projecting two bays to the east beyond the aisles. There is no clerestory to the main vessel and the aisles are made of equal height with it. The aisle vaults are of an extreme ingenuity, the aisle being crossed between each bay by an arch supporting a horizontal stone beam-like member from the centre of which the vault springs out in all directions. The main vault is one of the earliest examples in which, by the use of small additional lierne ribs, linking the main ribs which spring from the piers, an elaborate pattern is formed on the vault surface. At Bristol, and equally in all these fourteenth-century west-country vaults, this pattern is so disposed as to shift the interest of the vault de-sign from the divisions between the bays and so emphasize the continuity of the vault in length as against the orthodox con-tinental system of a well-marked series of vaulted bays. Some of the vault ribs at Bristol are given cuspings so as to make foiled figures standing bold from the surface of the vault and give an effect of depth and light and shade which seems to be another aspect of the fashion we have already noticed. In one of the sub-ordinate buildings at Bristol an even more fantastic vault is found, in which the ribs are boldly detached from the vault surface, almost like internal struts. Other examples are to be found on a small scale at St. David's and in the later fourteenth century on a comparatively large scale at St. Mary's, Warwick. At Wells the choir vault, which dates from the early 1330's, that is, perhaps about ten years later than the Bristol example, is an even more striking example of the use of ribs as a decorative

PLATE 86

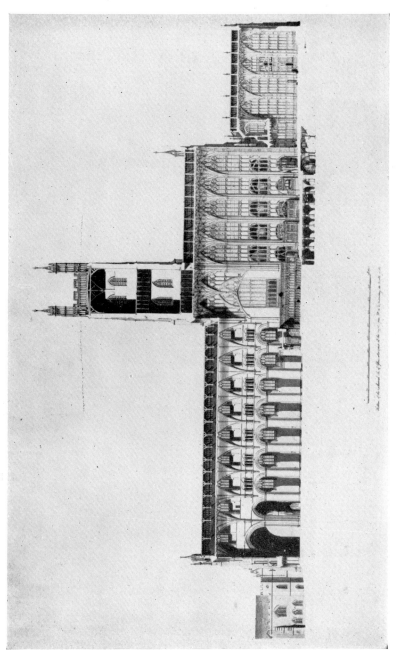

Gloucester Cathedral: longitudinal section

PLATE 87

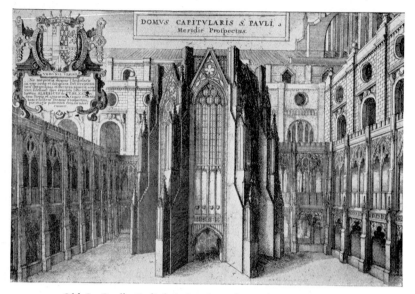

a. Old St. Paul's Cathedral, London: chapter house and cloister after Hollar

b. Sherborne Abbey, Dorset: nave

rather than a structural feature. All the main ribs except the transverse are interrupted by rectangular or kite-shaped foiled figures made up of these small subordinate ribs so that the vault, though a perfectly sound structural piece of masonry, no longer expresses its structure but appears like an elaborately decorated stone ceiling. At Gloucester the subordinate ribs are multiplied to such a degree that a tight mesh all-over pattern was produced, giving a continuous effect from the west side of the crossing to the east end of the church. The continuity of this pattern is strongly reinforced by no less than three parallel longitudinal ribs. At Tewkesbury, which is almost contemporary with Wells, the pattern is less elaborate but equally designed to subordinate structural expression to linear pattern used to reinforce the unity of effect. All these late vaults from the mid-thirteenth century onwards are natural, if in the later cases extreme, examples of the English tendency to exploit the springing of the ribbed vault as a sort of large stone-built corbel or bracket. This tendency reaches its full development in the later fourteenth century with the invention of the fan vault. In the fan vault the ribs are spaced equally and generally of equal curvature from the springing, so that a symmetrical part-conoidal-shaped bracket is achieved. The orthodox fan vault, of which the grandest examples date from the later fifteenth and early sixteenth centuries, covers the surface of these conoidal brackets with a system of panelling formed out of the ribs, and thereby achieves a continuity of pattern motif with the tracery of the later medieval windows and the stone panelling applied to wall surfaces and piers. Sherborne minster is perhaps the most complete example of this (Pl. 87 b). The early fan vaults, however, show this process just beginning. With reference to chronology, it seems that the earliest fan of which we have knowledge was built for the new chapter-house at Hereford and completed by 1371: this vault is only known from a drawing by the antiquary Stukeley, made in the early eighteenth century, but the surviving fragments of the building bear out the accuracy of Stukeley's detail. This is of extraordinary interest, for the tracery patterns formed by the ribs on the vault at

Hereford are not quite those of the orthodox later fan, but show markedly the influence of the court school of masons with their predilection for French-derived geometrical patterns. Almost contemporary with the Hereford chapter-house are the first bays of the cloister at Gloucester, in which the fan vault, though used on a slightly smaller scale, has already begun to assume the patterns with which the later examples have made us familiar.

The invention of the fan vault did not mean that the more varied type of patterned vault, of which the most extreme examples have been described at Wells and Gloucester above, was altogether superseded, though the tendency to make the vault conoids into symmetrically formed corbel brackets prevails in almost all important late-medieval vaults. The freer pattern-making of what is called the lierne vault, as opposed to the fan, however, continues in fashion right down to the early sixteenth-century vaults at St. George's, Windsor, a building which contains some of the most remarkable examples of late vaulting. In the last quarter of the fifteenth century there was developed, apparently first at Oxford, a type of vault which is sprung not from the piers nor the clerestory walls at the sides of the building but from two points being voussoirs of transverse arches thrown across the main space, each voussoir being about a quarter of the way across. In the earliest example, at the Divinity School at Oxford (chap. XV, Pl. 109 *b*), the great transverse arch is plainly visible and the voussoir consists of a huge stone from the upper part of which the vault is sprung and which hangs below the line of the arch in the form of a lantern pendant. The best known and most elaborate example of this type of vaulting is that of the great chantry chapel which Henry VII added to the east end of Westminster abbey, in which the pattern of vault ribs, an orthodox fan pattern, springs from the lower part of the voussoir stone just above the pendant lantern and the network of panels conceals the great transverse arch which passes across the church above it. A further refinement at West-minster is that the panels are largely openwork tracery through which a keen eye can just discern the great transverse arch.

The discussion of these later vaults has taken us beyond the point in the general history of architectural taste which we have reached in the account of the work on Gloucester choir, which was finished in the middle years of the fourteenth century. A profound change had come into being in the later years of the century which is possibly an example of the influence of the great constructional carpenters on the whole attitude to archi-tectural design. This is the vogue for the four-centred, rather flat arch, a form which comes naturally in wood, where a slightly cambered tie-beam roof gives a very spacious effect to the interior of a church while providing the slope to the outside of the roof which is suitable to the use of lead as a roof covering, a material which lies more easily on a low-pitched than a high-pitched roof. One of the finest early examples of this flat four-centred arch treatment that survives to us is in the parish church of Northleach in Gloucestershire, where all the arcades have this form. This gives an entirely different kind of space effect, at once broader and with less emphasis on the vertical direction, than the more acutely pointed two-centred arches which had prevailed up to that time. The later vaults, both lierne and fan, but especially the former, tend to exploit this form of arch and so give a broader space effect to the whole interior of the build-ing. It seems likely that the taste for pendant vaults which we have mentioned at Oxford and at Westminster may also owe something to the invention of the great carpenters, for in the later fourteenth century a type of open timber roof was de-veloped whereby the trusses spanning the building have on each side a series of great wooden brackets known as hammer-beams, the projecting ends of which are adorned either with sculpture or pendants. The earliest known hammer-beam roof is said to be a comparatively modest example in one of the sub-ordinate monastic buildings at Winchester, but the earliest surviving important example is the astonishing roof of 67 feet span built for Richard II in the 1390's at Westminster hall. This was the work of Hugh Herland the king's master carpen-ter, and superseded the aisled treatment of the hall, which dated from the late eleventh century. It seems likely that a great

hammer-beam roof had been built a few years before the work
at Westminster over the great hall at Dartington in Devon
for King Richard's elder half-brother. In the course of the
fifteenth and early sixteenth centuries the hammer-beam roof
became extremely popular both for parish churches—especially in eastern England—and for the halls of important domestic
buildings. Notable examples survive at Eltham palace of the
later fifteenth century and at Hampton Court dating from the
1530's and already showing signs of renaissance influence in its
carved details. The most extravagant examples of the hammer-
beam roof, however, are to be found in the East Anglian
parish churches such as Knapton in Norfolk and March in
Cambridgeshire. In these examples the trusses have two super-
imposed series of brackets, each terminating in angels with out-
spread wings, so that the view up into the roof seems to be filled
with a pattern of such angel figures. The ingenuity of such devices as these was exploited in the court architecture of the early
Tudor kings to express a taste which may be described as that
of artificial pageant chivalry, which can be traced from the
mid-fourteenth century onwards, a simple example of which
may be seen in the growing use of heraldry as a decorative motif
not only for tomb design, but as architectural decoration on a
major scale. This heraldic pageant chivalry taste reaches its
most extreme expression in the ante-chapel of King's College
chapel, Cambridge (Pl. 88), built under the terms of the will
of Henry VII, in his chantry chapel at Westminster, and at
St. George's, Windsor.

The most notable feature of the architecture of the later
middle ages in England is the number and splendour of the
parish churches.

The parish churches of the earlier middle ages (twelfth and
thirteenth centuries) are in general notable for the evidence
they provide of local building technique, and occasionally
for richness of decoration, rather than for size or architectural
ambition. The most common plan forms are a series of
rectangular spaces arranged axially: twofold—aisleless nave
and square, or more rarely apsidal, choir; or threefold—nave,

PLATE 88

King's College, Cambridge: ante-chapel from the east

PLATE 89

a. Leuchars Parish Church, Fife

b. Lawford Parish Church, Essex: from the south-east

square choir, and apsidal presbytery. In some instances the square choir of the threefold type formed the base of a tower, though generally the church bells were hung in a bell cote on the west gable. Examples where no expense has been spared to enrich the building decoratively are Kilpeck in Herefordshire, with its celebrated porch and chancel arch sculpture, Iffley in Oxfordshire, with a notable treatment of the west front, and Leuchars in Fife, a rather later example (Pl. 89 *a*). A variation of this type of plan is where a tower is added to the west of the nave, anticipating the usual form of parish church of the middle ages. A less usual plan form than the axially arranged series of 'boxes' is the aisleless cruciform church with a central tower, of which the remains of a fine and richly-decorated example dated 1124 is at Castor in Northamptonshire, and a remarkable thirteenth-century example at Potterne in Wiltshire. These are all examples of basic types of plan; most often early medieval parish churches have been enlarged or remodelled at various dates. The most usual modification is the addition of aisles to the nave, or, less frequently and generally later, to the chancel. This, as also with the addition of porches, western towers, transeptal chapels, &c., was done piecemeal, and it is this process which gives the parish churches their evidential value as documents in the religious and social history of the middle ages and also a great part of their picturesque appeal.

The number of early parish churches which have a truly architectural quality such as one finds in the great churches is comparatively small. They are to be found in large villages or small towns; the larger and more ancient towns were divided into a large number of small parishes, and even when they were very rich, as in Lincoln and Norwich, were, at any rate before the thirteenth century, remarkable for the number rather than the splendour of their churches, and this was particularly true of London. In such quickly grown seaports as New Shoreham or Hythe there are early churches of great magnificence; Melbourne in Derbyshire, a residence of the bishop of Carlisle, is a church with a great nave of five bays with two western towers, and at Long Sutton in Lincolnshire and Wal-

soken in west Norfolk there are other fine late twelfth-century
aisled naves. These last two, like the later West Walton, were
aisled from the beginning, but in the majority of cases aisles
were added to pre-existing churches, a most striking example
being Geddington in Northamptonshire where, above the
arcades on the face towards the aisles, the late-Saxon blind
arcading which ornamented the exterior of the original church
can clearly be seen. These early aisles are generally narrow and
often have been widened in the later middle ages. In the fen-
lands of Lincolnshire and west Norfolk a number of fine
towers were built in the first half of the thirteenth century, as at
Long Sutton and West Walton, and these form an early example of a regional group of parish church features such as
became frequent in the late middle ages.

    The earliest examples of the late-medieval movement for re-
building and beautifying parish churches date from the late
thirteenth and early fourteenth centuries and are to be found in
the great collegiate chancels added to many parish churches in
the midland counties. These buildings are called collegiate as
they were often occasioned by the endowment of chantries—
that is, provision for masses to be sung for the souls of the
founders—at the main altar of the parish churches, the chancels
of which were elaborately reconstructed to accommodate the
priests endowed to say these masses. The priests were either
formed into an association or college from the beginning, or
were subsequently organized in this way. Splendid examples
of such chancels are to be found in Huntingdonshire, such as
Fenstanton, Bassingbourne in Cambridgeshire, and, perhaps
the most elaborate of all, at Lawford in Essex (Pl. 89 b). But in
the course of the fourteenth and fifteenth centuries, notably with
the growth of religious guilds attached to parish churches and
reflecting the widespread prosperity of the country districts due
to the wool and cloth trade, the naves and other parts of the
parish churches shared in this movement for enrichment. That
is not to say that the parish guilds by themselves could afford to
undertake these great works, but they formed a vehicle direct-
ing the benefactions of the rich towards the parts of the church

which were peculiarly the property and responsibility of the parishioners.

An immense variety of enlarged and enriched parish churches were developed in the course of the fourteenth and fifteenth centuries. These can be considered on a regional basis, the regional schools being determined partly by economic considerations such as the availability and cost of transport of certain kinds of materials, and partly by the tendency to pre-scribe to the masons particular existing buildings as models which should be taken as a general guide to what was required by the clients. These examplars were generally chosen from some readily available example in the neighbourhood and tend to the formation of a regional school. One interesting example of this may be found in a type of church which prevailed both in Devon and in Kent. This is the prevalence of a plan of three almost equal vessels, the side aisles being of almost the same width as the central vessel. All three vessels are covered at an equal height and there is no clerestory; fine examples of this type of church are to be found in both these counties. A smaller and more striking example of the affinities between these two widely separated regions is to be found in the church of Chart-ham in Kent, built in the very first years of the fourteenth century or even a little earlier. This church consists of a broad, spacious chancel, broad but rather shallow transepts, and a wide, aisleless nave, the whole being covered with wagon roofs which meet at the crossing with four great diagonal wooden ribs, like a skeleton vault. A very favourite addition to make to a parish church in the late middle ages was a new and am-bitious tower, generally a western tower. There are clearly recognizable regional or local schools of design of which those of Somerset are the most famous, though many of the flint towers of Norfolk and Suffolk are of admirable proportions and great splendour. The eastern county churches are par-ticularly noteworthy for the elegance and slenderness of their arcades and the great spaciousness of their interiors. The slenderness of piers was probably a direct consequence of the need for economy in cut freestone. But above all the eastern county parish churches are notable for their elaborate lantern-like clerestories and the splendour and ingenuity of their open timber roofs, of which two of the most striking examples of the hammer-beam type have already been mentioned. In the later fifteenth and early sixteenth centuries the colourful pageantry taste we have already referred to produced in East Anglia a vogue for the use of brickwork and for elaborate patterned surfaces in specially cut flints inlaid with patterns in freestone. Inevitably, owing to their generally more modest scale, the parish church buildings do not give so clear examples of the changing taste as we have traced in the greater church buildings, but it can be claimed with some confidence that, broadly speaking, the story as we have traced it in the great buildings can be seen reflected and with increasing clarity in the parish churches.

WORKS FOR REFERENCE

BILSON, J. 'The Architecture of the Cistercians', *Arch. Jnl.* lxvi (1909).

BOND, F. *Gothic Architecture in England* (1905).

CLAPHAM, A. W. *English Romanesque Architecture before the Conquest* (1930); *English Romanesque Architecture after the Conquest* (1934); *Romanesque Architecture in England* (1950).

HARVEY, J. H. 'The Mediaeval Office of Works', *Jnl. Brit. Archaeol. Assoc.* vi (1941); 'The King's Chief Carpenters', ibid. (1948).

LETHABY, W. R. *Westminster Abbey and the King's Craftsmen* (1906); *Westminster Abbey Re-examined* (1925).

PANTIN, W. A. *Durham Cathedral* (1948).

PRIOR, E. S. *Gothic Art in England* (1900).

Royal Commission on Historical Monuments: *St. Albans Cathedral* (1952) (Inventory of the Historical Monuments in London: I. Westminster Abbey).

SALZMAN, L. F. *Building in England down to 1540* (1952).

THOMPSON, A. HAMILTON. *The Ground Plan of the English Parish Church* (1911); *The Historical Growth of the English Parish Church* (1913); *The Cathedral Churches of England* (1925).

WEBB, G. F. *Ely Cathedral* (1951); *Gothic Architecture in England* (1951).

WILLIS, R. *The Architectural History of Canterbury Cathedral* (1845).

XIV. ART

THE emergence of a genuine medieval art, a synthesis of barbaric and classical styles, took place in England at the close of the seventh century. Its greatest centre was Northumbria, following the synod of Whitby in 664, but at Canterbury also there was a new creative impulse. Celtic art had reached a fine skill in pattern, which is known to us in the scroll work of objects such as the Desborough mirror or the somewhat later, less vigorous and daring ornament of the Battersea shield, both of them to be seen in the British Museum. The Romans brought their tradition of monumental figure sculpture: their officers carried with them elaborately chased silver plates, such as the Corbridge lanx found in 1735 on the bank of the river Tyne, or the Mildenhall treasure discovered in Suffolk in 1946: above all, in their villas they laid out mosaic pavements whose abstract designs had a direct and easy appeal to native British craftsmen and underlie the great triumphs of Northumbrian book decoration. A Romano-Celtic phase produced works such as the small Gloucester head or the Bath gorgon, where classical forms are infused with a crude but intense barbaric emotionalism. The Anglo-Saxon Conquest brought new types of ornament, particularly used for metal work, drawn from a Celtic tradition, but transmuted through wanderings and contacts unknown to Celtic Britain. The great burial treasure found in 1939 at Sutton Hoo in Suffolk shows a range of artistic achievement which had never, before its discovery, been suspected. The metal work is of the highest quality, using stylized but recognizable human and animal forms (Pl. 90), and Frankish coins and two large Byzantine silver bowls prove that there were wide and prosperous external contacts. The burial itself, if the term can be used, for there was no corpse, is generally assigned on the evidence of the coins to the years 650–70, but an earlier date is not altogether excluded. The first great Anglo-Irish illuminated manuscript, the Book of Durrow (Trinity College, Dublin), also dates from the third quarter of the century. Its exact place of origin is uncertain. It is traditionally held to have been written at the monastery of Durrow in Co. Offaly, but its ornament, particularly its trumpet-pattern, suggests English motifs, and textually it is based on the Vulgate version of the Gospels current in the newly Romanized English Church. Whatever its prove-nance, it is the precursor, in its magnificent decoration, of the Lindisfarne Gospels, the great masterpiece of Northumbrian monasticism, written c. 700. But where the evangelist pages of the Durrow Gospels are still patterned abstractions, hardly recognizable as human, the Lindisfarne pages show seated author portraits, based on classical humanist models, with a genuine attempt to give proportion and roundness to the forms, a pictorial tribute to the return of Christian Rome (Pl. 91 a). The splendour of the book lies, however, in its glowing, in-tricate initials, where trumpet patterns swell and curve, ribbon animals ceaselessly interlace, bending birds appear, and closely woven patterns fill the background spaces with an ever-chang-ing, brilliant inventiveness (Pl. 91 b). The new classical feeling can be seen in two pieces of carving, the Bewcastle and Ruth-well crosses, the former datable by an inscription to c. 700, the latter undated but nearly contemporary work. Both crosses have figure-subjects; those of Bewcastle are somewhat flatter and stiffer. Both have affinities to the Lindisfarne evangelists and also to the figure of St. Cuthbert incised in 696 upon his coffin. On the Ruthwell cross the figures, worn and weathered though they are, still have a plastic sense and a noble dignity that stand comparison with the masterwork of any period. The huge, simplified gesture of the Magdalen at the feet of Christ has an expressiveness which transcends any crudity in the naturalism of its execution (Pl. 92 a).

Nowhere in north-western Europe has this union of the classical and the barbaric produced such striking work, and it was not long before its influence began to spread. Northum-

PLATE 90

Purse-lid from Sutton Hoo. Gold frame (7½ in. long), fittings, and ornamental plaques, decorated with garnets and mosaic glass. The man between two beasts is an Eastern design (the Master of the Animals) adapted in Christian art to the theme of Daniel in the Lion's Den, though here any Christian symbolism is unlikely

PLATE 91

b

a

a. St. Luke, Lindisfarne Gospels, British Museum MS. Cotton Nero D. IV, f. 137ᵛ. The Greek title in itself betrays the classical Byzantine origin of the design. The size of the page is 13½ × 9¾ in. The evangelist wears a mauve mantle over a pale purple tunic; the folds are indicated by red strokes on the mauve, green on the purple. The hair and beard are dull green, the cushion brick red, the seat dull green with a yellow centre. The ox is purple with blue wings

b. The beginning of the Gospel of St. Matthew, from the Lindisfarne Gospels (f. 27). The elaborate monogram is composed of L, I, and B, the beginning of 'Liber generationis Iesu Christi'. Several of the spandrels contain patterns made up of 'ribbon' beasts

brian manuscripts rapidly became known on the Continent. The famous copy of the Vulgate, the Codex Amiatinus, was taken by Abbot Ceolfrid of Jarrow (d. 716) to Rome as a present for Pope Gregory II, and as befitted a work for such a recipient its illustrations, based on a sixth-century original, probably the Codex Grandior of Cassiodorus, are the most fully classical of all the Northumbrian paintings. It was a return traffic, for, earlier, Benedict Biscop had brought paintings from Rome to Jarrow and Wearmouth, which no doubt were among the models on which this northern renaissance drew. At Echternach in Luxembourg, a house founded c. 700 by St. Willibrord, the Northumbrian-born missionary archbishop of Friesland, there was a scriptorium which carried on the Northumbrian tradition; the Echternach Gospels (Paris, Bibl. Nat. MS. lat. 9389), where a new decorative effect is achieved by setting the evangelist symbols against a background patterned only by black-line rectangular divisions, may be taken as an example of this artistic dispersion. This greater simplicity is a mark of the more restrained style of the middle years of the eighth century. In Mercia, however, in the second half of the century, under the prosperous rule of Offa, there is a full use of exuberant ornament, thinner and prettier than any as yet mentioned, which can be seen in the pages of the Vatican Gospels (MS. Barb. lat. 570), the English contemporary of the great Irish Book of Kells, and in the carvings preserved at Breedon and Fletton. This is a period where the arts are all too little known, and extant examples all too few. Offa's coins show a high ability in craftsmanship and compare favourably with any contemporary designs in north-west Europe. His contacts with the court of Charlemagne introduced new continental influences and motifs such as the scraggy, prowling lion that appears on the Rothbury cross in Northumberland and is to be found amongst the foliage of the Ormside bowl, one of the most admirable of our Anglo-Saxon pieces of metal work. The increased skill in figure representation, as shown in the evangelists of the Vatican Gospels and in some of the Breedon carvings, probably owes something to these foreign influences.

Southern England has on the whole less striking pieces to its credit. If the fragments of the Reculver cross are contemporary with its base, set in the pavement of a seventh-century Saxon church, then Kentish sculpture had reached a fluency and ease of representation unknown farther north; but stylistically these pieces would fit more easily with a late tenth-century date and the evidence they present is too problematic for any firm statement. Certainly the treatment of drapery in them is much more sophisticated than it is in two manuscripts of the mid-eighth century, the Codex Aureus at Stockholm and the Canterbury Psalter, now Cotton MS. Vespasian A.I in the British Museum. In them the figures are based on classical prototypes, beyond any question of relapse into barbaric formulas, though the native idiom can be seen in the decorative initials. In the kingdom of Wessex, steadily growing in importance in the ninth century, we have few certain pieces of evidence. At Codford St. Peter, between Warminster and Salisbury, there is a cross shaft with the figure of a man holding a branch in one hand and some small instrument in the other; it is probably an early example of one of the seasonal labours. It has a beautiful dancing rhythm and the whole design is most ingeniously adapted to the space. Nothing at all like it survives, but it is hard to place stylistically except as ninth-century work (Pl. 92 *b*). No doubt there were many other such imaginative works swept away in the destructive inroads of the Danes that filled the middle years of the century.

The return of better-ordered times under Alfred and his successors gave an opportunity for a renewal of the arts. The most famous object associated, though not certainly, with the great king himself is the Alfred Jewel, now in the Ashmolean Museum, inscribed 'Alfred had me made'. Here the elaborate setting is composed of barbaric motifs, though the technique of the cloisonné enamel may come from continental examples. Other influences are apparent: between 909 and 916 Ælflæd of Wessex, the wife of Edward the Elder, commissioned an embroidered stole and maniple, which later were given to the shrine of St. Cuthbert and enclosed in the saint's tomb, where they were found in 1827. The ornament includes acanthus sprays and standing figures of prophets and saints; the shape of the bodies under the draperies is outlined with curving folds; they are the product of a developed Romanesque style, where classical and Byzantine models have been fully understood and their meaning absorbed into the artist's own range of ex-pression (Pl. 93 *a*).

The second half of the century saw a great monastic revival in England. Aesthetically its most satisfying surviving product is the group of manuscripts of the so-called Winchester School, a misleading title, for Canterbury and the monasteries of the fenland certainly counted for much in the development of the style. The name, however, is a not unfitting tribute to St. Æthelwold, bishop of Winchester, the presiding figure, with St. Dunstan, in these monastic reforms. Here again there were close continental contacts, particularly with the abbey of Fleury. In a Psalter (B.M. MS. Harley 2904), probably written at Ramsey, the Crucifixion page is a famous masterpiece, and the same artist or a colleague who had closely absorbed his style illustrated a Fleury book, St. Gregory's Homilies on Ezekiel, which is now MS. 175 in the Bibliothèque Municipale of Orléans. The Harley Crucifixion, a work of the last quarter of the century, is a tinted outline drawing (Pl. 93 *b*), and it is for its drawings, executed with light, broken, impressionistic strokes, that the School today is particularly admired. To contempo-raries the magnificent fully painted pages of the Benedictional of St. Æthelwold (now at Chatsworth) were probably more prized. The Benedictional is indeed a memorable book. The heavy bars of the frames, the fleshy acanthus leaves, the stolid, somewhat flaccid figures, fall short of the monumental and are a not always happy reflection of Carolingian models of the 'Ada' group, but the relation of the figure scenes to the wide ornamental borders is altogether excellent, and the gay colours, gold, pinkish red, blue, purple, green, picked out here and there with opaque white, relieve the heaviness of some of the figure drawing. In the scene of the Marys at the Tomb the drapery of the women flutters away to merge with the ornaments of the frame, and the shields of the sleeping guards echo and blend with the decorative roundel behind them. The Benedic⁄ tional was illuminated either at Winchester or Ely between 975 and 980; a later book, the Missal (actually Sacramentary) of Robert of Jumièges (now MS. Y. 6 at Rouen), whose date must lie between 1008 and 1025, shows fully painted scenes treated with nervous, twisting lines, which invade even the backgrounds, squiggled with impatient brush strokes; the drapery bunches in small folds, giving a wrinkled outline to the figures, and its lower edges break into zigzag frills. This is the closest interpretation of 'Winchester' drawing in painterly terms; classical repose is far away; its odd, pulsating liveliness is the work of a notable and individual artist (Pl. 94 *a*).

The outline drawings, like the paintings of the Benedic⁄ tional, owe much to Carolingian models. Here the influence is that of the Rheims style, of which a famous example, the Utrecht Psalter, was at Canterbury by the end of the tenth century, when a copy of it was made there (B.M. MS. Harley 603). These crowded scenes, filled with small figures, seem to have awoken a ready response in English artists. The Psalter, now B.M. MS. Cotton Tiberius C. VI, is an example of work on a larger scale; its fine, uncrowded drawings measure $9\frac{1}{2}$ inches by $5\frac{3}{4}$ inches and the figures fill the space. It is a book with no provenance, but it clearly dates from the middle years of the eleventh century. The sensitive modelling of earlier work has now become stylized; the hair is set in formal curls, the features fixed in a rigid pattern; it has a fine remoteness and monumentality, but the emotional intensity of the Harley Crucifixion or the dazzling liveliness of the Sacramentary of Bishop Robert are no longer within its scope.

Of tenth⁄ and eleventh⁄century sculpture tantalizingly little is known. Bradford⁄on⁄Avon has two large angels, each about 5 feet in length, which must have been part of a great tenth⁄ century rood. Carved in comparatively low relief, they are very linear in concept, and their long albs have the frilled edges of the Winchester School. Some ivory carvings reflect more clearly the stylistic phases to be found in manuscript illumination,

PLATE 92

a   *b*

a. Detail of the Ruthwell Cross: Mary Magdalen at the foot of Christ. The cross is a little over 17 ft. high and is made of red sandstone. The figures are carved in deep relief

b. Codford St. Peter: stone shaft, about 4 ft. high. The two sides have decorative scroll work. The dating of this remarkable piece of carving is extremely uncertain. Kendrick places it on the evidence of its ornamental portions in the first half of the ninth century

PLATE 93

a   *b*

a. The prophet Joel from the stole of St. Cuthbert (2⅜ in. wide).   From an inscription on the stole it is known to have been made by the command of Queen Ælflæd (d. *c.* 916).   Silk and metal thread on silk

b. Crucifixion from MS. Harley 2904, f. 3ᵛ.   Probable dating, 970–90.   Drawing in red outline, heightened by black strokes; some blue is used in the folds and patterns of the drapery.   Size of page, 13½ × 9⅞ in.

and two ivory figures in the museum at St. Omer, a Virgin
and St. John from a Crucifixion, must be near in date to the
Psalter MS. Cotton Tiberius C. VI. But the main sculptural
achievement remains controversial, a controversy centring
round three celebrated works, the Romsey Rood, the York
Virgin, and the Chichester slabs of the Raising of Lazarus.
The first of these is almost life size, the figure is fairly fully
modelled, the loincloth, looped in a familiar Winchester
style, clings to and is moulded by the body beneath with no trace
of Winchester fluttering lightness: it is possible to regard it as a
contemporary parallel to the Harley Crucifixion, and to explain stylistic differences by the needs of the different mediums,
or to place it in the early twelfth century as part of a new wave of
humanistic feeling. The York Virgin, headless but beautifully
cut in hard, local stone, is claimed as eleventh century on account of its epigraphy, or as mid-twelfth on the treatment of its
drapery; it remains a puzzling piece, but the Chichester slabs,
both from the history of the cathedral and from their own stylistic
qualities, must come from the first half of the twelfth century.

In English ornament in the tenth and eleventh centuries
Viking influences steadily become apparent. Its earliest manifestations, the so-called Jellinge style, seem to have coincided with
and been part of a general revival of stylized animal carving,
where the animals are enmeshed in thick bands of interlace, a
revival that is particularly associated with the Danelaw and
with Northumbria. The second Viking style, the Ringerike,
is on the other hand mainly confined to southern England. Its
features are a reduction of the full-leaved Winchester acanthus
to a thinner, irregular foliate design, which sprouts unex-
pectedly from the tails and feet of the animals depicted, as in the
gravestone carved with a stag in the Guildhall Museum. In the
last phase, the Urnes style, beasts and plants dissolve into flow-
ing ribbon pattern, a curious barbarism beside the Winchester
humanism. The process can be seen at work on a fine tympanum preserved at Southwell. Tympana and fonts are in fact
the most numerously preserved examples of Anglo-Saxon
stonework, particularly in smaller, country churches; but they

are hard to date exactly and many of their carvings, vigorous
but crude, may be later products subject to a considerable provincial time-lag.

   In the graphic arts, as opposed to architecture, the Norman
Conquest made comparatively little break. The reforming influence which had created the Winchester style was already
losing its impetus. Normandy had its own school of illuminators and Norman books soon appear at Durham and Exeter,
but the Norman School owed much to England, and Anglo-
Saxons had been working in Norman scriptoria such as Mont-
St.-Michel. The Norman artists used harder outlines, which
never equal the expressive touch of the Winchester style at its
best, and had a liking for stronger, contrasted colours, greens,
yellows, and reds. They filled the trellis-work of their initials
with climbing figures, men hunting or being pursued by fantastic beasts; there is a fierceness, sometimes brutality, in their
imaginings which had not appeared in Anglo-Saxon art; but
their fluttering draperies and twisted poses recall Anglo-Saxon
models, and the two schools easily amalgamated (Pl. 94 *b*). In
sculpture the same strange beasts of this age of dragons soon
appear. Normandy seems to have had a less-developed practice
in stone-carving, but the capitals in the crypt and on the outer
arcades of the transepts at Canterbury, which must almost
certainly precede the consecration of 1127, show Norman
fancies interpreted with a new and very considerable skill (Pl.
95 *a*). They provided stylistic types for a whole school of southern carving, of which Romsey and Christchurch still have
notable examples. Moving northwards, Henry I's foundation
at Reading was another centre, more Anglo-Saxon in the
wiriness of its interlaces, gripped by cat's masks as in some
Winchester initials; here beakheads were employed as voussoir
ornament, and it may well be at Reading abbey that this char-
acteristically English motif was popularized. Leominster in
Herefordshire, a cell of Reading, provided a local centre for the
diffusion of the Reading style, and a local sculptor of originality
and force gave to Herefordshire carving, in churches such as
Kilpeck and Shobdon and on fonts such as those at Castle

PLATE 94

a   *b*

a. Adoration of the Kings, from the missal of Robert of Jumièges, MS. Rouen Y. 6, f. 37. The size of the page is 13¼ × 8¾ in. The quick brush-strokes give a curious shimmering effect of motion to this remarkable piece of visual interpretation

b. Initial from British Museum MS. Royal 12 E. XX (f. 124ᵛ). This small drawing, by a Canterbury or Rochester artist, where each beast bites its man, is an epitome of the inventive violence of the first half of the twelfth century

PLATE 95

a. Capital from St. Gabriel's Chapel in the crypt of Canterbury Cathedral. A fox plays the recorder and a griffin the harp. These represent a favourite medieval fable, the beasts mentioned by Boethius in his *Consolatio*, that despite their long ears do not understand the music that they make

b. St. Paul and the Viper. Wall painting in St. Anselm's Chapel, Canterbury Cathedral, *c*. 1160. Approximately 3 ft. 6 in. square. The saint is shown against a blue background, framed in a green border. He wears a buff mantle over a white garment; the folds are painted in red

Frome and Erdisley, a particular individuality which makes them the most interesting of the products of our provincial schools. Here and in many parts of England (the Yorkshire churches are a notable group) there is an inventive confusion of dragons, griffins, signs of the zodiac, symbols of the evangelists, wild huntsmen, and creatures from the bestiary. A great Bible in the Bodleian Library (MS. Auct. E. Infra. 1 and 2) has a remarkable gallery of such themes and brings to a high state of excellence this tangled, violent pattern making.

Figural representation of a naturalistic kind advanced more slowly. A Psalter made for St. Albans about 1130 (now preserved at St. Godehard's church in Hildesheim) shows a new wave of Byzantine influence, which possibly came through Ottonian versions, and in which the continental upbringing and contacts of the Empress Matilda may have had some part. The biblical scenes are still highly formalized, but are lucidly set out in a framed space, not enmeshed in whirling coils. The Bury Bible, painted at Bury St. Edmunds in the middle years of the century, is the greatest product of this phase, the work of an important artist who could create a sense of space around his figures, and whose deep-toned colours lend a new solemnity to his work. Close in style, possibly even by his hand, is the fresco of St. Paul and the viper at Canterbury (Pl. 95 b), the greatest surviving medieval wall-painting in England. Here a Byzantine style and pose has been fully absorbed and a singularly impressive and convincing work produced. Canterbury has other wall-paintings, in St. Gabriel's chapel in the crypt, probably dating from the 1130's, which are of fine quality and further evidence of the lost achievement in this branch of the arts, now little known except in shadowy remains or in the reduced scale of manuscript illumination.

Throughout the century there is a dual movement, naturalism, linked with Byzantine humanist conventions, and the old barbaric tradition of intricate and formalized patterns. Sometimes the two blend as in the brilliant pages of the Lambeth Bible, or in the work of some of the hands, in particular that of the so-called Master of the Leaping Figures, in the Winchester

Bible. But gradually naturalism triumphs. The draperies cease to cling in rounded folds, as though damp and moulded to the body beneath; instead they fall loosely round figures which, a little stiffly at first, have relaxed from their strained and twisted postures and are firmly seated, with some sense of perspective, in their chairs (Pl. 96 a). Narrative interest widens: a Psalter made for Gloucester, now in the Staatsbibliothek of Munich, has some eighty full pages of Old and New Testament scenes. It is a return to a classical, humanist style, worked out simul-taneously in England and northern France; it is in fact a Channel style, and it represents the interrelationships of the Angevin Empire rather than any national trend (Pl. 96 b).

In sculpture this classicizing movement was to lead in France to the great triumphs of the west portals of Amiens and Rheims and the south porch of Chartres. England, fertile and imagi-native in manuscript painting, had no equal sculptural achieve-ment, at least as far as can be judged from the existing remains, much battered by Puritan fanaticism and crumbled by English weather. When in 1146 Alexander the Magnificent, bishop of Lincoln, began the remodelling of his cathedral façade, he borrowed many motifs from recent work at St. Denis, and his carved columns show a curiously direct relationship with the French example. But there is no trace of the column figures which were the great innovation at St. Denis and were to have in France so distinguished a future. These do not appear in England till some years later, at Rochester, and they never be-came a common English feature. The museum of the York-shire Philosophical Society has a group of noble figures, prophets and apostles, almost life size, either from a doorway or the inside of the choir: they must date from the last quarter of the twelfth century, and have a real sense of form and a classical certainty in the fall of the drapery; but, impressive though they are, they are provincial work compared to their French contem-poraries. The same is true of the two reliefs of seated apostles at Malmesbury, precursors of York by probably some twenty-five years, robust and vigorous, memorable in the rhythm of their grouping, but somewhat coarsely cut (Pl. 97 a). English artists

PLATE 96

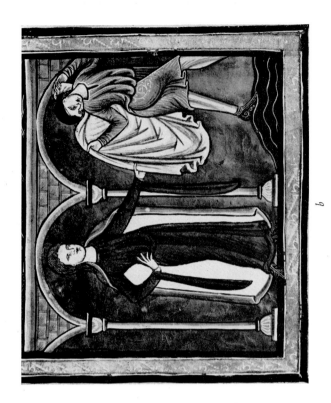

b

a

a. King David, from the British Museum Psalter, MS. Royal 2 A. XXII, f. 14ᵛ. The size of the painting is 6¼ × 4 in. This is a Westminster book, illustrated in the transitional style between Romanesque and Gothic. David wears a brown mantle over a violet tunic; the back of the throne is blue; the main background and some of the ornament on the garments are gilt; the frame is salmon pink

b. Joseph and Potiphar's wife, from the Psalter in the State Library, Munich, MS. lat. 835, f. 14. Note the attempt at realism with which Joseph seems to pass out of the picture space and also to be set back in it as compared to the lady, whose foot rests on the border of the frame. The pattern visible on Joseph's tunic at his hip is a popular 12th century convention

PLATE 97

a. The Malmesbury Apostles. One of a pair of tympana carved on either side of the south porch of Malmesbury Abbey, *c.* 1160. The figures are almost life size. On the right St. Peter can be identified by his large key. The figures are uncouth, the postures naïf, but the group has the strong linear rhythm that is one of the most characteristic qualities of English twelfth-century art

b. Detail from the Gloucester candlestick in the Victoria and Albert Museum. The candlestick is in gilt bell-metal and 23½ in. high. It was given to Gloucester by Abbot Peter between 1104 and 1113. It may be taken as a small-scale model of the large paschal candlesticks which are known to have existed in many of the greater churches

were happier in the decorative work of capitals and voussoirs, in the small trellised scenes of the outside of the Malmesbury porch or in the subtle variations of the simple foliage capitals that were the only ornaments tolerated by the strict Cistercian houses. A curious trend is noticeable in decorative art: the elaborate intertwinings, inhabited scrolls, and beakheads of the Reading school give way to a severely geometric, regular pat- tern, the finest example of which is perhaps Hugh du Puiset's doorway in the castle of Durham; this in turn is replaced by the new classicism, the magnificent acanthus capitals of the rebuilt choir at Canterbury, the freely curving foliage of Wells, inter- spersed with a three-petalled leaf that has a new naturalism of growth.

To contemporaries, however, if we may judge from the comments of the chroniclers, art meant above all the shining splendour of metal work, inlaid with enamels and jewels, the great candlesticks, the carved altars and shrines, that gleamed in the great cathedrals and were singularly adapted to their ill-lit mysteriousness. *Nitens*, 'gleaming', is the characteristic word; but all this admired output is hardly known to us, save for small models such as the Gloucester candlestick (Victoria and Albert Museum) (Pl. 97 *b*), or enamel plaques, mainly de- tached from the object they originally decorated. This love of sparkle and brilliance can, however, still be appreciated by us in one medium, that of stained glass, and in particular at Canterbury where there remains much late twelfth-century glass, displaced, restored, but sufficiently preserved to show its great beauty, the final flowering of our Romanesque style; and in the cathedral's later windows we can follow the develop- ment, in the panes of the miracles of Becket, of the new Gothic mannerisms.

For the classic phase of transition is not truly Gothic in its figural representation; rather was it striving after a sense of weight and dignity which was soon to find itself at variance with the narrow, pointed, crocketed tabernacles of Gothic art. These, whether the decoration was drawn or carved, demanded lightness and elegance rather than substance and gravity. In some manuscripts illustrated at Peterborough under Abbot Robert de Lindeseye (1214–22) we can see the new features appear: legs and arms are grotesquely thin and give a curious affected refinement to the poses; there is a graceful swaying movement throughout; the Cross itself is decorated with bands of English stiff leaf. In the works of one of our named illumi‑nators, William de Brailes, the scenes are set in ovals linked by decorative patternings which recall the tracery of a window; in a Psalter at Trinity College, Cambridge (MS. B. II. 4), some of the scenes used in the Gloucester Munich Psalter are repeated; probably some twenty‑five years only lie between them, but the thin‑limbed, mincing figures of the later version are a new world of fantasy, charming, tender, and ingenuous, fresh in inspira‑tion, lacking the less couth force and grandeur of the 1190's (Pl. 98 a).

In sculpture the main surviving English achievement of the first part of the thirteenth century is the west façade of Wells. Here a great army of statues, including 176 full‑length figures, interspersed with smaller biblical scenes in quatrefoil openings, were set in tiers of pointed niches covering the whole façade. When fully painted, as traces show that they originally were, it must have been a fantastically imaginative spectacle. It has no exact parallel in France, and the small size of the doorways, with their lack of emphasis, is a peculiarly English feature. Iconographically it is a great summary of the Church trium‑phant. The work seems to have been mainly completed be‑tween 1220 and 1242. Many different hands were at work on it, though there is little marked stylistic development and some of the more archaic, squatter figures are scattered amongst the finer examples. The Gothic counterpoised pose is sometimes apparent and in the higher ranges there are thin, elongated figures, which contrast strikingly with the finely proportioned deacons on the bottom range of the eastern gable. These latter are the work of a considerable master of the close of the classicist period: rarely has virile manhood been so vigorously portrayed as in these powerful heads, finely erect on their strong necks, the broad‑built frames curiously contrasted with the long, loose

PLATE 98

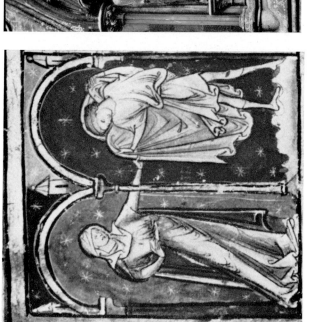

b

a

a. Joseph and Potiphar's wife from the Gospels in Trinity College, Cambridge, MS. B. 11. 4, f. 7. The page measurement is 11¼ × 8¼ in. with six compartments to a page in the opening narrative scenes, each compartment being approximately 3 in. square. The miniatures are alternately on blue and pink backgrounds: compare the treatment of the figures with the similar design in pl. 96 *b*. The book is not certainly dated, but must be early thirteenth-century work. Its calendar suggests a London provenance

b. North tower of west front of Wells Cathedral: statues of deacon saints. These are among the finest pieces of this great gallery of thirteenth-century sculpture. They are carved in freestone from the Doulton quarries, and are approximately life size. Traces of colour prove that they were originally painted

PLATE 99

a. The incredulity of St. Thomas: wall painting in the south transept of Westminster Abbey. The figure of Christ is about 9 ft. high. His mantle is red, that of the apostle dark green over a pale yellow tunic

b. Tomb of Eleanor of Castille, bronze cast by William Torel, 1291–2, Westminster Abbey

robes, in which the fine pleating of the linen is exactly rendered
(Pl. 98 *b*). There are no foreign models that can be exactly set
beside them, though resemblances of course exist. It is a
curiously unified and English school, whose influence can be
seen in some of the tomb effigies of the time and in some
scattered figure-carvings; an influence which lies behind the
sculpture of Westminster abbey, though here new and powerful contacts with France came into play.

The work on the abbey, the new choir, the chapter-house,
the crossing and transepts, was in progress between 1245 and
1269 and was contemporaneous with the building of the
Sainte Chapelle (1245-9) and the new choir of Amiens (*c.*
1240-69). Henry III and St. Louis were linked by marriage,
piety, mutual tastes, and rivalry. There can be little doubt that
the English king in his devoted patronage followed closely
the styles and fashions of France. Westminster was a great foyer
of all the arts. Some of its wall-paintings survive, and the Incredulity of St. Thomas and the St. Christopher, where the
figures are approximately nine feet high, are amongst the most
striking of our surviving Gothic wall-paintings. Rediscovered
in 1936, they still have some of the brilliancy of their colour
contrasts, and the great curve of St. Thomas's arm is a piece of
genuine visual expressionism (Pl. 99 *a*). Some of their characteristics recall the contemporary illumination of the St. Albans
School; they have the same curled hair and the exaggerated
sidelong glance of the eyes; the mannered elegance of the poses
is more French than English, but it is an elegance that was being rapidly assimilated by English artists. The Westminster retable comes from the same artistic phase and, though much
damaged, is a striking example of the high quality of the fittings of this sumptuous church. The mosaic paving of the
presbytery, still wonderfully intact, and the mosaic on the base
of the Confessor's shrine and Henry's own tomb are Cosmati
work by Italian craftsmen.

Henry's effigy was of bronze, cast in London by William
Torel in 1291-2. In the same years Torel had made the effigy of
Eleanor, wife of Edward I. This is a work of great beauty. The

head on its engraved cushions is formalized, with probably no attempt at natural likeness, and the hair is set in regular curves; but this severity is counteracted by the flow of the drapery, which has a suavity of line that had not yet been achieved in English stone-carving (Pl. 99 *b*). These bronze figures intro-duce a notable line of tomb effigies which continue throughout the later middle ages to represent much that is best in English craftsmanship. Purbeck marble was in the thirteenth century the fashionable material for the major tombs, and here the hardness of the material resulted in a simplified treatment of the features and a stiff rigidity of the drapery; both qualities can be seen in one of the finest examples, the tomb of King John at Worcester, probably about 1230. The sculptor of another splendid monument, the effigy of Archbishop de Gray at York, was more subtle in the use of his tools, more able to suggest the forms below the drapery. The archbishop lies beneath a pin-nacled canopy, also of Purbeck marble, and these canopied tombs, ever increasing in elaboration till they come to enclose a complete chapel, were to provide some of the happiest expres-sions of English plastic sense.

As compared with these tombs, but little religious sculpture has survived. The great doorway of the north transept at West-minster was rich in statuary but nothing now remains of it. The Virgin and the Angel of the Annunciation from the chapter-house show us the Wells tradition meeting with a new French civility, a subtlety in the sense of gesture, a modishness in the gathering of the drapery, which are outside the range of the provincial schools. But it is the angels of the transept spandrels that reveal Westminster sculpture at its best. Carved in such high relief as to be almost free standing, they have a liveliness of movement, a sureness of modelling, and a vigorous charm that can hold their own against any angelic rivalry. Hard to see from floor level, they remain, preserved from icono-clasm by their remoteness, one of the greatest treasures of our medieval inheritance (Pl. 100 *a*).

Beside them the angels of the choir at Lincoln are heavy, boorish-looking creatures, their robes treated in flat planes with

PLATE 100

a. Angel with censer: south transept, Westminster Abbey. There is no exact evidence for dating, but *c.* 1255 would fit the general progress of the building and be stylistically acceptable. Cleaning in 1933–4 revealed traces of the original painting and gilding, which doubtless made the figures tell more convincingly from the height at which they are placed

b. Angel of Judgement, from the Angel Choir, Lincoln Cathedral, *c.* 1270. Seen from below the distortion of the left arm is corrected by perspective

PLATE 101

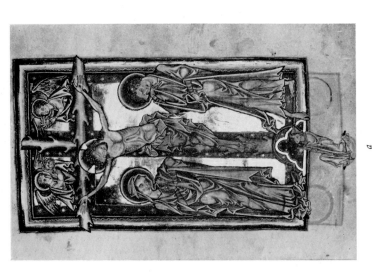

a. Crucifixion, from the Evesham Psalter, British Museum, MS. Add. 44874, f. 5: 12½ × 8¼ in. Painted on a patterned gold ground: the garments of the figures are tinted blue, red, brown, and green; the cross is green on a red background. At the foot kneels an abbot, probably Abbot Henry of Worcester (d. 1263). The book was written for the Abbey of Evesham, and had some connexion also with Richard of Cornwall, whose arms appear on one of the pages

b. Virgin and Child with Matthew Paris at her feet: tinted drawing from the *Historia Anglorum*, British Museum, MS. Royal 14 C. VII, f. 6: 14½ × 9½ in. It is very reasonable to assume that the drawing is by Paris himself

none of the delicate perceptiveness of the Westminster work. Elsewhere in Lincoln minster, Westminster sculptural influence is evident. The south door begun in 1256 may well be modelled on the north door of the abbey; the central tympanum has been sadly battered and somewhat sentimentally restored, but the little figures in the foliage scrolls of the arches have the poise and skill and gestures of the best Westminster work. Inside the new extension of the choir the angels already mentioned were, on the Westminster model, carved in the spandrels; as the scheme advanced, its meaning deepened, and instead of musical instruments one angel holds a naked soul, one a balance (Pl. 100 *b*), a third sternly expels the naked figures of Adam and Eve. Solidly and broadly made, they are intended to be seen from below, and it is from there, unlike Westminster, that their effect is most telling. This is a local school, to whom the graces of the porch carvings must have seemed strangely foreign. But the Lincolnshire stone on which the masons worked has a warmth of tint, and there is no lack of subtlety in the colouristic effects of contrasting Purbeck colonnettes and of the play of light and shade over these broad carved surfaces. The Angel Choir has rare beauties of its own, owing little to other examples whether English or French.

One feature of the rise of Gothic art is a new emphasis on simple, recognizable human emotions. In the Crucifixion, St. John leans his head on his hand, his face furrowed with grief (Pl. 101*a*). In the Nativity of the Missal of Henry of Chichester the Virgin gives the Child her breast, while a woman draws back the bed-covering to aid her (an original inventive touch typical of this humanizing movement). The seated Virgins no longer present the Child frontally to the congregation; it is their own relationship within the carved or painted scene that is stressed, as in the famous roundel at Chichester, work of the mid-thirteenth century.

It is in a group of manuscripts associated with Salisbury that this tendency can best be seen. While in France the ornateness of Gothic was being stylized and refined to a medium capable of wide ranges of indirect expressiveness, clear, rhythmical, precise as a piece of Mozartian music, England returned to a more frankly narrative style. The Amesbury Psalter (All Souls College, Oxford), the Missal of Henry of Chichester (John Rylands Library), and the Rutland Psalter (Belvoir Castle) are a trio of masterpieces, all from the middle of the century, Gothic in their diapered backgrounds, curving postures, softly falling drapery, but classicist in their sense of rounded forms and their strong feeling for the human implications of the story. Whereas in France the window tradition of splitting up the page into small scenes still held good, these English books have full-page Crucifixions, Nativities, and, in the Rutland Psalter, Old Testament scenes.

The great central school is, however, that of St. Albans. Here all the arts were practised: fresco paintings of the thirteenth century, a nobly posed series of Crucifixions, still survive on the pillars of the nave; a St. Albans craftsman, Walter of Colchester, made the shrine for the relics of St. Thomas Becket (translated 1220), and the scriptorium was in the thirties presided over by Matthew Paris, the historian, famous also to his contemporaries for his skill in illumination. Space does not permit here any attempt to distinguish between the many works that have at various times been claimed for him. In his *Chronica Minora* there is a full-page drawing of the Virgin and Child, with the inscribed figure of Matthew himself kneeling before her. It is a mature and powerful work; the sense of weight and volume in the figure, so securely posed upon the seat, would not seem out of place in the Giottesque painters of the Trecento (Pl. 101 *b*). Far less sympathetic and pleasing than her Amesbury sister, this representation of the Virgin shows a grasp of visual forms in advance of the technical level of the times. Tinted line drawings, to which English artists have always been so partial, were much favoured at St. Albans, and it is a medium which reveals all the skill of the draughtsmanship, the sense of proportion, the reasonable anatomy, the bunched and knotted drapery, carefully examined and no longer conventionally formalized. Hair and beards fall in rippling curls, the heads are slightly bent and often seen three-quarters full; the

PLATE 102

a   *b*

a. Abraham and Melchisedeck, from the Psalter in St. John's College, Cambridge, MS. K. 26: 11 × 7¼ in. These pictures (46 in all) are bound up with a late-fourteenth-century text, and nothing is certainly known of their provenance. Stylistically they seem to belong to the St. Albans style of the late thirteenth century, and are notable examples of it

b. Felbrigg brass, 1416, Felbrigg Church, Norfolk. Sir Simon Felbrigg and his wife Margaret (cousin to Anne of Bohemia) who died 1416, when the brass was made, the spaces for the date of his death being left blank. He is represented as standard-bearer to Richard II. Notice his palettes bearing St. George's cross, and the garter on his left leg. She wears kirtle, mantle, and crespine head-dress, and has a pet dog at her feet. Above are the arms of Richard II and his queen, and on the middle pinnacle those of Sir Simon and his wife, with his badge, a fetterlock, repeated. Richard II's badge, a white hart, forms the corbel from which the arches spring

PLATE 103

Page from the Ormesby Psalter, MS. Douce 366, f. 55ᵛ. In the initial D (blue and gold, pink background) is Christ before the high priest. In the bottom border is the story of the unicorn (symbol of the Incarnation) which loses its fierceness in the lap of a virgin. The main design of the border is in blue and gold, with details in pink and green

slanting eyes, with their strongly marked pupils, gaze always sideways. It was a centre with wide influences: certainly the painter of the frescoes at Westminster was well conversant with the style; a noble book, the Oscott Psalter, has similar echoes, and might almost be from the hand of the fresco painter; a group of Apocalypses, notably one in Trinity College, Cambridge (MS. R. 16. 2), and one in the Bibliothèque Nationale, Paris (M.S. fr. 403), also have stylistic connexions with the St. Albans School. The illustrated pages bound in with a later Psalter, MS. K. 26 of St. John's College, Cambridge, may be taken as the climax of this style before it loses its individuality in the general acceptance of the rhythm, poses, and physiognomies of French predominance (Pl. 102 *a*).

Illustrated Apocalypses, with their scenes of the terrors of the Last Days, the Rider on the White Horse, the Many-headed Beast, the Mouth of Hell, enjoyed a great vogue at the end of the century. Their sensational but symbolic incidents replaced in popular favour the bestiaries, which had long catered for similar interests and in the early years of the century had attracted some of the ablest artists. One of the Apocalypses (MS. Douce 180 in the Bodleian Library), partially composed of finished paintings, partially of uncompleted drawings, must receive special mention, for its angel scenes are among the loveliest of English conceptions and have a placid, dream-like beauty seldom equalled.

More genuinely Gothic in its small, swaying figures and its closely wrought tracery is the Windmill Psalter (now in the Pierpont Morgan Library, MS. 19). The calendar is missing and it is hard to date it at all exactly: but its vigorous figure-drawing suggests thirteenth- rather than fourteenth-century work, and its draperies have something of the metallic quality of an earlier age. The work of an able and original artist, its famous initial to the first Psalm, with its fine mesh of pen work, may be taken as bridging the passage from the Salisbury School to the great highly decorated manuscripts of the first half of the fourteenth century. These fall into three main groups, the East Anglian, with the Ormesby and Gorleston Psalters as examples; the York-Nottingham group, with Queen Isabella's Psalter and the Tickhill Psalter; and the so-called Queen Mary's Psalter and Psalter of Richard of Canterbury, these last two being decorated by the same hand, a very skilled draughts-man, whose tinted drawings are among the great examples of this particularly English convention.

It is in the East Anglian School that we find some of the most splendid page layouts of English art; script, historiated initial, line-ending, and endlessly elaborate borders are built up into intricate displays, which at times defeat their own object by be-coming fussy, wearisome, and a little pretentious. One of the most splendid, to judge from photographs, was the Douai Psalter, destroyed in the First World War; the St. Omer and Gorleston Psalters are characteristic examples; the Ormesby Psalter, a puzzling book by various hands, shows classical motifs from some Italian prototype woven into this English pattern with considerable gain to the firmness and clarity of the design (Pl. 103). Latest of the group, the Luttrell Psalter (c. 1335–40) has the same treatment of the page, but its grotesques, its large and ludicrous monsters, are crudely drawn and the line has almost been crossed between fantasy and buffoonery, though, as in all these manuscripts, there are some charming genre scenes of everyday agricultural life.

Elsewhere the countryside begins to bulk large in the artist's consciousness. The chapter-houses of York and Southwell have each a series of capitals, where the foliage is lovingly studied from the actual leaves of trees and hedgerows, studied with an accuracy that makes exact botanical identification possible (Pl. 104 a). This is a new relationship between visual experience and visual art, but these carvers, bred in a long tradition of pattern making, could still control these natural-istic growths which mask but never forsake the form of the capitals they so notably adorn. From now on these careful borrowings played a large part in English decorative art.

At the close of the thirteenth century the type of figure sculp-ture favoured by the court may be seen in the Eleanor crosses erected in the 90's. In the canopies the ogee curve is employed

PLATE 104

a. Hop-leaves capital: the chapter house, Southwell Minster, *c.* 1300. The leaves are carefully naturalistic in their treatment and belong to a style first popularized at Rheims Cathedral in the mid-thirteenth century. The sculpture of Southwell chapter house is closely related to that of the chapter house at York

b. Freestone effigy of a knight, early fourteenth century. There is no sense of death or repose. The knight draws his sword from its sheath, with little regard for his recumbent posture, but with a fine sense of curvilinear design

PLATE 105

The tomb of Lady Idoine Percy, Beverley Minster: detail of canopy. In the spandrels of the cusps of the ogee arch are the shields, held by knights (right) of Edward III (after 1340) and of Lady Idoine's family, FitzAlan; (left) of the Warenne family and of the lordship of Clun (this last held by a lady). Below the finial, God the Father holds the soul of the deceased in a cloth supported by angels. The larger angels, like those on the other face, may have held emblems of the Passion. Lady Idoine died in 1365, but the tomb may have been carved during her lifetime

(an early instance of it), and the crosses show in their figures
also an increasing sense of curving rhythms. They have a swaying motion, the head slightly bent in a contrary movement to
the hips; the drapery is flatly treated but is edged with small,
crumpled folds. The Virgin and Child in the York chapterhouse, though sadly mutilated, shows this mannered charm of
the first quarter of the century. Tomb effigies have again survived
more plentifully, and have in the female figures the same smooth
falling garments, though the recumbent attitude presents a
more rigid discipline. This in the male effigies was sometimes
avoided by the popular fashion of crossing the legs, so as to give
a coiling twist to the whole composition. On the knight's
tomb at Dorchester (Oxon.) the movement of legs, arms, and
head are conceived in a series of spirals, which give to it a
curiously modern, abstract appearance (Pl. 104 b). A new
material was now coming into use, alabaster, which was to play
a conspicuous part in English carving of the later middle ages.
An early example is the effigy of Edward II at Gloucester,
placed on his tomb some time after his death, one of the undoubted masterpieces of the century, though curiously oldfashioned in its stylized hair and beard and its sidelong glance
which recall the conventions of the St. Albans School. Above
the effigy rises a splendid canopy, and it is in these elaborate and
detailed works, and in the small-scale carving of bosses, that
fourteenth-century invention seems at its happiest. The Percy
tomb at Beverley (after 1339, possibly as late as the 60's), still
wonderfully complete and sharply cut, is a marvellously ingenious piece of pattern-making, and has a delicacy and elegance almost at variance with the stone from which it is
wrought (Pl. 105). The small figures on it have a sureness of
touch in their execution, whereas much of the large-scale
sculpture of the time, such as that on the west front of Exeter
(c. 1340–80), has a gauche clumsiness. There is in fact much
that is disappointing about English figure-carving as it has
come down to us from the last quarter of the fourteenth and first
quarter of the fifteenth centuries. At a time when France was
producing a new and vigorous realism and Claus Sluter was

working in Burgundy, there is nothing in England that shows
any real understanding of these neighbouring movements. The
well-known and much-admired Virgin and laughing Child
on the outer gateway of Winchester College has the smooth,
curving drapery of the international style but none of its suavity
of pose or expression. The best work is to be found in bronze,
but this from its expense was used only for the tombs of the very
great. The effigy of Edward III and the bronze mourners round
the tomb chest are works of genuine feeling, and the effigies of
the Black Prince, Richard II, and Anne of Bohemia make a
notable line of successors, where an actual likeness is more and
more vividly aimed at. This aim can be seen also in the alabaster effigy of Henry IV, cruder than the more stylized and individual 'laton' work, but with a convincing toughness of its
own.

The alabaster quarries of Nottingham, Lincoln, and York
provided much of the material for tomb effigies. They also provided the basis of a thriving English trade in small statues and
retables, many of which were exported to the Continent. From
the mid-fourteenth century till the Reformation, the industry
continued, growing more organized and less sensitive in its
productions. Some of the earlier pieces have considerable
quality, and are not unrelated to the much finer work that was
being done on an even smaller scale on ivory plaques, of which
the Grandisson triptych in the British Museum may be taken
as an example. But as the demand grew, it was met by readier,
more repetitive production, and a collection of English ala-
basters, unless most scrupulously picked, soon becomes wearisome, though even in the second half of the fifteenth century
works were produced as graceful and charming as the alabaster slab of the Annunciation inset on the tomb chest of
Thomas Boleyn in Wells cathedral, a wonderfully fresh
variant of a stock theme.

The carved effigy was not the only form of figural commemoration. England is pre-eminently the country of engraved
brasses, though the metal sheets seem mainly to have been
imported from Flanders and Cologne and the most splendid

brasses in England, those in St. Margaret's, King's Lynn, are by Flemish workmen. In England as opposed to the Continent the figures were cut out and bedded in stone, lettered surrounds and canopies being likewise cut out (Pl. 102 *b*). From the early fourteenth century till the late sixteenth this remained an extremely popular form of memorial, and even today many survive. At its best this is a medium of delicacy and distinction; in its economical lines a great survey of costume and armour is chronicled for us; but it lent itself to repetition and shop production and the later brasses reach a low level of insipid clumsiness.

The history of English painting is at this stage confused and hard to judge. From 1350 Master Hugh of St. Albans was in charge of the painted decorations of St. Stephen's chapel at Westminster. Something of the general design is known from early nineteenth-century copies, and a fragment, the scene of the children of Job, is now preserved in the British Museum. It is curiously Italianate in conception; the rounded modelling, the relations of the figures to the space are quite apart from Gothic conventions. Master Hugh is known to have had some painted 'Lombard' panels; certainly in some way Italian models were available. Their influence is visible not only in these wall-paintings but in the work of an English illuminator responsible for a series of illustrations to Genesis (B.M. MS. Egerton 1894) and to the so-called Derby Psalter. This was a Giottesque influence; Sienese models, more closely bound up with the general international style, can also be traced in pages such as the Gorleston Psalter Crucifixion. For a time it seems as though the English decorative school was submerged beneath an influx of continental styles. The English idiom of detailed, intricate surface patterning re-asserts itself, however, all the more intensely because on a small scale, in the psalters made for the Bohun family, where the Italian and English influences meet and blend.

English art was now losing its anonymity, at least to the extent that there are many known names of master masons, sculptors, painters, illuminators, and glaziers. It is not always, however, easy to attach particular works to particular names. Mr. John Harvey's researches have done much to bring these artists' names out of the oblivion of accounts and inventories and to associate them with relevant works, but when a great building was undertaken many hands were employed and we can rarely be sure that the genius visible in some work of art corresponds with the name that figures in the account roll. Such an artist with no identified paintings is Gilbert Prince, whose name figures frequently in the royal accounts between 1364 and 1396; the tasks noted are painting of banners, funeral pomps, festival decorations, but such were the normal employments of great painters from Leonardo downwards. The work that may with most likelihood be assigned to him is the large panel, 86 inches by 43 inches, of Richard II, probably painted for Westminster abbey and still hanging there. Gilbert, however, as he did not die till 1396, is a possible claimant for the most celebrated court painting of the time, the Wilton Diptych, for this famous problem piece of Richard II kneeling before the Virgin is generally dated, on heraldic grounds, to *c.* 1395. There has been much controversy as to whether its delicate and precise beauty, its convincing masterliness, are due to a French or English hand. Subject and provenance make it clear that it has an English origin; stylistic parallels are more easily found in France, but in the absence of English comparative material these cannot be considered conclusive. Many of the duc de Berri's treasures have survived. When the rebels burned John of Gaunt's palace of the Savoy in 1381, what may not have perished in the fire?

English painting at the close of the fourteenth and opening of the fifteenth centuries is in fact wonderfully varied in its styles. A series of paintings collected from a scrapbook and recon⁄ structed into a Carmelite Missal (B.M. MS. Add. 29704-5, 44892) shows Bohemian and Burgundian influences upon the various artists at work on it. A certain Hermann Scheere, an illuminator who had connexions with Cologne, was working in London in the opening years of the fifteenth century and was the leading artist amongst those responsible for the Bedford

Hours (B.M. MS. Add. 42131) painted between 1414–35. Doubtless other foreign artists were attracted to Lancastrian London and settled and practised there. John Siferwas, a Dominican friar, is a named English artist who reflects some of these foreign influences in his work in the Sherborne Missal (Alnwick castle) and the Lovell Lectionary (B.M. MS. Harley 7026); in the latter manuscript the presentation plate showing Siferwas offering his book to Lord Lovell is a striking instance of the new interest in portraiture, which seems to have resulted in a numerous production of small panels, showing the head and shoulders. It is a type common to France and Flanders, and in England seems to have been practised with no particular individuality or distinction; but the examples known are mainly, possibly entirely, sixteenth-century or later copies of earlier works. Now that the Portrait Gallery panel of Margaret Beaufort is known to have another head beneath its present surface, and the same gallery's portrait of Henry VII is generally attributed to a visiting Fleming, English panel portraiture, between Richard II and Henry VIII, can boast few extant triumphs. The countess of Salisbury (*c.* 1532–5) (National Portrait Gallery) is perhaps the best survival of this class of work and its rigid lines and flat head-dress and garments serve as a link with the decorative costume pieces of the Elizabethan age. Subject paintings on panel are comparatively rare. The Norwich retable (Norwich cathedral), a series of five panels of which the central one, the Crucifixion, has been cut down to form an even board, has been associated, from its heraldic ornament, with the suppression of the Revolt of 1381. Painted on a background of gilt-embossed gesso, the slender, brittle figures and the carefully painted clothes recall the work of the East Anglian miniaturists. The painting of the Crucifixion in the collection of the late Viscount Lee of Fareham is a work of uncertain provenance but of strongly English characteristics. It has many parallels with the fine miniatures of the Hours of Queen Elizabeth (Dyson Perrins Collection, Malvern), which probably dates from *c.* 1415–*c.* 1440. As compared with the Norwich retable the figures are more rounded and better pro-

portioned. The artist had certainly seen some contemporary
Flemish work, but he still uses a conventionalized rocky ground
space, and the blue background, now much flaked, can never
have conveyed much spatial illusion. It is, however, distinguished work and if it represents an active school of painters
their output would have taken a worthy place in north-west
European art.

In the most notable surviving painted cycle of the second half
of the fifteenth century, the Eton chapel wall-paintings (1479–
83), Flemish influence is dominant. The artist was William
Baker, a good English name, but iconographically and stylistically the frescoes are dependent on Burgundian manuscripts
of the Miracles of the Virgin, such as that which is now MS.
Douce 374 in the Bodleian Library. Their grisaille treatment,
their full draperies and experiments in perspective are found
some years earlier in the illustrations to Thomas Chaundler's
Liber Apologeticus, now in Trinity College, Cambridge.

One branch of Gothic art was peculiarly associated with
England, that of embroidery. The Cuthbert stole shows an
early proficiency in the medium. It had been recorded as far
back as the Norman Conquest that Englishwomen were very
accomplished with the needle and the Bayeux Tapestry,
whether made in England or Normandy, may be taken as an
example of this type of skill. By the second half of the thirteenth century, English embroidery, *opus anglicanum*, enjoyed
a wide continental repute. In the Vatican inventory of 1295 it
is mentioned 113 times. Many pieces, some of them papal gifts,
still survive on the Continent. One of the finest was the gift of
Clement V to St. Bertrand de Comminges, where the figure
scenes are set on a closely patterned ground. Some of them,
such as the education of the Virgin, have a delicacy of line,
which even in this material recalls contemporary works such
as the Douce Apocalypse. The Pienza cope, presented to the
cathedral by Pius IV in 1462, is probably work of the late
fourteenth or early fifteenth centuries, and is one of the most
magnificent of the surviving pieces. The better-known Syon
cope (in the Victoria and Albert Museum) cannot compare

PLATE 106

a. Light from Gloucester east window, 1347–9. Figure of St. Peter holding the abbey church which was dedicated to him. His nimbus is light blue, the diapered background dark blue. The rest is carried out in white and yellow stain. The window was erected as a memorial of Crécy

b. Light from a window in the north clerestory of the choir, Great Malvern, *c.* 1460–70. St. Wulfstan, Bishop of Worcester (1062–95), in white and gold vestments, with red dalmatic and apparels. Black-and-white checker pavement. The canopy is in white and yellow stain. Blue background for the figure, red for the canopy

PLATE 107

a. Opus Anglicanum. Panel from the orphrey from Marnhull Priory in Dorset-shire, now in the Victoria and Albert Museum. The figures are embroidered with silk on a ground of gold thread. The style is that of the early fourteenth century

b. Richard Beauchamp, Earl of Warwick: bronze, cast by William Austen from a wooden model by John Massingham. The tomb was commissioned in 1454, fifteen years after the earl's death, and therefore is in no way a likeness. It is in the Beauchamp Chapel, St. Mary's, Warwick

with some of the more splendid and individual vestments preserved on the Continent, but in the same museum the panels of the Marnhull orphrey show the range of expression and vivid narrative quality that was achieved (Pl. 107 a).

The colours which, somewhat faded, still glow on the embroidered vestments are more brilliant in the stained glass that survives in some quantity. Canterbury has the greatest collection of early thirteenth-century glass, but it is at York that the developments of the glaziers' art can best be studied. During the Civil War, a period very dangerous to pictured windows, those of the minster were protected by Fairfax; in the replacing of the glass after the war of 1939–45, much cleaning and re-grouping of scattered fragments was undertaken. York has been doubly fortunate; in preservation, and in the scholarly skill and devotion which has surveyed and re-interpreted its great possessions. In the Five Sisters window of the north transept the minster has a notable example of grisaille glass, where leading, tracery, and strips of coloured glass build up a trellis frame-work through which on a background of greyish glass runs a scroll and leaf pattern. The Five Sisters is work of the later thirteenth century. Early in the fourteenth century the discovery of the silver stain process (painting the glass with a preparation of silver, which when fired produced a yellow colour on white glass or green on blue) increased the range of details that could be secured without separate leading of each different colour. By 1338 when Robert the Glasier made the York west window this process was freely used. The type of design also had changed. Each light has a large single figure under an elaborate Gothic canopy against a single-coloured background, a type that was to be demonstrated even more finely in the huge east window of Gloucester, glazed between 1347 and 1349 to commemorate the victory at Crécy (Pl. 106 a). These stately individualized figures under their elaborate canopies reach their full development in the glass of the ante-chapel of New College, Oxford, where a new subtlety of colour, cooler and less vivid but with a brilliant shimmering effect, lends especial distinction. In the fifteenth century York was once more one of the great centres, and the one whose produce is best preserved, for, apart from York city itself, the rich collection of fifteenth-century glass in Great Malvern priory church is the work of the York glaziers. Very considerable realism had by now been achieved. The figures are rounded, the draperies fall in natural curves (Pl. 106 *b*); in the narrative scenes a genre element appears. This reflects an improvement in the cartoons; there is also noticeable a lack of originality in using them. At Malvern the same cartoon, sometimes reversed, was made to serve for various personages. By the close of the century the English tradition, which can be so clearly followed at York, was being modified by Flemish influences and free borrowing from fifteenth-century Flemish designs, a repertory which England could not equal. Henry VII's glazier was a German by origin, Barnard Flower (d. 1517), who contributed four windows to the great series of richly coloured and dramatic scenes in King's College chapel, Cambridge (1515–31), which marks the splendid close of our medieval glass.

English sculpture of the fifteenth century is also something pattern-ridden. The gallery of carved figures in Henry V's chantry at Westminster, completed in the middle years of the century, contains notable figures such as that of St. George, in which the problem of representing plate armour in stone is capably handled without any loss of movement and liveliness, but the smaller figures are squat, unexpressive, and repetitive, and the famous relief of the king on horseback, with its attempt to render a landscape background, is, for all its enterprise, clumsy work. The figures of the choir screen at York are almost grotesque with their frizzed hair and gauche poses. But much of the sculpture of the time has disappeared; the great reredoses with tiers of figures were left as shattered empty niches by waves of iconoclasm. Here and there fragments suggest that work of real quality has perished. Winchester has some striking heads, full of feeling and power. In the Beauchamp chapel at Warwick some charming figures surround the east window, and the great ceiling of the Oxford Divinity School includes in its pendent tabernacles some small figures vigorously cut.

It is in the Beauchamp chapel, referred to above, that England's greatest fifteenth-century statue is to be found, the recumbent bronze effigy of Richard Beauchamp, earl of Warwick. In full plate armour, the earl lies with his head on his helm; his eyes are open, gazing on the Virgin, carved in a corbel above the east window; his hands are not folded in prayer, but, apart, they seem to be welcoming the celestial vision. The bronze is treated in smooth, broad planes, but wrinkles and veins are clearly marked. In its finality and conviction it rises above the English idiom as we know it elsewhere into the company of European masterpieces (Pl. 107 *b*). It was cast by William Austen of London, and the wooden pattern for it was commissioned from John Massingham. It is tempting to see in Massingham a knowable artistic personality; he had already been working for three years in the Beauchamp chapel, and the carved figures of the window and the models for the moving and expressive bronze weepers round the tomb are probably his. Ten years earlier he had been working at All Souls. Here only the general framework, reset with later figures, remains in position, but the statues of Henry VI and Archbishop Chichele, which formerly stood above the main gateway, are preserved and, despite much weathering, can be seen to be works of unusual ability; the cloaked, restricted figures, adapted for narrow niches, are given movement and variety by the slight but emphatic fall of the drapery.

The Warwick effigy stands by itself, the climax of our bronze figures, till, some sixty years later, the Italian Pietro Torrigiano (1472–1528) designed the tomb of Henry VII and Elizabeth of York and that of Lady Margaret Beaufort, using the old Gothic convention of recumbent pose with joined hands raised in prayer, but modelling the faces with a new truth to nature and spreading the drapery in full, pliant folds, that belong to the high renaissance in their luxuriant sense of form. Between Massingham and Torrigiano, however, many fine tombs were produced, of which one must stand as an example, that of Alice, duchess of Suffolk, at Ewelme, cut in alabaster. She lies under a canopy with a frieze of angels, crowned by standing angels carved in wood, while more angels hold heraldic shields on the side of the tomb chest. Beneath lies the lady's corpse, almost a skeleton, somewhat gruesomely shown; above it on the chest's foot, invisible except by bending down to floor level, is painted the Annunciation, the colours still well preserved in their obscurity. The thin ascetic face of the duchess, the eyes half-closed, is clearly a likeness, the portrait of a woman of character who has known and suffered much; now death has come; already the cheeks are half-sunken; the smooth sheen of the alabaster, smoothly carved with little modelling, increases the impression of the final moment (Pl. 108 *a*); there is none of the deep lines, the round indentations, the humorous half-smile which Torrigiano gives to Lady Margaret.

The last great series of our Gothic standing figures is in Henry VII's chapel. This assemblage of saints is by many hands, some probably not English: there is a German look about these reading prophets, with their fantastic headgear and their voluminous, sharply indented cloaks; the group of St. Sebastian between the archers is set on Gothic pedestals under crocketed canopies, but a renaissance example, from Italy if at some removes, lies behind this straining, youthful nude (Pl. 108 *b*). It was, however, mainly in decoration, in friezes and roundels fixed on Gothic frames, in new classical motifs, rams' skulls and cornucopias, that the renaissance influence became apparent, and the Gothic style was still powerful when in 1538 the first iconoclastic blow was struck by Thomas Cromwell's injunctions ordering the destruction of 'such feigned images' as were 'abused with pilgrimages'. Of the cult images of England many of the most revered were of wood: a holocaust began, the first of many in which our medieval wooden figures perished, so that we only know this great branch of carving in the superb work of screens and choir stalls, such as those worked under the direction of William Brownfleet of Ripon (*fl.* 1489–1520) or the angels of the roof of Westminster hall carved by Robert Grassington in Richard II's reign. Gold and silver work had cupidity as an added foe. The great silver shrines such as that of Becket were melted down, and there are

PLATE 108

a. Alabaster effigy of Alice de la Pole, Duchess of Suffolk (d. 1477) from her tomb at Ewelme

b. St. Sebastian between the Arche: Henry VII Chapel, Westminster

few pieces of our ecclesiastical metalwork that have survived. The crozier of William of Wykeham, piously preserved at New College, is a rare reminder of this gap in our artistic heritage.

The history of English iconoclasm has never yet been fully written. Medieval builders were none too nice about their treatment of the art of previous generations. When they rebuilt the choir of St. Mary's abbey, York, the great column figures, only some seventy years old, were buried in the new foundations. But in the sixteenth and seventeenth century religious fanaticism was added to the mere utilities of changing taste. As Thomas Cromwell's engineers blew up Reading abbey or Lewes priory, whole chapters of English carving were lost, and the scattered stones, less valuable than the squared ashlar, were roughly hacked to serve what building use they could. Torn leaves from illuminated missals blew about college quadrangles, and vestments, the prized *opus anglicanum*, were ripped in pieces or set to vile purposes. But even as destruction took its course, with a thorough violence almost unparalleled on the Continent, palliatives appeared. John Leland in 1533 was made 'king's antiquary'. He noted many things now lost to us and some he was able to preserve. The age of collecting began, and something was saved, though little could be done for the great statuary schemes of the abbeys and eventually of the cathedrals also. The weather has joined with man in the destruction of our medieval achievement; but enough remains to show its accomplishment, its varying history, its moments of originality, its times of decline, its adoption of foreign fashions, and its recurrent assertion of peculiarly English qualities.

WORKS FOR REFERENCE

Boase, T. S. R. *English Art 1100–1216* (*O.H.E.A.* iii, Oxford, 1953).

Bond, F. *Fonts and Font Covers* (London, 1908); *Screens and Galleries in English Churches* (London, 1908), *Wood Carvings in English Churches*: i. Misericords; ii. Stalls and Tabernacle Work (London, 1910).

Borenius, T. and Tristram, E. W. *English Medieval Painting* (Florence and Paris, 1927).

BRIEGER, P. H. *English Art 1216–1307* (*O.H.E.A.* iv, Oxford, forthcoming).

CHAMOT, M. *English Mediaeval Enamels* (London, 1930).

CHRISTIE, A. G. I. *English Mediaeval Embroidery* (Oxford, 1938).

CROSSLEY, F. H. *English Church Monuments 1150–1550* (London, 1921).

DODWELL, C. R. *The Canterbury School of Illumination* (Cambridge, 1954).

EGBERT, D. D. *The Tickhill Psalter and Related Manuscripts* (Princeton, 1940).

EVANS, J. *English Art 1307–1461* (*O.H.E.A.* v, Oxford, 1949).

KENDRICK, SIR T. D. *Saxon Art to 900* (London, 1938); *Late Saxon and Viking Art* (London, 1949).

KEYSER, C. E. *Norman Tympana and Lintels*, 2nd ed. (London, 1927).

LONGHURST, M. H. *English Ivories* (London, 1926).

MILLAR, E. G. *English Illuminated Manuscripts from the 10th to the 13th Century* (Paris and Brussels, 1926); *English Illuminated Manuscripts of the 14th and 15th Centuries* (Paris and Brussels, 1928).

MOLESWORTH, H. D. *Mediaeval Sculpture in England* (London, 1951).

OAKESHOTT, W. *The Sequence of English Medieval Art* (London, 1950); *The Artists of the Winchester Bible* (London, 1945).

PRIOR, E. S. and GARDNER, A. *An Account of Mediaeval Figure Sculpture in England* (Cambridge, 1912).

RICE, D. TALBOT. *English Art 871–1100* (*O.H.E.A.*, ii, Oxford, 1952).

RICKERT, M. *Painting in Britain: The Middle Ages* (London, 1954).

SAUNDERS, O. E. *A History of English Art in the Middle Ages* (Oxford, 1932); *English Illumination*, 2 vols. (Paris and Florence, 1928).

SAXL, F. and SWARZENSKI, H. *English Sculpture of the Twelfth Century* (London, 1954).

STONE, L. *Sculpture in Britain: The Middle Ages* (London, 1955).

TRISTRAM, E. W. *English Medieval Wall Painting*: i, The Twelfth Century (Oxford, 1944); ii, The Thirteenth Century, 2 vols. (Oxford, 1950).

WOODFORDE, C. *English Stained and Painted Glass* (Oxford, 1954).

WORMALD, F. *English Drawings of the Tenth and Eleventh Centuries* (London, 1952).

ZARNECKI, G. *English Romanesque Sculpture 1066–1140* (London, 1951); *Later English Romanesque Sculpture 1140–1210* (London, 1953).

XV. LEARNING AND EDUCATION

1. *Anglo-Saxon Period*

WHEN Augustine made Canterbury the head-quarters of Pope Gregory's mission to the English, he and his fellow monks had from the outset to apply themselves to a great educational undertaking. They had to make intelligible a religion, the scriptures, theology, and service-books of which were written in a foreign tongue. What provision Augustine made for the instruction of converts is not recorded. It must have been, however, partly to serve an educational need that the monks sent by Gregory in 601 to reinforce his mission brought with them a large number of books. Thomas Elmham, the fifteenth-century historian of Augustine's abbey of SS. Peter and Paul, outside Canterbury, termed these volumes with some truth '*primitiae librorum totius ecclesiae Anglicanae*'. The existence of a school at Canterbury prompted Bishop Felix in 631 to ask Archbishop Honorius for *pedagogi* and *magistri* with whom to staff the one that he wished to set up at Dunwich for the benefit of his East Anglian converts. As this request was for professional teachers and masters, it may be inferred that at Canterbury, in accordance with the growing practice of western Christendom, there was already an archbishop's school in addition to the cloister-school for novices which Augustine's monks must have instituted. The work of Irish missionaries soon proved no less important than that of the Roman in transforming the pagan culture of the English peoples. The need for the re-establishment of Christianity in Northumbria after the fall of King Edwin and the flight of Paulinus gave Irish missionary enterprise its greatest opportunity in England. Monasteries founded under Irish influence quickly became as important for the spread of Christian learning and education here as they were already proving to be in western Europe. The cultural influences of Ireland were not confined to Northumbria. Glastonbury has claim to be regarded as hardly less fertile in its propagation of Celtic tradition.

With the advent of Archbishop Theodore and Abbot Hadrian in 668 a new chapter opened. Their prestige soon drew students to Canterbury from all parts of England and from Ireland too. Even though an elementary knowledge of Greek was one of the distinctive accomplishments of contemporary Irish scholarship, no Irish monk could compare in classical and theological learning with these two scholars who were as familiar with the heritage of Byzantium as with that of Rome. The most distinguished offspring of the union of the continental and the Irish traditions was St. Aldhelm, 'the father of Latin poetry in England', the first Englishman to win fame as a scholar in western Europe. Dr. M. R. James has reckoned that 'quotations from some forty Latin authors, pagan and Christian, may be traced in his works, made in such a manner as to imply acquaintance with their writings'. In a well-known letter excusing himself on account of his studies from spending Christmas with Bishop Hedde at Winchester, Aldhelm mentions, in addition to classical exercises, his preoccupation with mathematics, astronomy, and Roman law.

Such an advance in learning could not have been made without a considerable collection of books being available. The distinction of being an outstanding benefactor in this respect is given by Bede to Benedict Biscop (d. 690), friend and successor of Abbot Hadrian, who endowed his twin foundations of Wearmouth and Jarrow with a notable library, which in the course of many years he had collected on the Continent. Without the use of this library his pupil, Bede (d. 735), could never have won his exalted reputation in the middle ages as theologian and scholar. In Bede's lifetime and for a century after his death Northumbria gave the lead to the remarkable con tribution made by English scholars and scribes to the revival of learning in Europe. The labours of English mission/ aries like SS. Willibrord, Boniface, and Willibald, greatly in/ creased intellectual intercourse between western Europe and their homeland. Great as was the achievement and influence of Bede, the scholarly activities of eighth/century England were by no means confined to the monasteries. The northern episco/ pate notably fostered the cause of education. Bishop Acca (d. 740), founder of a fine library at Hexham, was taught in the household of Bosa (d. *c.* 705), bishop of York. There were schoolboys in the household of Bosa's successor, St. John of Beverley (d. 721). Under Archbishop Ecgberht (d. 766) this practice was further developed, and the school of York took shape with Æthelberht (d. 780) and, after his accession as archbishop, his pupil Alcuin (d. 804).

Alcuin has left a memorable poem descriptive of the school and the library of York, a school where instruction in the seven liberal arts led on to study of the Scriptures. Such a school was more than a grammar school. It aimed at the education of a well/equipped clergy. A single teacher was essaying to cover a curriculum which five hundred years later would have been appropriate to a university. It was a school of this sort that Alcuin wished might be re/established at Canterbury, when in 797 he wrote from abroad urging the clergy and nobles of Kent to obtain 'doctors and masters of holy scripture, lest the word of God be lacking among you'.[1]

While Alcuin was writing these words, ruin threatened Christian civilization in England. In 793 Lindisfarne was plundered by Viking war/bands: in the following year Jarrow. A hundred years later King Alfred was moved to lament that such was the decay of learning on account of the ravages of the Danes that very few clergy south of the Humber, none in Wessex, not many beyond the Humber knew enough Latin to understand the meaning of their service/books or to translate a letter from Latin into their mother/tongue. In setting himself the task of reviving educational standards he aimed at ensuring

[1] *Councils and Eccl. Docts., &c.* (ed. Haddan and Stubbs), iii, p. 797.

that all clergy of his kingdom could read Latin and all young freemen English. With heroic application he himself took the lead in providing translations of such books as he deemed it 'most necessary for all men to know'. In so doing he inaugurated the literary use of English prose.

Owing to the collapse of monasticism throughout England caused by the Danish invasions, the main task of educational reconstruction fell to the bishops and clergy during the first fifty years after Alfred's death. The school at Glastonbury, where St. Dunstan received his education, was under the control of a community of secular priests. A similar connexion seems to account for the few other schools that are known to have existed in the tenth century. Eventually under the inspiration of St. Dunstan (d. 988) and his disciples St. Oswald (d. 992) of Worcester and St. Æthelwold (d. 984) of Winchester monasticism revived; it was, however, the influence of Alfred that was reflected in the works of Ælfric, author of the earliest Latin grammar of medieval Europe. Ælfric wrote for the instruction of a wide circle: his *Dialogue* was designed for the benefit of English schoolboys whether they were to be monks or not: his translations of Scripture and his homilies were composed with the thegn as well as the parish priest in view. In the hands of Ælfric (*fl.* 1006), Byrhtferth (*fl.* 1000), Bishop Wulfstan (d. 1095), and other writers, the English language was made a noble literary instrument for prose and verse and a remarkable vehicle of education during the last century before the Norman Conquest and was unsurpassed by any other European vernacular. With the coming of the Normans the English language was displaced and confined to humble usage for the next three hundred years.

2. *AngloNorman Monasticism and the Twelfthcentury Renaissance*

The Norman régime imparted new intellectual stimulus to monastic life in England. But whereas the intellectual activities of AngloSaxon monasteries had redounded to the advantage

of the nation at large, the notable literary productivity of monastic cloisters during the century following the Conquest was
more self-centred. The histories invaluable for subsequent historians and the lives of saints were composed primarily for the
benefit of individual houses. The schools of Anglo-Saxon
monasteries had been open to external scholars, but those of the
Anglo-Norman generally were not. Within the greater houses,
notwithstanding the importation of a number of monks from
Normandy, Old English traditions survived. Their hagio-
graphy was largely concerned with Old English saints, and
their best histories reflected the influence of Bede. The most
notable Anglo-Norman historians, Osbern (*fl.* 1090) and
Eadmer (d. *c.* 1124) of Christ Church, Canterbury, William
of Malmesbury (d. *c.* 1143), Simeon of Durham (*fl.* 1130), and
Orderic Vitalis of Saint-Evroul (d. *c.* 1143) were English or
half-English by birth. Notwithstanding their separation from
society the black monks acted as the chief medium through
which England made contact with the intellectual renaissance
that was stirring clerical life on the Continent during the
twelfth century. The reputation of Lanfranc and Anselm as
theologians was won before they came to England and belongs
rather to Norman history; but in the professional field England
is specially indebted to Lanfranc for his introduction of the
standard western text of the Vulgate and for the foundation that
he furnished for the new study of canon law. The cultural distinction of the monasteries during the first century after the Conquest lay in other directions, in the growth of their libraries, in
the literary activity of their scriptoria, in the knowledge of
classical authors, and in the polished latinity of their ablest
monks.

The addition of a considerable number of French-speaking
foreigners to the landed and trading classes in England and the
rapid growth of the towns after the Conquest greatly increased
the need of school education, and effected a revolution in the
curriculum, as Norman-French replaced English as the everyday speech of the upper orders of society. Evidence for ascertaining the number of schools and their location at any period

during the middle ages is insufficient; and for the first two centuries after the coming of the Normans it is very meagre indeed. Nevertheless, there are enough grounds to warrant the surmise that every fair-sized town had a school at some time during these two centuries but not always continuously, and that schools existed for a time at least in places where none might have been expected. Early in the twelfth century Theo-bald of Étampes, the first master known to have lectured at Oxford, expressed the opinion, albeit in a rhetorical context, that 'throughout Normandy and England not only in the cities, but also in small towns, there are as many practised schoolmasters as there are tax-collectors and other royal offi-cials'.[1] Reginald, a monk of Durham, writing in the second half of the century about the miracles worked by St. Cuthbert, tells how the key of the church of Norham, in which a priest held classes for boys living near the Scottish border, was found in the gullet of a great salmon netted in the Tweed, having been pitched into a deep pool by young Haldene, who was due for a beating on account of idleness.[2] Early in the fourteenth century there were as many as eight grammar schools in the county of Lincoln.

Song-schools attached to cathedral and collegiate churches continued throughout the medieval period to teach small boys 'to synge and to rede'. But the standard, as one of the elder boys in the song-school described by Chaucer in the *Prioresses Tale* (ll. 84–95) explains, was elementary: 'I lerne song, I can but smal grammere.' He did not pretend to understand the Latin words of a service book, but learned them by heart.

> And than he song it wel and boldely
> Fro word to word acording with the note.

In the nine secular cathedrals the primary responsibility for the choristers and the song-school rested with the precentor who also might suppress unlicensed song-schools, kept by 'divers chaplains, holy water-carriers and others', from competing with that of the cathedral. Great interest was shown in the

[1] *Collectanea* (Oxf. Hist. Soc.), ii, p. 158.
[2] *Reginaldi monachi Dunelm. Libellus* (Surtees Soc.), p. 149.

development of church music, and song-schools rendered an important service in that connexion. They helped, too, to serve the more general educational purposes of the modern primary or preparatory school.

The provision of masters to teach grammar and the liberal arts was made an episcopal charge by papal decree in 826. Subsequent legislation to this same end was reinforced by the Lateran Council of 1215, which required every cathedral and every sufficiently endowed collegiate church to provide free schooling in grammar for all clerks by attaching a prebend to the mastership, and every metropolitan church to provide a theologian. In the secular cathedrals this responsibility came to be vested during the course of the twelfth century in one of the canons, generally known as *magister scholarum*, but by the end of the century as chancellor. In the eight dioceses where the cathedral churches were under monastic administration the bishop usually retained the appointment of a schoolmaster in his own hands, leaving the prior and convent to provide a theological lecturer; and so, too, at Carlisle where the cathe-dral church was linked with a priory of Austin canons.

In some towns the appointment of the master of the grammar school is found in the twelfth century to rest with a house of Austin canons. At Bristol the grammar school had ancient association with 'the guild or brotherhood of the community of the clergy and people of Bristol' or the Guild of Kalendars, as it was better known. London, as might be expected, was not restricted to a single school. In addition to St. Paul's school there were two other privileged schools, one attached to the church of St. Mary of the Arches, the other to the college of St. Martin's-le-Grand. For any additional school the licence of the master of the cathedral school was required.

While the revival and extension of grammar schools was taking place in England, an educational movement of greater import was gathering momentum among the secular clergy of Normandy and France where cathedral schools, such as those of Chartres, Laon, and Paris, were rapidly winning fame for their concern not only with the liberal arts but also with theology and law. The influence of these developments was soon felt in England, as scholars crossed overseas to avail themselves of the better facilities for study, and as scholars trained in continental schools came to win a livelihood by opening schools in England where clerks might study these subjects. There were bishops in twelfthcentury England, who by their own eminence in learning or by their employment of trained scholars from abroad in their households, were in a position to lend encouragement to the growth of a similar movement in this country. Archbishop Theobald (d. 1161) by his choice of able scholars for his *familia* stimulated the study of ecclesiastical law. The *familia* of his successor, Archbishop Becket, which was noted for its *eruditi*, included John of Salisbury (d. 1180), one of the greatest scholars of his age, and Herbert of Bosham, the hebraist. During the course of the century the secular cathedral churches were all influenced by this new movement. The study of law at Lincoln was in sufficient repute by 1160 to attract St. Thorlak from Iceland; but with the appointment of William de Monte as chancellor about 1190, Lincoln became more noted for theology. The study of law prospered at Exeter during the time of Bishop Bartholomew. Gerald of Wales (d. *c.* 1220), who studied theology at Lincoln when he could not cross to France, was told on his appointment as a canon of Hereford that the liberal arts were better studied there than elsewhere in England.

These promising developments were not confined to the cathedral cities. Other towns more favourably placed were sought by masters who were minded to set up schools in this country on the lines of those in which they had received their training abroad. For this purpose, owing to the centrality of their position, Northampton and Oxford offered ideal alternatives. Towards the close of the twelfth century there were schools at Northampton of sufficient repute to attract lecturers of the calibre of Daniel of Morley, who had studied at Paris and Toledo, and Geoffrey of Vinsauf, the accomplished author of a treatise on the art of poetry. Oxford had other advantages besides its central position at the crossing of two important highways. Masters might well have expected to receive encouragement there from the religious houses of the town, St. Frideswide's priory and the collegiate chapel of St. George's-in-the-castle, both notable in the middle years of the twelfth century for canons of considerable reputation. Moreover, close by there were two royal residences. Beaumont, outside the north gate, and Woodstock manor about eight miles away. With the exception of King John, medieval English kings were to prove powerful protectors of Oxford as a seat of learning.

In these circumstances a sequence of notable lecturers at Oxford from the early years of the century is explicable: by 1117 Theobald of Étampes, who boasted of having an audience of from 60 to 100 clerks; in 1133 Robert Pullen, a leading theologian and later a cardinal; in 1149 Vacarius, a Lombard jurist of repute. This auspicious beginning may have received fresh impulse from scholars returning from Paris, when, about 1167, Henry II, as a measure against Becket, then sheltering in France, banned Englishmen from studying abroad. Gerald of Wales, in recounting his visit in 1184 to give public readings of his *Topographia Hibernica*, describes Oxford as the place where the clergy in England 'flourished and excelled in clerkship', and records that on the second day he read his work to 'all the doctors of different faculties and such of their pupils as were of greater note'. Evidence is forthcoming from other sources to confirm the conclusion that in Oxford a *studium generale* was already forming. A charter executed in 1201 preserves the name of the first graduate known to have presided over its schools: *Magister J. Grim magister scolarum Oxonie.*[1]

3. *Growth of the Universities of Oxford and Cambridge*

For a long time the future of the Oxford schools remained precarious as one crisis followed another. In consequence of grave trouble with the townspeople in which King John sided with the town, masters and scholars dispersed in 1209 for four years.

[1] *Snappe's Formulary, &c.* (Oxf. Hist. Soc.), p. 309.

This *suspendium clericorum* had historic consequences, for some of the masters, who with their scholars found accommodation in other towns, moved to Cambridge and, deciding to stay there, originated a second English university. Cambridge, a small town of no great consequence at this period, might seem to have little to offer a settlement of clerks. The Austin canons there had left their house a century earlier and moved to a larger site at Barnwell. But the relatively large population of East Anglia may sufficiently explain the choice of towns like Cambridge, and, later, Stamford, by migrant masters.

Both universities experienced severe troubles, sometimes due to bitter disputes with townspeople over rents and the price and quality of victuals, sometimes to internal disorder caused by student factions, and sometimes to strained relations with their respective spiritual overlords, the bishops of Lincoln and Ely. The problem of securing a *modus vivendi* as between town and gown vexed successive generations of masters. The position in both towns was exceptional. Nowhere else in England were townsmen required to accommodate a large extraneous concourse of clerks who had everything to buy and nothing to sell. The temptation to exploit this advantage was great. Furthermore relations were constantly embarrassed by the follies and factiousness of young students. It was fortunate for both universities that they early received royal support. Henry III, for all his faults, proved himself a good friend to Oxford, not only by his grants of privileges, but also by his plainly expressed interest in the rise of an important university in his kingdom. He sent relatives of his own to study there, including the unpopular Aymer de Valence (d. 1260), bishop of Winchester. When in 1229 the masters and scholars of the university of Paris were in trouble with the Parisians, he invited them to England: it was a memorable gesture.

At Oxford the most serious clash between town and gown occurred on St. Scholastica's day (10 February) 1355, as the result of a tavern brawl. During the revolt of 1381, the townsmen of Cambridge took their revenge upon the university in their midst by indulging in a riot of destruction which has left its mark until the present day. In the course of it all academical muniments stored in the University church were burned in the market-place. By the close of the middle ages both universities were so well fortified with privileges as to form, ecclesiastically and civilly, two exceptionally independent clerical communi- ties, directly responsible to the Crown. Neither university was in origin, despite the claims of their medieval champions, a royal foundation: but each became a royal university (*universitas nostra*) by grace of royal patronage.

Until the fifteenth century the university of Cambridge seems to have been largely dependent on the eastern counties for its support; but Oxford soon attracted clerks from all parts of Great Britain and Ireland: and the rapidly-growing prestige of its schools rendered the continued resort of English secular scholars to the university of Paris something of a luxury. The days had passed when able Englishmen, like Archbishop Langton (d. 1228) made their reputations as theologians in the schools of Paris. Langton's successor, St. Edmund of Abing- don (d. 1240) studied at both places. Until the outbreak of the Hundred Years War placed the French universities out of reach, connexion between Oxford and Paris was maintained, but by friars rather than by secular scholars. In medieval times neither Oxford nor Cambridge drew scholars in appreciable numbers from the Continent. Again the chief link was fur- nished by foreign friars assigned to study theology in the Eng- lish *studia* of their orders.

Although at Oxford and Cambridge racial differences did not affect the constitutional organization of the university to the same extent as at Paris, regional loyalties and prejudices neces- sitated at an early stage the recognition of two 'nations', Northerners and Southerners. In addition there were explosive groups of clerks from Wales and Ireland, who for the purpose of faction-fights ranked as Southerners. As late as 1334 a party of aggrieved northern masters seceded to Stamford and, being minded to establish themselves there, had ultimately to be dis- lodged by royal writ. Feud between North and South bit deep into the social life of the universities and outlasted the medieval period. As the early masters of Oxford and Cambridge did not live under the shadow of a cathedral church they were spared many of the conflicts with ecclesiastical authority in which the masters of Paris engaged; but, even so, they were not without their disputes over claims of exemption and independence. By 1221 the bishop of Lincoln had accorded to the *magister scolarum* at Oxford the title of chancellor, and by 1226 the bishop of Ely had followed suit at Cambridge: but only after longdrawnout disagreement was each university acknowledged free to elect its own chancellor without seeking episcopal confirmation: Oxford by 1370, Cambridge by 1400.

During the course of the thirteenth century the number of students in Oxford rose rapidly and probably reached its peak before the end of the century. In 1315 it was computed that there were 1,500 clerks in residence. By that date a decline was setting in which was greatly accelerated by the Black Death and subsequent outbreaks of plague. Some recovery had taken place by the beginning of the fifteenth century when the resident university, it has been computed, numbered about 1,200. The academical population of Cambridge remained relatively small, amounting to about a third of that of Oxford, until the fifteenth century when a substantial increase began. The early masters were obliged in the interest of law and order to bring the miscellaneous aggregation of students under some control. In 1231 it was required by the king that all clerks at Oxford must be attached to a master. By the close of the century it had become the general practice in both universities for masters to rent premises to serve as boardinghouses where undergraduates or young graduates could lodge and be under tuition. Halls (*aulae*) for students reading arts, inns (*hospicia*) for those reading law, as they were called at Oxford, and hostels (*hospicia*) as they were usually called at Cambridge, came to be regarded as approved places of residence where all students might live under the rule of a Principal at their own charges. At Oxford lodging in the houses of townsmen was forbidden by statute *c.* 1410 owing to the indiscipline of *chamberdekyns* as such lodgers were termed. Students of high birth and ample means rented halls of their own in which to reside with their house/ holds.

4. *The Earlier Oxford and Cambridge Colleges*

Before the Black Death a large number of clerks coming to the universities were rectors of benefices who were given leave of absence by their bishops for the purpose of study, provided that they appointed curates to discharge their parochial duties. This procedure was regularized by the constitution *Quum ex eo* of Boniface VIII. There must have been many scholars who were too young to accept a benefice, or who had no wish as yet to commit themselves to proceeding to Holy Orders. The grade of 'first tonsure' sufficed to secure all clerks 'benefit of clergy'. Then as now many looked to their parents or relatives for their support; others were fortunate in receiving from a benefactor an exhibition for their maintenance, as, for example, Adam of Usk, ecclesiastical lawyer and chronicler, who owed his educa/ tion at Oxford to Edmund Mortimer, earl of March (d. 1409). Medieval testators turned this form of charity to reciprocal ad/ vantage. At the suggestion of Bishop Grosseteste, Alan Basset, an Oxfordshire landowner, founded by his will, about 1243, scholarships for two priests studying at Oxford or elsewhere who were to say mass daily for the souls of the testator and his wife. William of Kilkenny, bishop of Ely, made a similar benefac/ tion in 1256 at Cambridge. In 1249 William of Durham, who had distinguished himself as a master at Paris, bequeathed, with the same intention, 310 marks to the university of Oxford for the maintenance of ten or more masters of arts studying theo/ logy. Out of this legacy there grew University College, but not before the precedent for a collegiate hall for the residence of graduates had been set by Walter of Merton (d. 1277), bishop of Rochester and chancellor of England. A rarer form of academical benefaction at this early period was the provision of an annual sum for the support of scholars in atonement for an ecclesiastical offence. Under the legatine award of 1214 the citizens of Oxford were obliged to pay 52s. a year to Oseney abbey *in usus pauperum scolarium*. About 1260 John Balliol in part compensation for an outrage against the Church in the diocese of Durham was required by the bishop to maintain a certain number of poor scholars at the university. Out of this, with the added munificence of his widow, Devorguilla, there grew Balliol College. But it was Merton College, founded about 1260, furnished with statutes in 1270 and 1274, that became the prototype for subsequent collegiate foundations. A few years later, about 1280, Cambridge received her first college, Peterhouse, founded by Hugh Balsham, bishop of Ely, and provided by a subsequent bishop, Simon Montacute, with statutes on the model of those of Merton.

In days when residence was required as a qualification for the higher degrees a scholar was faced with a lengthy and expen- sive sequence of study. The early founders of colleges were prompted, in the main, by a desire to provide means for a suc- cession of select scholars to pursue post-graduate studies in arts or theology: in some colleges a small proportion of the fellows were allowed to read canon or civil law or medicine. Very often the choice of these scholars was limited to parts of the country in which a founder was interested. By the middle years of the four- teenth century six secular colleges (University, Balliol, Merton, Exeter, Oriel, and Queen's) had been founded at Oxford, and eight (Peterhouse, King's Hall, Michaelhouse, Clare, Pem- broke, Gonville, Trinity Hall, and Corpus Christi College) at Cambridge. King's Hall and Trinity Hall are noteworthy: the former because it was 'supported by public funds, founded in the first place for laymen connected with the Court' and the latter because it was the first college in either university in- tended for study of canon or civil law. Nine of these colleges were founded by ecclesiastics, three by women (the lady De- vorguilla, the lady Elizabeth of Clare, and Marie Valence, countess of Pembroke); two of those founded by ecclesiastics were fortified by royal patronage (Oriel and Queen's). Corpus Christi College was the singular achievement of two Cam- bridge guilds which combined to found it.

Although constitutionally not colleges, the convents of the four orders of Friars, Dominican, Franciscan, Carmelite, and Augustinian, that were established in Oxford and Cambridge by the end of the thirteenth century served a similar object. The Dominicans settled in Oxford in 1221, and in Cambridge by 1238; the Franciscans arrived in Oxford in 1224, and in Cambridge about two years later. Their activity in the erection of buildings for their convents must have imparted an encour￹aging sense of stability and permanence at a time when the secular masters and scholars still only described themselves as staying (*commorantes*) at Oxford or Cambridge. Their con￹vents, moreover, pointed the way to the provision of more en￹during residential societies for secular clerks in the form of colleges. The other religious orders were slower to associate themselves with the new movement. By the end of the thirteenth century, however, a group of Benedictine houses was support￹ing a combined *studium* in Gloucester College; and the monks of Durham had established Durham College. In the following century the student monks of Christ Church, Canterbury, were accommodated in modest premises until Archbishop Islip founded the dual establishment for monks and secular clerks over which John Wyclif unsuccessfully presided. In 1348 Canterbury College was reconstituted by Archbishop Langham and placed under monastic administration. At Cambridge the student monks of Ely were provided with a hostel by Prior Crawden (d. 1341); but it was not until 1428 that the student monks of other Benedictine houses in the eastern counties were given a combined *studium*, later known as Buckingham College. Cistercian monks assigned for study at Oxford were granted separate accommodation in Rewley abbey, founded in 1281, until the erection of St. Bernard's College in 1437. No similar arrangement was made at St. Frideswide's priory or Oseney abbey for Austin canons. Such student canons usually resided in colleges as 'sojourners' before St. Mary's College was founded in 1435. Gilbertine canons were housed in St. Edmund's hostel at Cambridge. No special arrangements seem to have been made for the residence of the few Cluniac or Carthusian monks or Premonstratensian canons who came to study at either university.

5. Curricula in Universities and Inns of Court and of Chancery

With the rise of the universities the monk's carrel in the quiet seclusion of the cloister (Pl. 109 a) was no longer the chief seat of learning. It had been replaced by the master's chair set in the public forum of the schools; and with the change a revolution took place in the conditions under which learning was pur' sued. The educational method developed at the universities was one of question and answer. Lectures prepared the student for engagement in disputations and determinations appro' priate to the successive stages of his course. Every course of study had an immediate professional objective, the licence to teach (*licencia docendi*). Whatever ultimate career a scholar might have in view, he was required to deliver lectures at given stages in his academical progress. If he reached the degree of master in any faculty, he was under oath to lecture for two years as a necessary regent before he was free to leave the university.

The original organization of a curriculum and the institu' tion of a system of degrees were effected at Oxford and Cam' bridge by masters who for the most part were familiar with the precedents set by Paris. Degrees were granted in Grammar, Arts, Theology, Law (canon and civil), Medicine, and, from the fifteenth century, Music. Study of the Seven Liberal Arts formed the broad foundation on which the other subjects were based. It was divided, in accordance with ancient tradition, into two parts, the *trivium* (grammar, rhetoric, and logic) and the *quadrivium* (arithmetic, geometry, astronomy, and music). Grammar and rhetoric, which covered classical literature, had received enlightened attention under the stimulus of the twelfth' century renaissance; but the intense concentration on logic and philosophy which characterized the study of arts during the thirteenth and fourteenth centuries resulted in a depression of linguistic and literary studies and a lowered standard of latinity until the influence of Italian humanism reached England in the fifteenth century. Meanwhile Donatus and Priscian reigned in

English schoolrooms. Even so, the grammar schools of the country soon came to depend largely upon the universities for their better qualified schoolmasters, and the grammar schools of Oxford to be noted for their masters. John Cornwall (*fl.* 1345) and Richard Pencridge (*fl.* 1365) were credited with having brought English back into the schools in place of French. It was said of John Leland (d. 1428) '*ut rosa flos florum, sic Leland grammaticorum*'.

The importance of classical studies, including a knowledge of Greek and Hebrew was appreciated by Robert Grosseteste (d. 1253), first chancellor of Oxford and founder of its European reputation for the study of philosophy and theology. But there were few after him, as Roger Bacon complained, who followed his lead. Besides Bacon himself, William de la Mare, also a Franciscan, deserves to be remembered as a thirteenth-century student of Hebrew. The Convocation of Canterbury in 1320 gave orders for the carrying out of the decree of the council of Vienne (1311) that the leading universities should make provision for the teaching of Greek and Hebrew; Worcester priory is known to have complied with this order by contributing its quota towards the salary of a *magister grecorum* at Oxford. Latin translations, and indifferent ones at that, were accepted as adequate media for the introduction of the greater knowledge of the works of Aristotle and his Arabian commentators that revolutionized philosophical and theological studies in the universities in the course of the thirteenth century. St. Edmund of Abingdon, later archbishop of Canterbury, is credited with having been the first to lecture on Aristotle's *Sophistici Elenchi* at Oxford. Not much later (*c.* 1209) John Blund was lecturing on the *libri naturales*. But at Paris the opinions of Aristotle soon came under suspicion; public lectures on his *libri naturales* and Metaphysics were banned by 1210. Nevertheless the 'reception' of Aristotle continued to make progress at Oxford, greatly to the benefit of the studies of Oxford masters in arts and theology. In this development, as in many others, the potent influence of Grosseteste is discernible. The first surviving list of works set for the arts course at

Oxford well illustrates the extent to which the study of logic and philosophy rested on Aristotle by 1268. No coincidence of greater moment for the advance of philosophy and theology in Oxford could have occurred than the advent of the Dominicans and Franciscans just at the time when Grosseteste was at the height of his academical career. His decision to associate himself closely with the newcomers by consenting to act as the first lector at the Franciscan convent had great historic issue. Several outstanding masters of arts became friars in the early days of the mendicant movement. Robert Bacon became the first Dominican master at Oxford about 1230; his famous namesake, Roger, entered the Franciscan order about 1257, and Alexander of Hales (d. 1245) while lecturing at Paris as master of theology stepped down from his chair with dramatic effect to assume the Franciscan habit.

At the time of the arrival of the friars theology at Oxford was still closely identified with the study of the Bible; but by the second half of the century a separation, based on Parisian practice, was being made between commentary with its moral emphasis and the discussion of theological problems. The latter were being given their appropriate place in the bachelors' necessary lectures on the *Sentences* of Peter Lombard. The way was opened for the development of theology as a speculative science and for the more strictly exegetical treatment of Bible study. The friars rapidly outclassed the secular masters in both these fields and maintained this lead for the next hundred years. During this period Oxford had no superior in Europe as a school of theological learning. The friaries at Cambridge played a no less important part in the faculty of theology there, being reinforced for many years by able friars from Oxford.

It was inevitable that the intellectual ferment which the friars did so much to promote should beget controversy. Disputes with the university authorities soon broke out at both universities on account of their claim, by reason of previous training in their convents, to be free to proceed to degrees in theology without having previously incepted in arts. The question of the meaning of evangelical poverty became a much vexed topic as between Dominicans and Franciscans, and between the mendicants of all four orders and the secular clergy. Differ-ences of approach to abstruse problems common to philo-sophers and theologians such as the principle of individuation and the unity of form tended to divide Dominicans and Fran-ciscans into two schools of thought. Aristotle continued to prove a stumbling-block to many mendicant and secular theologians; consequently the Aristotelian complexion of the thought of St. Thomas Aquinas provoked condemnations at Paris in 1277. These were followed by no less severe condem-nations at Oxford promulgated by Archbishop Kilwardby (d. 1279), himself a Dominican, and renewed by his Fran-ciscan successor, Archbishop Pecham (d. 1292) in 1284. But Thomism found bold supporters among Oxford Dominicans. Oxford, too, was one of the main battle grounds of the realist disciples of John Duns, the first great Scottish philosopher and theologian. Duns Scotus, *doctor subtilis*, was followed by an-other great Franciscan leader of thought, William of Ockham, *doctor invincibilis*.

In the fourteenth century, the secular masters, most of them fellows of Merton College, became prominent. In the main, their great contribution was made in the study of logic (*subtilitates anglicanae*) and philosophy: but the most famous of the Merton scholars was Thomas Bradwardine, the greatest English secular theologian since Grosseteste. The same period is notable for the new interest shown, outside the religious orders, in the collection of books. Richard Bury (d. 1345), bishop of Durham, whose love of books is commemorated in his *Philobiblon*, intended that his fine library should have a home in Oxford, but, owing to his debts, his executors had to dispose of it. The university was furnished by Thomas Cob-ham (d. 1327), bishop of Worcester, with its first library-building; Merton College by William Rede (d. 1385), bishop of Chichester, with a building even more spacious and with books.

The Black Death carried off Bradwardine within a few weeks of his promotion to the see of Canterbury. This scourge did great damage to the cause of education throughout the country: but in the universities, the ill consequences of the long-protracted war with France were more lasting. It interrupted the free interchange of ideas between English and French universities that had hitherto proved one of the most fruitful and salutary features of academical studies. The decline in papal prestige added a further disturbing factor. John Wyclif (d. 1384), the reforming theologian, embodied the confident individualism, the nationalist bias, and the high-minded scepticism that flowed from these events. The firm measures taken by Archbishops Courtenay and Arundel to eradicate his teaching from Oxford were calculated to discourage further challenge to traditional theology. The Wyclifite crisis was productive of some apologetic by mendicant theologians, notably the *Doctrinale* of the Carmelite, Thomas Netter of Walden; but by the time the superb Divinity School was completed about 1470 (Pl. 109 *b*), Oxford theology had never been at so low an ebb.

Unlike Paris, Oxford and Cambridge developed flourishing faculties of law in which both canon and civil law were read. At Oxford, as is evidenced by the visit of Vacarius, legal studies have their origin in the middle years of the twelfth century. By the thirteenth century a legal degree, whether in canon or civil law, or both, had become a much-desired qualification for all clerks who wanted to be ecclesiastical lawyers rising to become important diocesan officials or clerks in the royal service carrying out diplomatic missions and other responsible duties. It is likely that Henry Bracton (d. 1268) acquired his knowledge of civil law as a student at Oxford. From the middle of the fourteenth century the majority of bishops were graduates, and many of these graduates in law. The training in civil law given at Oxford and Cambridge met the professional needs of English clerks, but never compared with that to be obtained in the law schools of Italy. William of Drogheda (d. *c.* 1245) was the only civilian in either university to be quoted by the doctors of Bologna. In canon law, on the other hand, both universities developed schools of importance, and

PLATE 109

a. Cloister, Gloucester Cathedral, showing carrels

b. The Divinity School, Oxford

PLATE 110

a. Winchester College, founded 1373

b. New College and its hundred clerks
(New College, Oxford, MS. 288)

produced the two best-known English authorities on the subject, John Atton (d. 1350) and William Lyndwood (d. 1446), bishop of St. David's. The ecclesiastical courts of the various dioceses and the chancellors' courts in the two universities formed essential finishing schools for canonists. At the episcopal visitation of the Exeter consistory in 1323 there were five graduates in law described as *studens*.

By the close of the thirteenth century the growth of English law necessitated the organization of a system of training for lawyers who were to practise in the king's courts. Although the origins of the Inns of Court are obscure, enough is known to warrant the conclusion that the provision made for the teaching and housing of the *apprenticii* of the law centred in *hospicia* similar to those which had multiplied in the universities. By the fifteenth century four chief Inns of Court were in being, Lincoln's Inn, Gray's Inn, the Inner Temple, and the Middle Temple, containing, according to Sir John Fortescue, 200 students each. These Inns were administered by masters of the bench. The curriculum, as at the universities, consisted of lectures delivered by readers, whom the benchers appointed, and of the discussion of debated points of law in moots. The licence to practise took the form of the call to the bar. In the second half of the fourteenth century *hospicia* of similar character were established in the same quarter of London by chancery clerks for the training of their pupils in the intimate knowledge of writs required of those who wanted to qualify for administrative service in the chancery. As the common lawyers also needed this knowledge these smaller Inns of Chancery seem to have been drawn into association with the Inns of Courts and eventually to have been dominated by them. Educationally the rise of the Inns of Court and of Chancery are of particular interest, as they were the first professional schools in England for laymen. As described by Sir John Fortescue they included, in the middle of the fifteenth century, other subjects than law, such as history, scripture, music, and even dancing, in their curriculum, and were attracting many young men of social standing who were not looking to a legal career.

6. *The Later Middle Ages*

William of Wykeham (d. 1404), bishop of Winchester and chancellor of England, was moved to his notable munificence in the cause of education by the general decay of the *militia clericalis* which he attributed to 'the pestilences, wars, and other afflictions of the world'. In his twin foundations at Winchester and Oxford (Pl. 110 *a*) he not only erected a great school and a great college, but, in so doing, initiated a revolutionary de/ velopment in the provision of university and school education. The number of fellows in Oxford colleges was nearly doubled by the founding of New College: the quadrangular layout and size of its buildings set a new standard for collegiate architec/ ture. It was the first college in which undergraduates were in/ corporated on a large scale; and,consequently, the first to adopt and make famous the tutorial system which the halls had de/ veloped. The dependence of New College on a sister founda/ tion at Winchester for all its fellows was also an innovation. And Winchester College has the distinction of being the earliest fully endowed school in England. In Oxford Wyke/ ham's example inspired two subsequent benefactors: Henry Chichele (d. 1443), archbishop of Canterbury, who founded All Souls College in 1438, and a collegiate school at Higham Ferrers in Northamptonshire; and William Waynflete (d. 1486), bishop of Winchester, who founded Magdalen College, in its first form, ten years later. Waynflete, who had been head/ master of Winchester and provost of Eton, followed Wyke/ ham's example further by founding a school in association with his college at Oxford and another at Wainfleet, his native place. Waynflete introduced two important innovations in his statutes for Magdalen. He provided three lectureships in theology, moral philosophy, and natural philosophy, thereby making his college largely self/sufficient for the purpose of teaching. As the lectures were to be open to other members of the university, he pointed the way to the endowed university professorships which were eventually to supersede the regency system. He also made provision for the admission of the sons of noblemen as commoners (*commensales*), setting a precedent for the participation of fee-paying students in the teaching facilities and common life of a college.

Henry V is credited with the intention of founding a 'noble college' in the castle at Oxford: but his son looked to Cam-bridge as freer from the taint of Wyclif's 'damnable errors', and with truly royal munificence founded King's College in 1441, and linked it, in the manner of Wykeham's twin foundations, to the 'College Roiall' which he had erected the previous year at Eton to be 'the lady, mother, and mistress of all other gram-mar schools'. The promotion of theology as a defence against heresy prompted the foundation of Lincoln College at Oxford by Richard Fleming, bishop of Lincoln, in 1429, and St. Catharine's College at Cambridge by Dr. Robert Woodlark, provost of King's, in 1475. The foundation of Godshouse (later Christ's College) at Cambridge in 1439 calls for separate mention. With the establishment of Jesus College at Cambridge in 1497 on the site of the nunnery of St. Rhade-gund's by John Alcock, bishop of Ely, the impressive se-quence of colleges founded in the fifteenth century is brought to a close.

By the middle of the century it is possible from extant uni-versity registers to form some rough estimate of the number of students at both universities who left with degrees; but at no period in the middle ages is it possible to judge how many left without. Even so, there is reason to suspect that the proportion was large. The great majority of those who graduated remained celibate and proceeded to clerical careers: but there is no means of ascertaining how many of the non-graduates became laymen and married. In this connexion the evidence available for New College, although it does not furnish an answer to the last question, is significant, as it appears that on the average about half of the scholars who entered the college from Winchester did not graduate.

The parlous state into which grammar schools had fallen during the first half of the century is reflected in the foundation of Godshouse. It was founded by a London rector, William of

Byngham, as a training college for grammar schoolmasters, as he had been shocked to find in the eastern parts of England no less than seventy grammar schools closed for lack of masters that had been flourishing fifty years before. This scarcity of school- masters may in a measure be attributed to the fact that the stipends attaching to the masterships of the free grammar schools dependent upon a bishop's or a chancellor's licence were no longer adequate. But with the need there came at least a partial remedy in the form of free grammar schools endowed by private benefaction. As with the colleges at the universities, the fifteenth century witnessed the exercise of remarkable enter- prise on this account. Several collegiate schools, in addition to those already mentioned, were founded by noblemen and prelates; schools were promoted by town guilds like that at Stratford on Avon; and chantry schools were multiplied. In London the monopoly of the three privileged schools was broken when in 1441 John Carpenter, sometime provost of Oriel, later bishop of Worcester, founded St. Anthony's school, which became for many years the leading school in the city.

The most important development in English learning and education in the fifteenth century resulted from the awakening interest of English scholars in the revival of classical studies in Italy. Classical scholarship had made little progress in England since the days of John of Salisbury and Robert Grosseteste. The first contacts with Italian humanism were due to Lancas- trian patronage. Although the visit of Poggio to England from 1418 to 1422 at the invitation of Cardinal Beaufort bore very little fruit, the concern of Humphrey, duke of Gloucester, for the humanities set English learning and letters moving in new channels, particularly at Oxford. In deference to him the uni- versity revised its Arts course in 1431 so as to include the *Nova Rhetorica* of Cicero, the *Metamorphoses* of Ovid, and the works of Virgil as alternative texts for the study of rhetoric. There fol- lowed his princely gifts of books which made accessible to scholars translations from Greek authors that served to direct attention to Greek literature. Timely encouragement was given by men of scholarly influence like John Whethamstede, abbot of St. Albans: but more fruitful were the visits of the fortunate few to study in Italian universities and in the school of Guarino da Verona at Ferrara. John Tiptoft (d. 1443), earl of Worces⁄ter, and John Free, his literary assistant, were, each in his own way, masters of the new cult: Tiptoft, the English nobleman who came nearest to the Italian princely patron of the renais⁄sance and Free 'the first Englishman to become a professional humanist and reach the standard of the Italians'.

By the second half of the fifteenth century humanistic studies were beginning to win interest in Oxford, under the stimulus of Thomas Chaundler, warden of New College and chancellor (Pl. 110*b*). John Farley and William Grocin, both fellows of the college, when acting as registrars of the university left memorials of their newly won accomplishment by writing their names in Greek characters in the margins of official letter⁄books. Stefano Surigone, a Milanese scholar, had given courses on Latin eloquence at Oxford by 1470. The seal of Chaund⁄ler's fostering interest was set when as an old man he came up from Hereford where he was dean to reply to a Latin oration delivered by another Italian scholar, Cornelio Vitelli. The range of neo⁄classical literature in Oxford was enlarged by the benefactions of two distinguished Oxford scholars who had studied in Italy: William Grey, bishop of Ely (d. 1478) to Balliol College, and Robert Fleming, dean of Lincoln (d. 1483) to Lincoln College. Christ Church, Canterbury, introduced to humanism by its monks studying at Canterbury College, became a noted centre of the revival where the study of Greek was encouraged under the direction of its accom⁄plished prior, William Selling (d. 1494). Reading abbey is associated with the activities of the Greek scribe, John Serbo⁄poulos, in the transcription of Greek books for academic clients. The verdict that 'a utilitarian conception of the human⁄ities is the main feature of humanism in England during the fifteenth century' is borne out in the careers of a succession of ambassadors and high officials such as Thomas Bekynton (d. 1465), bishop of Bath and Wells, Andrew Holes (d. 1470) archdeacon of Wells, Adam Moleyns (d. 1450), bishop of Chichester, John Gunthorpe (d. 1498), dean of Wells, George Neville (d. 1476), archbishop of York, and William Shir' wood (d. 1494), bishop of Durham. The publication of the *Compendium Totius Gramaticae* by John Anwykyll, master of Magdalen school, printed at Oxford in 1483, prepared the way for the revolution in the teaching of Latin grammar that was to mark the educational revival of the next century. The wider diffusion of the New Learning was now well assured.

WORKS FOR REFERENCE

HOLDSWORTH, SIR WM., *History of English Law*, chapter on the Legal Profession in volume ii.

KNOWLES, D. *The Monastic Order in England* (1940), chap. xxviii–xxxi; *The Religious Orders in England*, i (1948); ii (1955).

LEACH, A. F. *The Schools of Mediaeval England*, 2nd edn. (1916); allowance needs to be made for his prejudice against the monasteries; his articles on schools in the *Victoria County Histories*.

LEVISON, W. *England and the Continent in the 8th century* (1945).

LITTLE, A. J. and PELSTER, F. *Oxford Theology and Theologians c. 1282–1302* (Oxf. Hist. Soc., 1934), Introduction.

POOLE, A. L. *From Doomsday to Magna Carta*, chap. viii.

RASHDALL, H. *The Universities of Europe in the Middle Ages*, ed. F. M. POWICKE and A. B. EMDEN (1936).

SALTER, M. E. *Medieval Oxford* (Oxf. Hist. Soc. 1936), lecture 5.

SMALLEY, B. *The Study of the Bible in the Middle Ages*, 2nd edn. (1952), chaps. v and vi.

STENTON, F. M. *Anglo-Saxon England* (1943), chaps. vi and xiii.

TOUT, T. F. 'The English Civil Service in the Fourteenth Century', in his *Collected Papers* (1934), iii, pp. 191–221.

WEISS, R. *Humanism in England during the 15th century* (1941).

XVI. HANDWRITING[1]

THE handwriting of the middle ages is one of its greatest achievements: comparable with its architecture, and, for the historian, even more fundamental and important. For although palaeographers study it primarily as a great art, we must never forget that most of our knowledge of the period rests upon written records. They are the very stuff of history; and the student is even more concerned with what is in his manuscripts than with their beauty. For this double approach we are rather better off than our medieval ancestors, most of whom were illiterate; and just because we all use a pen today we can appreciate, even if we cannot copy, the calligraphy, or fine writing, of the middle ages. Contrariwise, we have a lot to forget; for we must think ourselves back into a period when printing—not to mention the typewriter—was unknown: when men wrote with quills instead of steel pens, on sheepskin instead of paper, and in Latin instead of English.

A bald contrast between the handwriting of medieval and of modern society is, however, something less than a half-truth. Between, say, A.D. 500 and 1500 the extent and the function of handwriting were both transformed. In the barbarous centuries which followed the disintegration of the Roman Empire the practice of writing was increasingly confined to the Church, whose 'clerks' copied the great books written in better times—the Bible, the works of the fathers, and the classics—and in their chronicles kept a brief record of the more important contemporary events. They were acutely aware of the general collapse, and fearful lest the memory of the great days behind them should fall into oblivion. In these dark ages

---

[1] The writer wishes to acknowledge the expert assistance of Dr. R. W. Hunt who, as Keeper of Western manuscripts in the Bodleian Library, has so many of the oldest and finest manuscripts in his charge.

society rested largely on an oral and customary basis. Justice was done verbally in large assemblies, and the transfer of land or rights became a ceremonial act accompanied by a symbolic 'livery of seisin' and witnessed by neighbours. With the coming of the tenth century these primitive arrangements slowly gave ground, as wellknit states arose governed by autocratic rulers. Impressed by the changes of the last four centuries, we are apt to forget that between A.D. 500 and 1200 Europe changed at least as much as between A.D. 1200 and 1900. This revolution, for it is no less, is reflected in the history of medieval handwriting, which beginning in England as an occasional accessory of the monastic life gradually became the basic and indispensable instrument both of the central government and of ordinary business. Its finest triumphs as a pure art lie in the earlier centuries, but its importance in the history of society increases to the end of our period and, indeed, far beyond it. Much more attention—not unnaturally—has been devoted by palaeographers to the earlier centuries and therefore to Book hand or Text than to its 'poor relation' Court hand or Cursive. But Domesday Book and Magna Carta are also landmarks, though of a different kind, for they are stages in the gradual transition from oral custom to written record.

Because handwriting is at once a fine art and a daily utility, its history is governed by the broad distinction between text and cursive. For instance, it lies at the root of that slow and subtle development of writing at its best over the centuries, since as Dr. Lowe puts it, 'scripts like populations recruit chiefly from below'.[1] Yet the distinction oversimplifies the facts; for while calligraphic writing tends at any given moment to follow a single, fixed pattern (though with local variations), utility scripts of differing types and sometimes of real excellence coexist with it, often in great numbers. Indeed, by the fifteenth century most of the great departments of government, like the

---

[1] Thus, the letterforms of the ordinary writing of classical Rome (Pl. III b)—preserved for us on waxedtablets and wallinscriptions—are basically those of the square capitals (Pl. III a), disguised and modified by being written *currente calamo*. But from these modifications over centuries fresh formal hands evolve and ultimately a new and smaller calligraphic, or beautiful, writing—the minuscule.

a. Roman Square Capitals. Inscription of A.D. 222, commemorating the provision of a water-supply for the fort at South Shields (Co. Durham) Eph. Epigr. ix, 1140

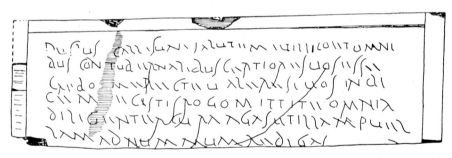

b. Roman Cursive. Writing-tablet from London

Rufus callisuni salutem epillico et omni | bus contubernalibus certiores vos esse . . .

(Antiquaries Journal, vol. xxxiii, p. 206)

PLATE III

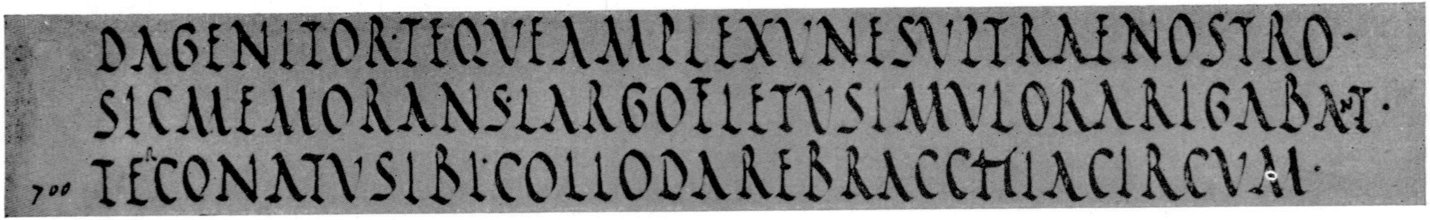

PLATE 112

a. Rustic Capitals. Vergil, Codex Palatinus. Fourth–fifth century. (C.L.A. Pt. i. no. 99)

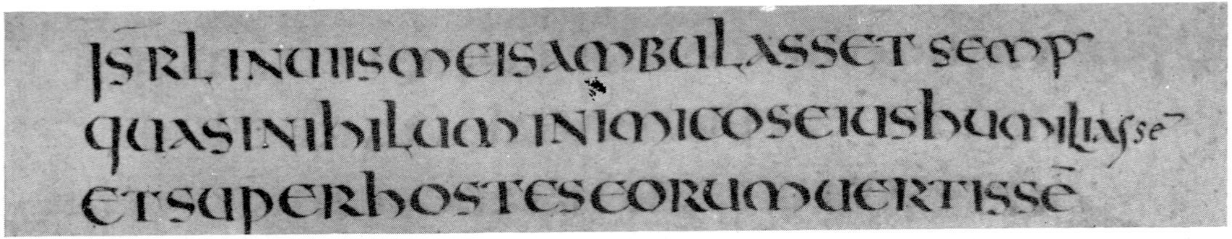

b. Uncial. Codex Amiatinus written at Jarrow by order of Abbot Ceolfrid (A.D. 690–716). (C.L.A. iii. 299)

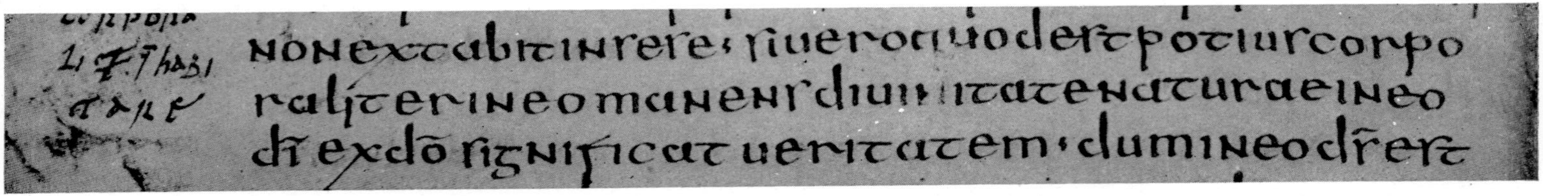

c. Half-uncial. Hilarius de Trinitate. Fifth–sixth century. (C.L.A. i. 1a)

chancery, the exchequer, and the law courts had each evolved its own highly artificial and intricate hand, uniform in execu-tion and recognizable at a glance. For this reason the historians of court hand tend to draw a further distinction between the set and the free hand, that is between writing according to the copy-book and what the professional scribe—often pressed for time —makes of it in practice. For writing throughout the middle ages was in general a matter for experts and a profession. Of the products of the 'literate layman' or amateur we encounter very little until the later part of our period.

I

The fundamental hand of all medieval writing, as well as modern, is the square Roman capitals (Pl 111*a*), the supreme legacy of Roman art, which has persisted unchanged for nearly two thousand years. Here already is the alphabet we use today, and though 'an inconvenient form of writing', except for titles, it was employed for important books as late as the fourth or fifth century. Not very much survives, apart from inscriptions on stone, in this script. For whole books it was wasteful both of space and of time; and in Pl. 112*a*, the full severity of the basic script is relaxed. The name of this fine script, Rustic Capitals, is, in fact, a misnomer, for the evidence suggests that it was the true book hand of classical times: but by the fifth century, its place was being filled by Uncials (Pl. 112*b*) and a century later by Half-Uncials (Pl. 112*c*). In both these scripts the angularity of writing in capitals is systematically rounded off into curves, more suited to penmanship, and both arose under the influence of the cursive forms used in everyday writing. To British students the half-uncial is of particular interest, for it is the basis for the script of the Irish 'Book of Kells' and older manuscripts, almost equally famous, written in England (Pl. 114).

These four large or majuscule scripts embody the highest achievements of writing until about the eighth century, and each, as it were, has a foot in antiquity. The centuries in which they flourished were the twilight of the ancient world, and their history is very imperfectly known. So long as the Empire held

together they seem to have been written with surprising uniformity throughout its whole extent. After that, barbarian invasions and the decline of the Roman *imperium* in western
Europe slowly brought to birth a new world. The widespread
secular culture of Rome was replaced by a society in which
writing (together with learning) inevitably became the specialized function of the Church. Writing, in consequence, began
to show more and more regional variations, associated for the
most part with important monasteries, which appear to us now
as islands of civilization in the general welter of the times. The
importance of Christian literature, and more especially of the
Bible increased, and decisive changes occurred in both the
form and materials of writing. In classical antiquity the normal
writing material was papyrus, a material manufactured from the
plant and made up in the form of a roll (*volumen*). By the fourth
century papyrus was giving way to sheepskin or parchment,
and there was a growing tendency more and more to substitute
for the roll the *codex* or book, made up in quires. The replacement of the papyrus roll by the parchment book effected a
revolution in the history of writing. Parchment gives a better
surface than papyrus for writing, and gradually a new pen
made from goose quills took the place of the reed pen of the
classical world. Parchment, moreover, is tougher and much
more durable than papyrus, and to this fortunate fact we owe
the survival of our medieval books. Hence our knowledge of
writing steadily increases as the use of papyrus declines. For
instance, the papacy, always a conservative institution, retained papyrus as the material for its 'bulls' or letters until the
eleventh century, and so few originals have survived, that we
are today better informed about the charters of the Carolingian
or the French monarchy, than about the more sophisticated
products of the papal chancery.

By the eighth century the majuscule scripts were dying out.
All over Europe their place was being taken by new and
smaller book hands, generally described as minuscule. Among
the complex causes of this transition must certainly be included
the need for economy, which could best be achieved by getting

PLATE 113

populusaudiensetrepublicani·iustaficauerunt dm· amen

EXPLICIT LIBER SECUNDUS·

INCIPIT LIBER TERTIUS·

SANCTISSIMA MARIAE PAENITENTIS HISTORIA QUARTI]
nofat in lucam caput elibri· et fio blaborem legentaum minuendum
Anouo inchoatur exordio rerum tamen secundi libri nectura finem retspicit

Carolingian minuscule. About A.D. 820, Tours writing. The second and third lines are in rustic capitals, the fourth in uncial
populus audiens et publicani iustificaverunt deum. amen. (Bodleian MS. Bodley 218, f. 62ʳ)

PLATE 114

Irish majuscule. The Book of Kells. Eighth–ninth century
Et crucifixerunt[t eu]m (Manuscript in Trinity College, Dublin)

more writing on to the skins available. Sheepskins and calf/skins, properly prepared, were hard to come by, and when, as often, Christian texts were written over those of the Latin classics (palimpsests) no disrespect was intended to what was erased. The scribes, in their poverty, were simply putting first things first. Our knowledge of how all this came about is one/sided, since so little is known of the writing which the minus/cule displaced—the scripts of the notaries and the traditional products of a fading classical culture. The only learning known to us in the eighth century is that of the monasteries, and the only scripts, apart from the exiguous remains of the Frankish and Italian chanceries, are those connected with particular regions or monasteries. In south Italy, for instance, a local minuscule arose, which we call Beneventan, associated particu/larly with the abbey of Monte Cassino: in Spain another, the so/called Visigothic, and in Frankland another, the Merovin/gian. Still earlier, Ireland and northern England had evolved a highly distinctive, if crabbed, minuscle with its own charac/teristic system of abbreviations based, like all abbreviations, on those used in Roman law/books. The insular scribes, however, with whom parchment seems to have been especially scarce, were pioneers in admitting abbreviations into the text of their writings. Different as these local scripts are from one another, they share the common fault of being extremely difficult to read. This defect was at last overcome by a new script with a great future (Pl. 113). This was the Caroline minuscule, a hand of great beauty and supremely legible, the emergence of which is closely associated with the great religious revival of Charles the Great's reign. Smaller than majuscule writing, it achieved its affect, Dr. Lowe tells us, 'by a rigorous elimination of cursive elements and by keeping letters distinct and properly aligned'. It was no sudden discovery, but the achievement of a new clear style, approaches to which go well back into the eighth century in various monastic centres. The earliest recognizable specimens come from Corbie, but it was the great abbey of St. Martin of Tours which was responsible for its diffusion over Europe in the ninth century, though rather after the time of its

famous abbot, Alcuin of York (796–804). This process was
speeded by its august parentage: but in the last resort the new
script won its way on its merits. Of all minuscules, it was the
Caroline that survived though here and there the older varieties
persisted for centuries. Beyond all other scripts it is the medieval
legacy to handwriting. Though transformed by the modifications of generations of scribes into the Gothic script of the
thirteenth century, it was rediscovered by the Italian scholars of
the Renaissance, and by the invention of printing, given permanent preservation.

By the middle of the tenth century the new script had reached
England, where for the next three centuries the finest Latin
books were written, with local English idiosyncrasies, in the
Caroline minuscule. But its triumph was qualified and limited
in England by earlier historical developments. The majuscule
scripts were, of course, brought into England by Augustine and
the other Roman missionaries after the year 597, but the origins
of *native* handwriting in the British Isles are entirely obscure. It
is only certain that by the seventh century there is evidence of
a definitely 'insular' type of half-uncial writing, and of the
pointed minuscule mentioned above, unique in being derived
from half-uncial, instead of being elaborated from cursive like
the minuscules of the Continent. The insular half-uncial, like
other majuscule scripts, died away leaving behind a number of
splendid manuscripts. Of these the most perfect example is the
'Book of Kells' which remains, both for its illumination and
its script, 'the admiration and despair of succeeding ages'. But
the insular minuscule remained; and the missionaries of the
eighth century who passed over to the Continent took their
minuscule with them. Indeed, the best evidence of their activities, which did so much to stimulate the great reform of
Charles the Great's reign, is supplied by the books they wrote
in famous abbeys like Bobbio, St. Gall, and Fulda. Meanwhile
at home the insular minuscule enjoyed a growing popularity
owing to the extraordinary development of a precocious vernacular literature in England before anything of the kind
developed abroad. We can only suppose that Ireland and Eng-

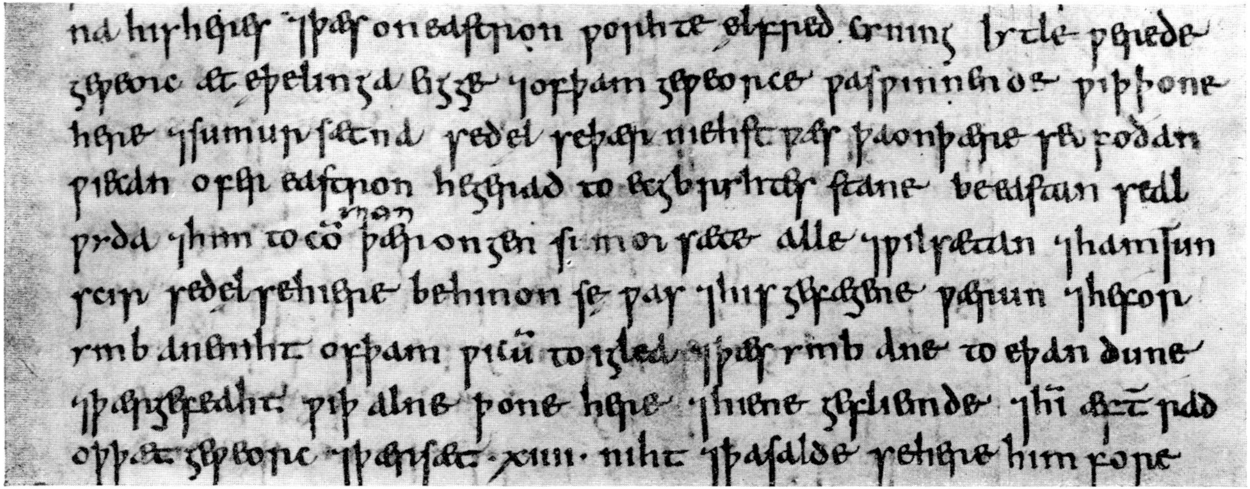

PLATE 115

Insular minuscule. Anglo-Saxon Chronicle written at Winchester about A.D. 891

na his heres and þæs on eastron worhte ælfred cyning lytle werede

(Maunde Thompson Fac. 145. Manuscript at Corpus Christi College, Cambridge)

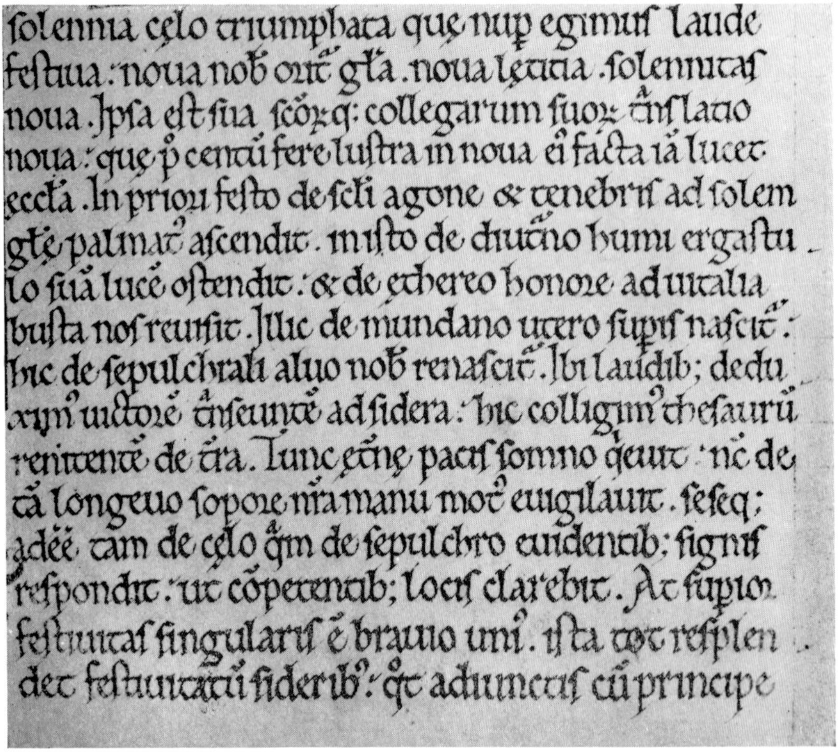

PLATE 116

solennia celo triumphata que nup egimus laude
festiua : noua nob ortu gra . noua leticia . solennitas
noua . Ipsa est sua scor q : collegarum suor translatio
noua : que p centu fere lustra in noua ei facta ia lucet
ecca . In priou festo de scti agone & tenebris ad solem
gre palmat ascendit . mixto de diurno humi ergastu
lo sua luce ostendit : & de ethereo honore ad uitalia
busta nos reuttit . Illic de mundano utero supis nascit :
hic de sepulchrali aluo nob renascit . In laudib ; dedu
crin uictore inseunte ad sidera : hic colligim thesauru
renitente de tra . Tunc etne pacis somno queut : nc de
ca longeuo sopore nra manu mor euigilaut . seseq ;
adee tam de celo qm de sepulchro euidentib : signis
respondit : ut copetentib ; locis clarebit . At supior
festiuitas singularis e brauio uni . ista tot resplen
det festiuitatu sideribs : qt adiunctis cu principe

Latin book-hand. Life and Miracles of St. Augustine by Goscelin, a monk of St.
Augustine's, Canterbury. Early twelfth century

Solennia cęlo triumphata quę nuper egimus laude

(Maunde Thompson Fac. 176. British Museum, MS. Cotton Vespasian B. xx)

land, lying on the outer fringe of Latin civilization, were driven to this course by the dearth of scribes who knew Latin. We still have at Corpus Christi College, Cambridge, a copy of the Anglo-Saxon Chronicle written at the end of the ninth century (Pl. 115), and in the Bodleian Library a contemporary manuscript of King Alfred's translation of Gregory's *Pastoral Care*. It is not therefore surprising that in the tenth century, the Old English insular script, with its special letters [ƿ (*w*), þ (*th*), ð (*th*), ȝ (*gh*)] was able to hold its own, for all vernacular manuscripts, against the competition of Caroline minuscule which was henceforth reserved for Latin books. In the royal charters of the tenth and eleventh centuries—superb specimens of calligraphy—the two scripts appear together: the Latin text written in Caroline, the Old English 'boundaries' of the property granted, in the native minuscule. Thus for centuries to come we have two streams of palaeographical development in England; two distinct book hands depending on language; and the strife of tongues was further complicated after the Norman Conquest by the introduction of Norman French, though this, of course, followed the Latin tradition.

These English peculiarities, though of great historical interest to us today, were not so important at the time, when the Latin language reigned supreme. Vernacular manuscripts are only a small fraction of what has survived, and it is probable that they were written as the only alternative to sheer illiteracy. Latin manuscripts alone had much scholarly repute and for these the Caroline minuscule reached the heyday of its development in the eleventh and early twelfth centuries. The specimen given in Pl. 116, which was written in the first quarter of the twelfth century, is taken from the Life and Miracles of St. Augustine by Goscelin, a monk of St. Augustine's, Canterbury. By this time the minuscule was a faultless script—supremely legible, with the words at last carefully separated, the sentences punctuated, and a still growing yet systematic scheme of abbreviations. Punctuation was not, as with us, grammatical but a guide to the reader who normally spoke aloud or muttered to himself as he read, while the abbreviations

and contractions were intended to lighten the labour of copying. In manuscripts of late antiquity the abbreviations are confined to b; (bus), q; (que), ū (um), and the contractions of the
holy names: e.g. D̄S for Deus, ĪHS, X̄PS for Jesus Christus,
but as time passed the practice was greatly extended, until in
the twelfth and thirteenth centuries the chief difficulty in
reading manuscripts lies in the correct extension of the
abbreviations. Roughly speaking, words were shortened in
four different ways:

1. By *suspension*, or the omission of the final letters of the
   word, shown either by a dot (e.g. *R.* for *Rex*) or a horizontal line above the last letter written (e.g. *hostē* for *hostem*).
2. By *contraction*, or the omission of medial letters, shown by
   a horizontal line (e.g. *d̄ns* for *dominus*, *ap̄li* for *apostoli*).
3. By *superior letters*, such as *qᵃm* for *quam*.
4. By *special signs*, some of which go right back to the Roman
   system of shorthand: e.g. 7 for *et*, and to the abbreviations
   used in legal and non-literary manuscripts: e.g. *p̄* for
   prae, *āt* for *autem*.

These methods of abbreviation used either singly or in combination certainly present great difficulties to the student more
especially if his Latin is weak. But when once they are mas-
tered good manuscripts (at any rate until the end of the twelfth
century) can soon be read with almost the same ease and at the
same pace as modern print.

    The development of abbreviations was, of course, deter-
mined by Latin manuscripts which alone used a fixed spell-
ing; but they were also applied, so far as could be, to books in
French and English, the history of which in England was profoundly affected by the events of the year 1066. Very soon after
the Norman Conquest the status of English, hitherto the
language of all classes and of government, was depressed, and
for nearly three centuries everyone except the serfs (the over-
whelming majority) spoke French. The writing of English
books almost, though not quite, ceased in the twelfth century,
and its place both in education and polite literature was filled

by the new French literature, which was now spreading like
wildfire across Europe. The French language has no great place
in the specialized history of handwriting, but its social importance in medieval England was immense. So French indeed did society become that a local offshoot arose in England,
with a literature of its own, known as Anglo-Norman: and
this, we may suspect, meant more to the tiny minority who
then aspired to 'education' than all the Latin learning of the
period. Yet in the long period, the most important of post-Conquest developments was the increased knowledge of Latin
which had always been 'in short supply' among the Anglo-
Saxons. Learning and letters in England were at last caught up
into the main stream of European civilization, and at the very
moment when the religious life of medieval Europe was at its
highest pitch of fervour. The new monastic orders—the Cluniacs, the Cistercians, the Canons Regular, and the Gilbertines—were heavily endowed by the new French nobility.
Scores of new monasteries were founded, which not only collected great libraries, but were themselves, not seldom, writing
centres of repute. The old Benedictine houses of Anglo-Saxon
times, soon full of French-speaking and Latin-minded monks
—foundations like Canterbury, Worcester, Durham, and
Winchester—continued to produce Latin books in their
scriptoria, which were masterpieces of calligraphy, though the
French minuscule in which they were now written was rather
different from that of pre-Conquest days. In the twelfth century the best elements of continental learning were thus fused
with the older English tradition, while in the thirteenth a new
foreign stimulus was supplied by the mendicant orders of
Friars, especially the Dominicans and Franciscans, whose
houses became centres of learning and writing. In the British
Museum, the Bodleian, the college libraries of Oxford and
Cambridge, our old cathedrals, and even in private hands,
finely written Latin manuscripts of these centuries survive in
thousands: a great field for palaeographers, still less than half-
explored.

Yet, though today we value the middle ages chiefly for their learning, scholarship, then as now, was a world apart, and, if possible, even more remote. The 'educated Englishman' of the twelfth century was, in fact, nearly a Frenchman who enjoyed listening to romances, like the *Song of Roland*, and took his English history from French translations of the romantic Geoffrey of Monmouth. On the other hand, he was more or less bilingual, which few of us are today, and if he happened to be a clergyman and knew Latin, trilingual. But the number of those, whether native or foreign, who spoke French can never have been more than some thousands in a population approaching two millions; and although the aristocratic structure of society preserved the vogue of French for centuries, it was English which inevitably prevailed as the spoken tongue. Nor did the written tradition fail, a fact attested by the survival into the late middle ages of the letters peculiar to the Old English script. Before the final resurgence of the mother tongue, enriched and transformed by foreign influences, French gave way altogether, while Latin steadily weakened. Already in the early fifteenth century Henry V was sending home English dispatches from Agincourt (1415), though the final victory of English was only achieved in the sixteenth century.

These developments, however, were still undreamed of in the tenth century, when the new minuscule from Tours was spreading all over the west. The European dominance of the Caroline minuscule for nearly four centuries is a potent reminder of the unity of civilization and culture in this period. One must not however think of it as either uniform or stationary. Within the general pattern there were endless local variations, and all the time, writing, like other forms of art, was changing, though with glacier-like slowness. For these reasons the modern scholar can generally tell where his manuscripts were written and—within half a century or less—fix their date simply by looking at them. At last, about the end of the twelfth century, and just when Romanesque architecture developed into 'Early English', the rounded minuscule gave way, quite suddenly, to a difficult and angular script which for lack of a better name

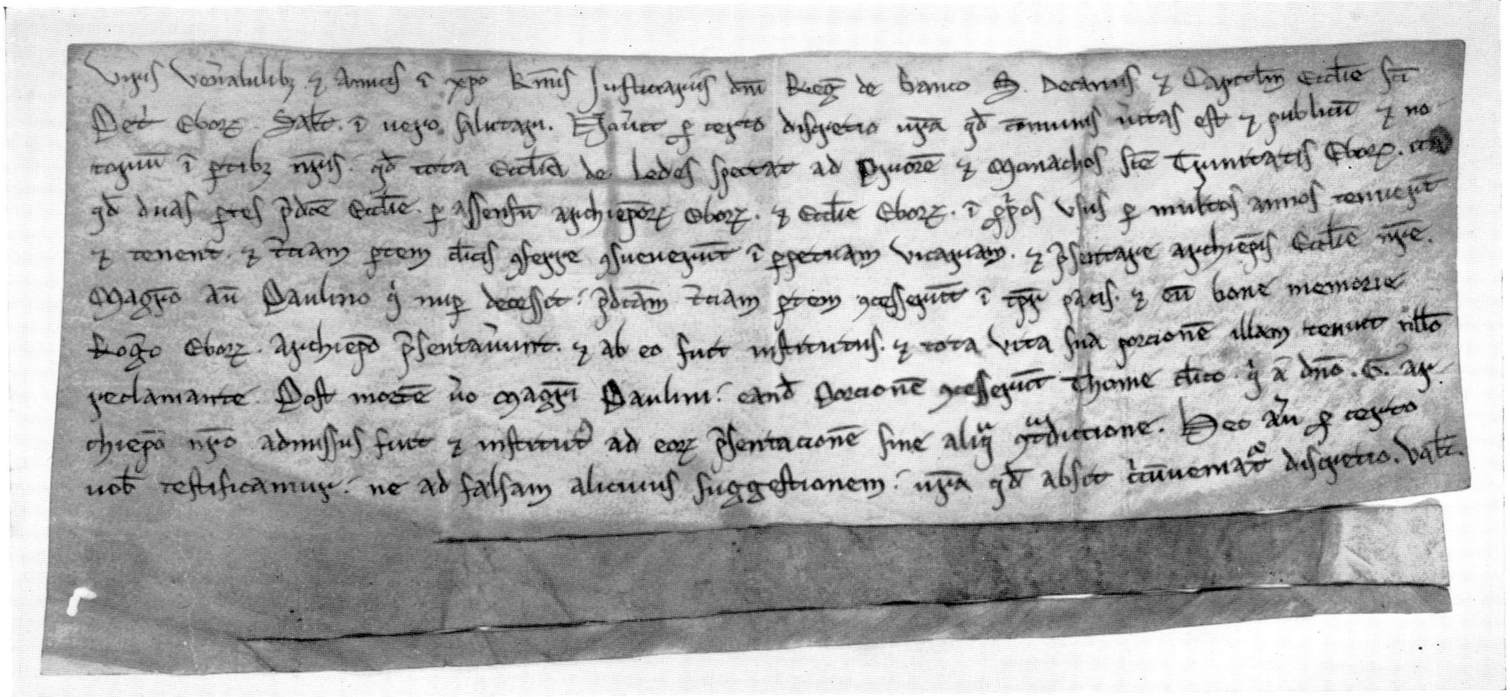

Cursive. Letter from Stephen, the Dean and the Chapter of St. Peter's at York to the Justices of the Bench. A.D. 1202–1212

Viris venerabilibus et amicis in Christo Karissimis domini Regis de Banco S. Decanus et Capitulum ecclesie sancti Petri Ebor' Salutem

(Bodleian Library, MS. Ch. Yorks. 540)

PLATE 117

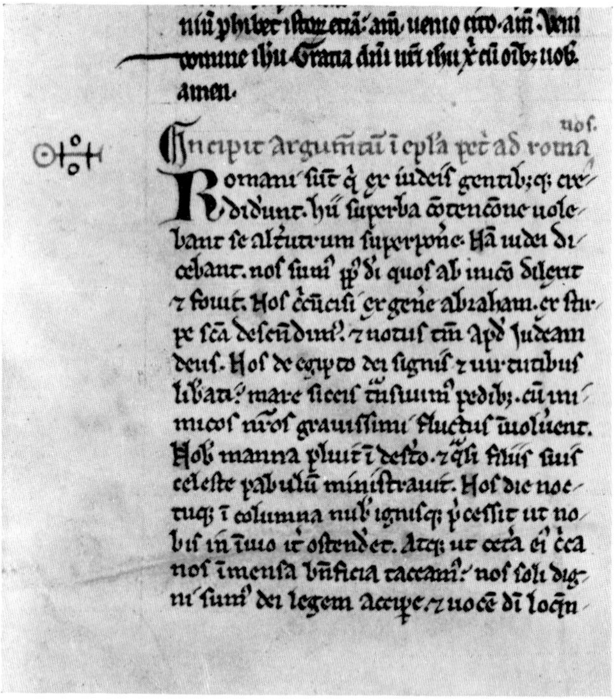

PLATE 118

a. Latin book-hand. Thirteenth century. The beginning of the
Argumentum in epistola Petri ad Romanos which Matthew Paris himself
added to a Bible written by a scribe

Romani sunt qui ex Judeis gentibusque crediderunt

(Corpus Christi College, Oxford, MS. 2, f. 369ᵃ)

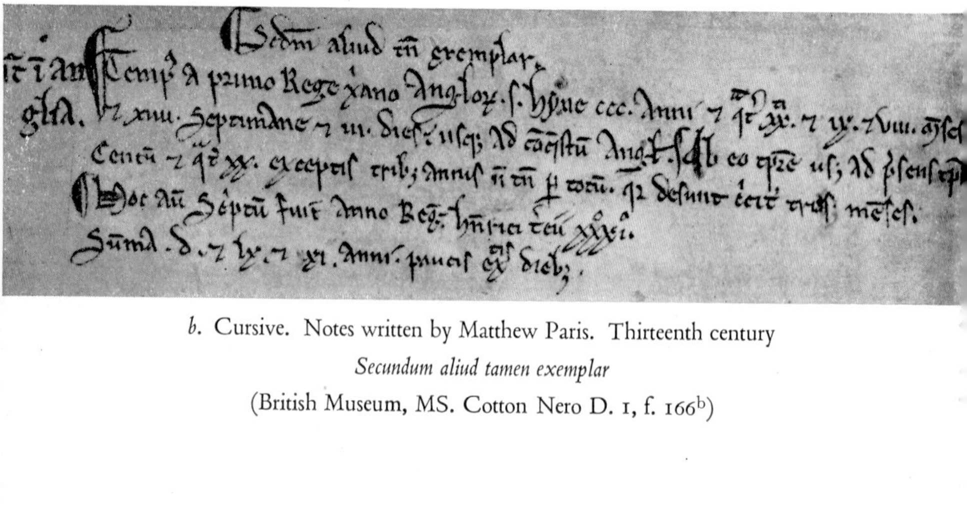

b. Cursive. Notes written by Matthew Paris. Thirteenth century

Secundum aliud tamen exemplar

(British Museum, MS. Cotton Nero D. 1, f. 166ᵇ)

we may call Gothic (Pl. 119). This change from the 'grand style' to one of 'general minuteness' was universal and perhaps deplorable, for despite the beauty of the new script, it fails in the fundamental quality of legibility. The falling off is all the more serious, since with the coming of the thirteenth century the number of surviving manuscripts increases in an almost geometrical progression. This too was the great age of the medieval universities, so that the whole academic learning of scholasticism must be read in highly abbreviated close scripts most trying to the eyes. Here none the less is a vast field for study and one in which scholars today are making great discoveries.

The very finest examples of the Gothic style are, of course, found in important religious books—bibles, the works of the great 'scholastics' like Peter Comestor, and, above all, in service books, especially psalters, missals, and breviaries. These were the *de luxe* volumes of the age, written without regard for expense, by scribes of unusual skill and often superbly illuminated. For mere 'literary' works, like chronicles, the full vigour of the new style was generally much mitigated, as in Pl. 118*a*, which shows the pleasing hand of Matthew Paris, the historian. Indeed, there was now so much bookhand writing on all levels, that collectively there are today probably more manuscripts written in modified Gothic, like that of Matthew Paris, than in the script of Pl. 119. Nevertheless, it was the hand of the missals and breviaries that was most esteemed at the time, and we can still admire the fantastic skill required to write it. Perhaps too it had a scarcity value, for it is hard to believe that the supply of such skilled scribes even then was enough to meet the demand. It could thus be only a matter of time until a reaction set in and the scholars, if not the scribes, strove to recover the splendid simplicity of the older writing. This movement in which Italy played a leading part brought about the archaistic and artificial revival of the *littera antiqua* (i.e. the post-Caroline minuscule of Italy) in the humanistic script of the fifteenth century, a variety of which, the italic, is shown in Pl. 120. With the simultaneous discovery of printing from movable type, further development was arrested and both the Gothic and the humanistic script became models for the printed book. Thus began a new 'battle of the books' which after a strife of centuries, ended everywhere (except in Germany) in the victory of the humanist letter-forms; and to this result, of course, the very type of *Medieval England* bears witness. But in England at least, the invention of printing did not immediately curb the inventiveness of scribes, and early in the sixteenth century a new hand, based partly on English models, makes its appearance. This is the script which the writing masters call 'secretary hand' (Pl. 121 *b*) which was developed and perfected as the century proceeded. It is, in Denholm-Young's words, 'the native, current hand for everyday purposes'; the hand, for example, of the great collection of *State Papers*, and as such of great practical importance to students of the period.

2

The history of medieval handwriting at its best is pre-eminently that of the Latin language and of the Catholic church: and it falls naturally into three periods. Of these the first is concerned with those splendid majuscule scripts, whose roots lie in antiquity, and their gradual replacement, under the influence of cursive writing, by the minuscule, the especial contribution of the middle ages to calligraphy. In the second period, which is conveniently dated by the appearance of the Caroline minuscule about the year 800 and lasts for four centuries, the new script reigns supreme for all literary writing. The third, beginning about 1200, is that of the Gothic script which after rather less than three centuries was in its turn discarded in the humanistic revival of the fifteenth century. In the second of these periods England was bound up more closely with the Continent than ever before or since, and shared a common Latin civilization that was truly European. For native and vernacular writing the periods, we have seen, need alteration, the first closing in 1066 and the third beginning early in the fourteenth century: the middle period—almost a blank—representing the price paid for internationalism. Yet, however, we distinguish periods, an underlying unity is found in the material used for writing, and therefore in technique. The classical world had employed papyrus: the modern world writes, and prints, on paper which 'came in' during the fif-teenth century. The medieval world in all three periods used sheepskin or parchment or vellum—three names for varieties of the same thing—which lasts longer than either papyrus or paper and gives a better surface for the pen.

The sketch given above is, however, something of an abstrac-tion for in treating writing as a form of art, it inevitably neglects history. But writing is, after all, only a synonym for history and art for art's sake a poor motto for the scribe since even the most exquisite manuscripts were written to serve useful purposes. There is, when all is said and done, a greater thrill in reading a manuscript than in merely looking at it, and the historian finds significance in the script—often beautiful—of manuscripts ignored by the student of writing as an art. The earlier centuries from which, relatively, so little has been preserved present little difficulty, for historians and palaeographers are equally in-terested in all that survives. But from the twelfth century on-wards—our third period—we enter a new world. The monks to whom we owe the finest manuscripts of the middle ages were, even then, a privileged class, to whom neither time nor money was important. Then, as now, there was also the world of affairs—the correspondence of kings, bishops, and barons, the writing of the law-courts, the tax rolls of the bureaucrats, private conveyancing and the accounts of business men. Not much is known about either the nature or volume of all this in the largely oral society of the early middle ages: but in the century after the Norman Conquest there was a rapid expansion of the written document, and by the late twelfth century there had developed a new cursive or semicursive, the 'court letter' (*littera curialis*) or as we say court hand. This new writing sur-vives in baffling variety and ever growing quantity, but Pl. 117 will suffice to show its origin in the Caroline minuscule written *currente calamo*. A large and mixed body of secular, professional writers sprang up, ranging from the half-illiterate scribe who compiled the manorial court-rolls to the highly-skilled clerks of the royal chancery, the notaries, both papal and imperial, and above all the Scriveners Company of London whose 'Com⁄mon Paper' or entrance book survives from the year 1390. Into this book for more than two centuries every member entered in his own hand his name and his acceptance of the company's rule—a unique record of the development of professional yet secular handwriting in its 'set' form.[1]

As the middle ages advance the classification of handwriting becomes increasingly difficult. Particularly well⁄written official documents of the twelfth century are often said by cataloguers to be written in 'charter hand', and by the end of that century the new cursive is already well developed. There was a growing tendency to link letters together; and their forms were greatly modified as the set hand taught to the apprentices became, under pressure of time, a free hand. These developments pro⁄foundly affected the development of book hand. The sudden change to smaller writing in the thirteenth century, as we have seen, reflects the influence of the new court hand, while the chronicles, and the ever⁄growing mass of vernacular writing (as English slowly came into its own) tend to be written more and more in hybrid scripts half⁄way between book hand proper and cursive. In this confusion of scripts we can, perhaps, distinguish a standard court hand which reaches its height to⁄wards the end of the thirteenth century. In the fourteenth and fifteenth centuries it slowly deteriorated, and at the same time the spread of education and the appearance of the 'literate lay⁄man' gave rise to a miscellaneous mass of documents as ill written as those of today. None the less there was throughout our period a body of highly trained professional scribes capable of writing well the standard court hand. But this is not all: for perhaps the most interesting feature of later medieval writing, as has been said above, is the emergence of elaborate and artificial set hands in the various departments of the 'civil service', which soon became fixed and traditional, and lasted for centuries. One of these, the new chancery hand of the late fifteenth and sixteenth centuries, is illustrated in Pl. 121 a. And there were

[1] See H. Jenkinson, *Late Court Hands in England* (Cambridge, 1927).

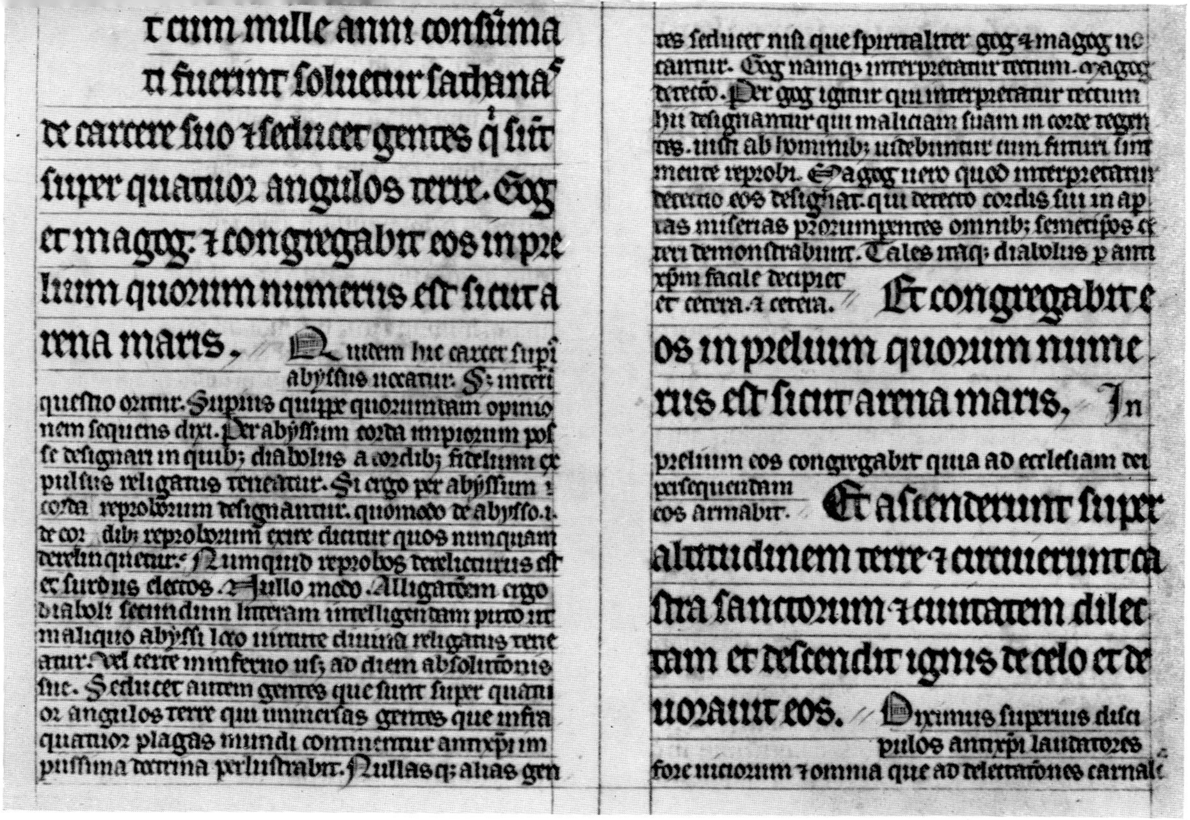

PLATE 119

Gothic script. Douce Apocalypse. Probably written before 1272. English
[E]t cum mille anni consummati fuerint
(Bodleian, MS. Douce 180, p. 87)

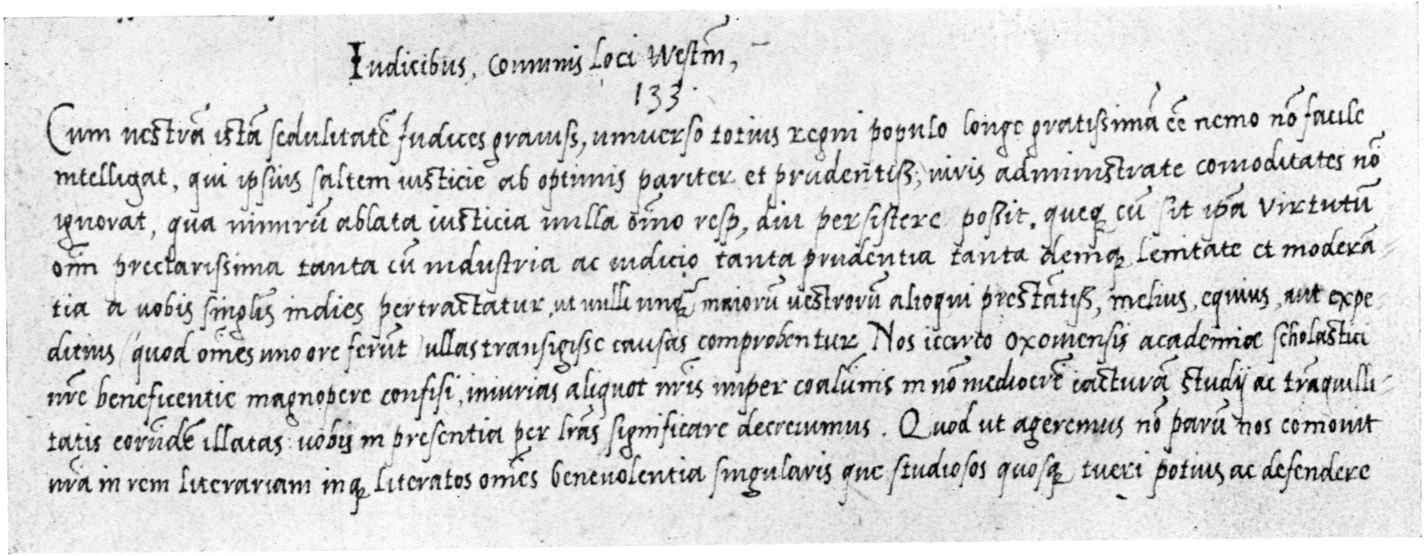

PLATE 120

Iudicibus, communis loci Westm,

133

Cum nestra ista sedulitate Iudices graues, innocens totius regni populo longe gratissima ee nemo no facile intelligat, qui ipsius saltem iusticie ob optimis partem et prudentiss: uiuis administretate commoditates no ignorat, qua nimirū oblata iusticia nulla ōmo res, aut perfectere posset, quaeq cū ista Virtutu ōm beatarissima tanta cū industria ac iudicio tanta prudentia tanta dēmq lenitate et modestia tia ac uobis singulis indies geritur tractatur ut nulli nunq maiorum nostrorum aliorum presentius, melius, equius, aut expedicius, quod omes nunc are ferīt nullas transfugisc causas comprobentur. Nos iccirco Oxonienses academie scholastici hoc beneficentie magnopere confisi, iniurias aliquot nres nuper coalumis in no mediocre cōttura Studii ac tranquilli tatis eorunde illacas: uobis in presentia per lras significare decreuimus. Quod ut ageremus no parui nos comonet iniuria in rem litterariam inq litteratos omes beneuolentia singularis qme studiosos quosq tueri potius ac defendere

Humanistic script. Letter from the University of Oxford to the Judges at Westminster. A.D. 1524

Iudicibus communis loci Westm'

(Bodleian, MS. Bodley 282 (S.C. 2949) f. 70ᵛ)

many others in the various departments of the exchequer and the courts of law, which survive literally by the ton in the Public Record Office. This official writing was done, generally speaking, not in books, but on great parchment rolls, the membranes being either gathered at the head, or sewn end to end, and then rolled up. In England the roll was as normal for government records as the 'book' for literary manuscripts.

For more than four centuries handwriting has fought a losing battle against the printing press; to which, we must now add, the typewriter. Yet in the general degradation one of its oldest functions remains in full force, and even grows in importance. For however much we print or type our documents they have still to be authenticated, and guarded against forgery. This is done by the signature, which is not merely a name, but a name written in an individual and personal way that carries conviction at sight. As such, it goes right back to the ancient world, and the notion of signatures was never entirely lost in the medieval world: indeed in the twelfth century the most solemn 'privileges' of the papal chancery were signed (or supposed to be signed) personally by the cardinals. But signatures were, after all, only intelligible to clerks while the written commands of kings and princes had to be recognized at a glance by their illiterate subjects. Thus, the conditions of the time were against the use of signatures at any rate in the earlier part of our period, when lay magnates—*pro ignorantia litterarum*—never aspired to do more than to add the sign of the cross (+) at the foot of a charter—and even this seems to have been done more often than not by the scribe. Feudal Europe therefore fell back upon another device, also classical in origin—the use of seals. By the sixth century the popes were sealing their letters with a twofaced leaden 'bulla', bearing on one side the pope's name and number and on the other the heads of St. Peter and St. Paul. A little later we find the Merovingian and Carolingian kings impressing on the face of their charters a wax seal, which, however, involved cutting the parchment to give it a grip and was in any case too easily removed. At last in the eleventh century the chancery of King Edward the Confessor evolved the pendent, 'coin' seal in wax, attached on a parchment strip cut at the foot of the document. This adaptation of the 'bulla' was rapidly copied in every European chancery, royal, baronial, and episco-pal. For the rest of the middle ages writing and seals were in-separably connected in men's thoughts, and at Runnymede King John accepted Magna Carta by affixing his seal to the 'petition' of the barons, not because he could not write (he probably could), but because medieval government in 1215 was government by seals. By the close of the middle ages the king possessed, in addition to the Great Seal employed in his Chancery, both a Privy Seal and a Signet, each with its own separate secretariat. Every department of government—the exchequer, the wardrobe, the law courts—had also its depart-mental seal, and the methods of government were copied by merchants and almost all owners of property. Like most medieval institutions, the system reached its height in the thir-teenth century, after which period, as a result of the develop-ment of cursive writing and the spread of education, the use of seals by the middle class slowly decayed. In the fifteenth century we find jurors signing their names to inquisitions: and it was left to that very educated dynasty the Tudors to introduce the personal signature or sign manual into the busi-ness of state. From the sixteenth century onwards the use of seals by high and low to authenticate documents has grown steadily less. The Signet still survives: but the Privy Seal was abolished a century ago (though not its Keeper, the Lord Privy Seal), and the Great Seal itself is only an antiquarian survival used for creating peers by letters patent.

The history of handwriting has been studied by its greatest exponents as an aspect of artistic evolution guided by natural selection: and with good reason, for we can certainly put our undated manuscripts in a rough sequence, merely by looking at their script. But we must not carry this approach too far. One recalls the old canon of Dunstable who proved a document to be a forgery by testifying in open court that he had written all their charters for the past forty years. Even if it be true that writing has never been a 'thing at the mercy of individual

PLATE 121

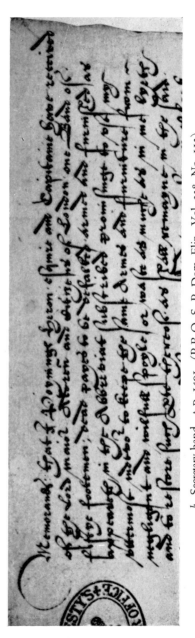

a. Chancery set hand. Sixteenth century. *Rex omnibus ad quos etc salutem.* (P.R.O. Patent Roll: 34 Henry VIII pt. 2)

b. Secretary hand. A.D. 1591. (P.R.O. S. P. Dom. Eliz., Vol. 238, No. 113)

whim', the notion of the survival of the fittest is only acceptable with large qualifications. The very reasons we advance for the triumph of the Caroline minuscule make it difficult to explain the vogue of the Gothic script for three whole centuries. At all times handwriting has been influenced by the taste of individual scribes, and also—like the history of costume—by the vagaries of fashion. We shall do well, then, to think of it as an art, governed by rules of course, but still as an activity of individuals some of whom, did we but know it, may have decisively changed its history. Wise men only date undated manuscripts within very wide limits, and even so, provisionally. But caution, too, can be carried too far for no subject better illustrates the blind operation of conflicting tendencies in history. Against the virtue of legibility must always be set the urge for greater speed in writing. The need to be easily intelligible is offset by the tendency to contract the writing, either to save space or the labour of the scribe. Most curious of all is the well-attested instinct to raise writing to the status of a 'mystery', which in the past has given rise to scripts of deliberate intricacy, and lingers on in the prescriptions written by our doctors. The same motives, allied with others, explain the revival of Latin in the public administration at the Restoration, and the retention of Law French well into the eighteenth century.

WORKS FOR REFERENCE

DENHOLM-YOUNG, N. *Handwriting in England and Wales* (Cardiff, 1954).

GRIEVE, HILDA E. P. *Some Examples of English Handwriting* (Chelmsford, 1949); *More Examples of English Handwriting* (Chelmsford, 1950).

JENKINSON, H. *The Later Court Hands in England* (Cambridge, 1927).

JOHNSON, CHARLES, and JENKINSON, H. *Court Hand Illustrated* (Oxford, 1914).

KENYON, F. G. *Books and Readers in Ancient Greece and Rome* (Oxford, 1932).

LOWE, E. A. *Codices Latini Antiquiores*. Parts i–vi (Oxford, 1934–53); 'Handwriting', in *The Legacy of the Middle Ages*, ed. C. G. CRUMP and E. F. JACOB (Oxford, 1926).

STEFFENS, FRANZ. *Lateinische Palaeographie*, 2nd ed. (Fribourg, 1907; French ed., R. COULON, 1908–10).

THOMPSON, E. MAUNDE. *Handbook of Greek and Latin Palaeography* (Oxford, 1912).

WARNER, G. F., and ELLIS, H. J. *Facsimiles of Royal and other Charters in the British Museum* (1903).

Facsimiles

Facsimiles of Ancient Charters in the British Museum. 4 vols. 1873–8.

Facsimiles of Anglo-Saxon MSS. 3 vols. (Ordnance Survey, 1878–84).

New Palaeographical Society, *Facsimiles of Ancient MSS.* First and Second Series (1903–30).

Palaeographical Society, *Facsimiles of MSS. and Inscriptions.* First and Second Series (1873–1901).

XVII. PRINTED BOOKS, THE BOOK-TRADE, AND LIBRARIES

1. *Printing*

THE introducer of printing into England, William Caxton, was born in Kent about the year 1421. Most of his life was spent in business on the Continent, where he became Governor of the English Nation in the Low Countries.[1] By the year 1469 he had also entered the service of the duchess of Burgundy, for whom he made various translations. His work proved popular, but the task of copying becoming burdensome he decided to multiply copies of his translations by the novel art of printing. Caxton seems to have learnt this in Cologne, but it was at Bruges that he printed, with the assistance of Colard Mansion, in 1475, the *Recuyell of the Historyes of Troye*, the first book printed in the English language. Caxton returned to England in the following year, and set up a printing press at Westminster. In 1477 his first dated book, the *Dictes or Sayengis of the Philosophers*, appeared (Pl. 122). From that date to 1491 Caxton printed ninety-six separate books, the most notable being Chaucer's *Canterbury Tales*, Malory's *Morte d'Arthur*, and the *Golden Legend*.

Caxton died in 1491 and left all his materials to his apprentice, Wynkyn de Worde, who printed over one hundred books in the fifteenth century. In 1500 De Worde moved from Westminster to London, where he continued working until 1535, by which time he had printed nearly 800 different books. The other fifteenth-century printers of Westminster and Lon-

---

[1] The Governor was an official of the association of Merchant Adventurers; he was elected by the members who resided in the Low Countries. His headquarters were at Bruges. He acted as an arbitrator in disputes between English merchants and represented them in correspondence with the home government.

don were Julian Notary, John Lettou, William de Machlinia, and Richard Pynson.

Oxford was the first provincial town in which a press was set up. Its earliest production was Rufinus's *Expositio in sim-bolum Apostolorum*, which, although dated 'MCCCCLXVIII', was almost certainly printed in 1478, the figure X having accidentally dropped out of the date. The name of the printer is not given, but it is generally assumed that he was Theodoric Rood of Cologne, whose name appears in 1481 as printer of the Oxford edition of Alexander de Hales's commentary on the *De Anima* of Aristotle. Four years later Rood is found associated in his business with Thomas Hunte, a university stationer. Seventeen books are assigned to the fifteenth-century Oxford press, but some of them are known only from fragments.

St. Albans had a printing press in 1480; the printer's name is unknown. He is generally called the Schoolmaster Printer, because of a reference to him by Wynkyn de Worde, who states in one of his books that it had also been printed by one sometime 'scole master of saynt Albons'. The most notable production of the press is the famous *Boke of St. Albans*, which treats of hawking, hunting, and heraldry. Eight books are known to have issued from this press, which ceased working, with the Oxford press, in 1486.

In London alone was there any continuity of printing; Wynkyn de Worde, Pynson, and Notary carried on their work into the sixteenth century, Copland, Faques, Redman, Berthelet, and Rastell being the more notable of their contemporaries or successors. The Oxford press resumed work from 1517 to 1519, and then broke off again till 1585. St. Albans also had a press working from 1534 to 1538. Other towns at which books were printed before 1550 were York (1509), Cambridge (1521), Tavistock (1525), Abingdon (1528), Ipswich (1547), Worcester (1549), and Canterbury (1549). Printing was introduced into Scotland by Walter Chapman and Andrew Myllar, who issued in 1508 a few poetical tracts. No press existed in Ireland before 1551, in which

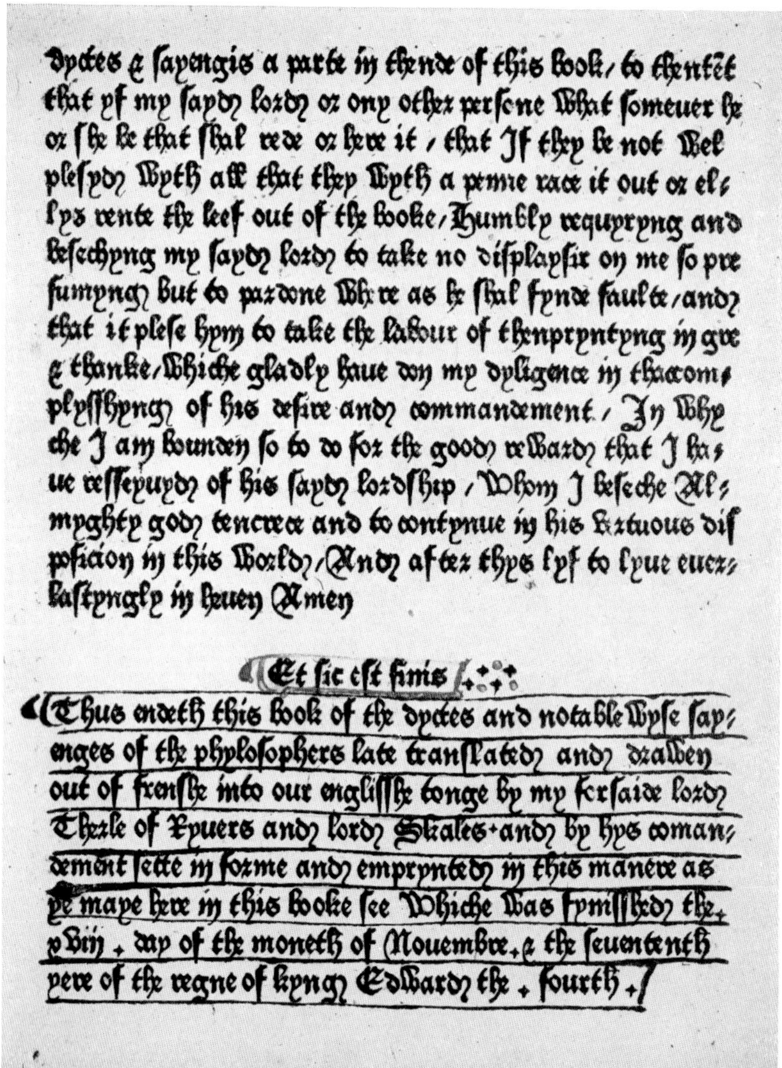

PLATE 122

dyctes & sayengis a parte in thende of this book, to thentent
that yf my sayd lord or ony other persone What someuer he
or she be that shal rede or here it, that If they be not Wel
plesyd Wyth all that they Wyth a penne race it out or els
rys rente the leef out of the booke, Humbly requyryng and
besechyng my sayd lord to take no displaysir on me so pre
sumyng, but to pardone Where as he shal fynde faulte, and
that it plese hym to take the labour of thenpryntyng in gre
& thanke, Whiche gladly haue don my dylygence in thaccom
plysshyng of his desire and commandement. In Why
che I am bounden so to do for the good reward that I ha
ue resseyuyd of his sayd lordshyp, Whom I beseche Al
myghty god tencrece and to contynue in his vertuous dis
posicion in this World, And after thys lyf to lyue euer
lastyngly in heuen Amen

Et sic est finis

Thus endeth this book of the dyctes and notable Wyse say
enges of the phylosophers late translated and drawen
out of frenshe into our englisshe tonge by my forsaid lord
Erle of Ryuers and lord Skales, and by hys coman
dement sette in forme and emprynted in this manere as
ye maye here in this booke see Whiche Was fynysshed the .
xviij . day of the moneth of Nouembre, & the seuententh
yere of the regne of kyng Edward the . fourth .

Colophon of Caxton's *Dictes or Sayengis of the Philosophers*, from the copy in the
John Rylands Library, Manchester

PLATE 123

Lectern desks in the Old Library of Trinity Hall, Cambridge

year Humphrey Powell printed an edition of the Book of Common Prayer in Dublin.

It is an interesting fact that the majority of books printed by Caxton, including his first, were in English, many being of a popular character. His successor, De Worde, also issued a large number of small popular poems and tracts. Besides this popular literature, service-books, law treatises, and minor theo-logical and scholastic books were printed in considerable numbers by the earlier English printers, but for editions of the Bible, Latin and Greek classical texts, and works of scholarship generally, England was dependent on the Continent.

The first classical text published in England is an edition of Cicero's *Pro Milone* printed by Theodoric Rood of Oxford about 1480 (Fig. 105). The earliest specimen of Greek movable type is found in a motto on the title-page of a book printed by Siberch at Cambridge in 1521. De Worde had previously used a few Greek words in some of his books, but they had been printed from wood-blocks. A Chrysostom printed by Wolfe of London in 1543 is the earliest Greek text printed in England.

The *editio princeps* of the English Bible was printed on the Continent in 1535 at some place unknown (Fig. 106). This was Coverdale's translation. The first Bible actually printed in England was produced by James Nycolson of Southwark in 1537. In the same year appeared 'Matthew's Bible', another continental printed version. This was followed by the 'Great Bible' of 1539, printed partly in France and partly in England. In 1560 the Geneva version was published. This, the first popular edition of the Bible, is noteworthy for its compact form, the use of Roman type, and the division of chapters into verses. The next important versions were the 'Bishops' Bible' (1568) and the Authorized Version (1611).

The press used by printers of the fifteenth century was made of wood, and of similar construction to the small platen presses of today. Two men sufficed to work it, one laying the paper and 'pulling' the press, the other 'beating', i.e. inking the type with ink-balls.

Very many books printed in the fifteenth century are without name of printer, place of printing, or date. When these are given

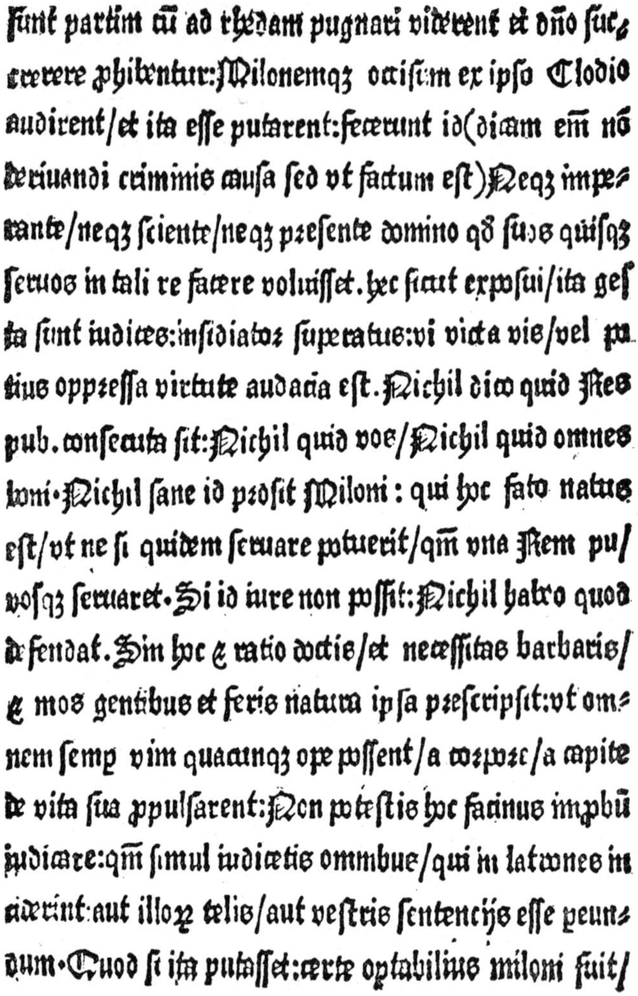

funt partim cu ad rkedam pugnari viderent et dño suc,
cætere philentur:ſMilonemq3 occiſcm ex ipſo Clodio
audirent/et ita eſſe putarent:fecerunt id(dicam em nõ
deriuandi criminis cauſa ſed ut factum eſt)Neq3 impe,
rante/neq3 ſciente/neq3 præſente domino qð ſuos quiſq3
ſeruos in tali re facere voluiſſet.hec ſicut expoſui/ita geſ
ta ſunt iudices:inſidiator ſuperatus:vi victa vis/vel po_
tius oppreſſa virtute audacia eſt.Nichil dico quid Res
pub.conſecuta ſit:Nichil quid vos/Nichil quid omnes
boni.Nichil ſane id proſit Miloni : qui hoc fato natus
eſt/ut ne ſi quidem ſeruare potuerit/qm vna Rem pu/
voſq3 ſeruaret.Si id iure non poſſit:Nichil habeo quod
defendat.Sin hoc & ratio doctis/et neceſſitas barbaris/
& mos gentibus et feris natura ipſa præſcripſit:ut om,
nem ſemp vim quacunq3 ope poſſent/a corpore/a capite
de vita ſua ppulſarent:Non poteſtis hoc facinus impbū
iudicare:qm ſimul iudicetis ommbus/qui in latrones in
ciderint.aut illos telis/aut veſtris ſentencijs eſſe peuni,
dum.Quod ſi ita putaſſet:certe optabilius miloni ſuit/

FIG. 105. Cicero's *Pro Melone* (Oxford, c. 1480)

they are usually found in the colophon, that is, a paragraph at the end of the book giving details about its production. A printer's device, if found in a book, can normally be accepted as the mark of the printer who actually printed the book,

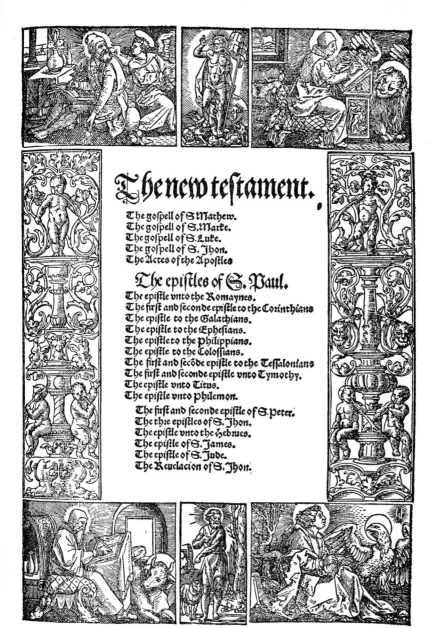

The new testament.

The gospell of S. Mathew.
The gospell of S. Marke.
The gospell of S. Luke.
The gospell of S. Jhon.
The Actes of the Apostles

The epistles of S. Paul.

The epistle vnto the Romaynes.
The first and seconde epistle to the Corinthians
The epistle to the Galathians.
The epistle to the Ephesians.
The epistle to the philippians.
The epistle to the Colossians.
The first and secöde epistle to the Tessalonians
The first and seconde epistle vnto Tymothy.
The epistle vnto Titus.
The epistle vnto philemon.

The first and seconde epistle of S. peter.
The thre epistles of S. Jhon.
The epistle vnto the hebrues.
The epistle of S. James.
The epistle of S. Jude.
The Reuelacion of S. Jhon.

FIG. 106. Coverdale's Bible, 1535. Title-page of the New Testament

Caxton, however, first used his device in the *Sarum Missal* of 1487, which was printed for him by W. Maynyal of Paris. Title-pages are uncommon; the earliest English book with a title-page is the *Treatise on the Pestilance*, printed by Machlinia about 1486.

In the lower margin of certain leaves in a printed book will generally be found a series of letters or numbers on the first pages of each 'gathering'. These are called 'signatures', and are intended to guide the binder when he 'gathers up' the sheets of the book he is about to bind. The first printer in England to use signatures was Theodoric Rood of Oxford. When a sheet is folded once it forms two leaves (a folio or fol.); when twice, four leaves (a quarto or 4to); when thrice, eight leaves (an octavo or 8vo). These are the normal sizes of early printed books.

2. *Binding*

Leather has always been the usual covering for books in western Europe, although in early times manuscripts were sometimes cased in precious metals decorated with jewels. The earliest extant English leather binding is on a copy of the Gospel of St. John at Stonyhurst, and is supposed to be tenth-century work. The bindings produced at Durham and Winchester in the twelfth century are remarkable for the beauty of the dies used to stamp the leather. Fifteenth-century bindings have very distinct characteristics, and it is possible to identify a considerable number of them by means of the dies used for their decoration. The use of small stamps was continued until the beginning of the sixteenth century when a large stamp, called a 'panel', came into general use. This was succeeded by a tool of wheel shape called a 'roll', which by revolution could repro-duce indefinitely the design cut upon it. The use of gold on bindings was popularized in England by the King's Printer, Thomas Berthelet (died 1555), who produced some notable bindings in leather and velvet. The 'boards' of bindings of the medieval period were invariably of wood.

3. *Book Trade*

Before the introduction of printing into England our knowledge of the production and selling of books depends largely on
isolated facts gathered together from a variety of documents.
The transcription and binding of manuscripts were carried on
at most monastic foundations, and at literary centres such as
Oxford, scribes, illuminators, binders, and parchment-sellers
are found in considerable numbers from the twelfth century
onwards.

Although it was an Englishman who introduced printing
into England, yet it must not be assumed that Englishmen at
first held any important place in the book-trade in England.
Caxton is, in fact, the only known native fifteenth-century
printer in England; De Worde, Lettou, Machlinia, Notary,
and Rood were all foreigners. And so it was with the book-trade
generally. From 1476 to 1535 the majority of those engaged in
the book-trade in England were foreigners. This influx of
aliens was largely due to an Act of 1484 which allowed 'any
artificer, or merchant stranger of what nation or country he be
. . . or any scrivener, alluminor [illuminator], binder, or
printer' to exercise their trade and to reside in England.

These foreign stationers not only had books printed for them
on the Continent for sale in England, but established themselves at literary centres and attended fairs where any considerable trade in books was likely to be done. An account-book of
John Dorne, an early sixteenth-century Oxford stationer, is still
preserved, and shows that a large part of his trade was done at
the Oxford book fairs, and that he made periodical visits to the
Continent to replenish his stock of books.

The book-trade flourished in England from the passing of
the Act of 1484 until 1534, when another Act was passed,
placing severe restrictions on foreign printers and stationers,
and on the importation of ready-bound books. The Act was
ostensibly for the protection of native workmen; it was, however, also directed against the importation of prohibited books,
for which there was a great demand. The first edition of Tyn-

dale's New Testament, printed on the Continent in 1525, is known to have consisted of 3,000 copies. Others quickly followed, but so efficiently was their suppression carried out that of the editions known to have been printed before 1532 not one-quarter has survived either as copies or fragments. From 1535 the book-trade in England rapidly declined and did not permanently revive until the reign of Elizabeth.

4. *Libraries*

References to collections of books in the British Isles are frequent from the seventh century, but there is little information about the manner in which the earliest collections were stored. We read, for instance, of manuscripts at Canterbury in the age of St. Augustine, and of a library administered by Alcuin at York in 778. In the twelfth century there were more than 300 works at Durham priory and the secular library at Christ Church, Canterbury consisted of over 200 volumes. In the latter collection were works by Cicero, Plato, Terence, Sallust, Vergil, Horace, Lucan, Statius, Juvenal, Persius, Cato, and Ovid. These collections were probably kept in presses in the cloisters, where they were also read. In the cloisters of Gloucester cathedral may be seen little alcoves, called carrels, where the monks of the Benedictine abbey of St. Peter pursued their studies. Later, when monastic collections increased in size, special book-rooms were provided. In the book-room of Christ Church, Canterbury, at the end of the thirteenth century, the books were arranged in two *demonstrationes* (large general divisions), and then into *distinctiones* (probably bookcases), each *distinctio* having a certain number of *gradus* (shelves). The books were classified under groups such as Theology, History, Philosophy, Music, Medicine.

A considerable amount of information about the arrangement and classification of books in monastic libraries can be derived from their catalogues, of which several are extant. The illustration shows a portion of the catalogue of the priory of St. Martin, Dover, compiled in 1389. This library was divided

PLATE 124

a. From the Catalogue of Dover Priory, 1389 (Bodleian, MS. Bodley 920)

b. The west wing of Merton College Library, Oxford

into nine *distinctiones*, designated by the nine first letters of the alphabet, each being divided into seven *gradus* numbered with Roman figures. Each entry in the catalogue has six divisions (see Pl. 124*a*): the first gives the shelf/mark A. v. 1 (Case A, shelf v, book 1); the second, the book (an old glossed Psalter); the third, the leaf on which certain opening words, selected for the identification of the volume, occur (i.e. on leaf 6); the fourth, the two first words on that leaf (*apprehendite disci*); the fifth, the number of leaves in the volume (i.e. 105); and the sixth, the number of works contained in the volume (viz. one).

The provision of a special building for a library seems not to be found before the fourteenth century. The aspect favoured by the early builder of collegiate libraries was one with the walls facing east and west, so that advantage might be taken of the morning sun, light rather than warmth being essential to the student. With the decline of asceticism and a greater desire for physical comfort a warmer aspect was often chosen. The light/ing of the building was secured by lancet windows placed closely together.

The earliest libraries were probably fitted up with bookcases in the shape of lecterns, to which the books were chained on either side. When books and readers were few this was con/venient enough, but, when they multiplied, the lecterns became crowded and one reader hindered another. The development of the lectern was a case (still having counters on either side) with a flat top, above which two or three shelves were fixed. Along the shelves ran a rod, to which were attached chains, the other ends of which were secured to the manuscripts. This method, which has been styled the stall system, naturally accommodated a much larger number of books and left the counters free for those actually in use. The practice of fitting cases against the walls of a library and carrying them from floor to ceiling is in England a late development of library economy. The Arts End (1612) of the Bodleian Library at Oxford is the earliest example of the style in this country.

No early example of the lectern system any longer exists in England. The lecterns at Trinity Hall, Cambridge, probably date from about 1600 (Pl. 123). The cases in Queen's College library, Cambridge, show traces of having been converted from lecterns, and there is documentary evidence to show that Pembroke College library, Cambridge, was fitted with lecterns until 1617. Apparently the only early surviving ex' ample of the style is the library of the Church of SS. Peter and Walburga at Zutphen, in the Netherlands.

Several excellent examples of the stall system still survive. One of the finest is the west wing of the library of Merton College, Oxford, the best example of a medieval library in England (Pl. 124*b*). The bookcases, each with four shelves on either side, are placed in the intervals between the windows. On each side of a case are sloping counters, and between each pair of cases is a thick wooden bench. The building itself dates from 1378, but there is reason to believe that the bookcases are of the late sixteenth century. Other good examples of the stall' system are the libraries of Corpus Christi College (1517) and St. John's (1596) at Oxford, and the Old Reading'room of the Bodleian Library (1602).

Of the two great English university libraries that of Oxford has priority of foundation, while that of Cambridge can claim a longer continuous history. The university of Cambridge re' ceived its first important gift of books in 1424. Its earliest library was on the first floor of the west side of the Schools' Quadrangle, but the room seems to have been employed for the purpose for no great length of time. The chief library (*Libraria communis*) was built in 1470 on the south side of the Quadrangle; five years later another library was erected on the east side by the chancellor of the university, Archbishop Rotherham. This smaller room was reserved for the archbishop's own library and the more valuable books possessed by the university. In the sixteenth century the fortunes of the library declined to such an extent that the *Libraria communis* was disfurnished in 1547. When, however, the university received large gifts of books from Archbishop Parker and others towards the close of the century, the library was restored to its former use.

Some idea of the routine of a medieval library may be gained by reciting some of the statutes framed for the library (*Libraria communis*) of the university of Oxford, which was founded by Thomas Cobham, bishop of Worcester, between the years 1320 and 1327. The library, which was built above the Congregation House adjoining St. Mary's church, was to be in the charge of two chaplains, one of whom was to be on duty before dinner, the other after. The books were to be secured by chains, and no one was to be admitted unless one of the chaplains was present. It was the duty of the chaplains to see that no reader entered the library in wet clothes, or having pen, ink, or knife; if notes had to be taken they were to be made in pencil.

Bishop Cobham died in 1327 heavily in debt, and there was some delay in securing the use of the library for the university, but by 1337 its history may be said to begin, and by the beginning of the fifteenth century it was fully established. In 1412 a new code of statutes was formulated. It provided that the librarian, who in addition to his ordinary library duties said masses in St. Mary's church for the souls of benefactors, should once a year hand over to the Chancellor and Proctors the keys of the library. The librarian's salary was fixed at £5. 6s. 8d. a year, to be paid half-yearly. In addition he might also claim a robe from every beneficed scholar at graduation. Should he desire to resign his office, a month's notice was required. Admission to the library was restricted to students who had studied in the Schools for eight years, an exception being made in the case of the sons of lords who had seats in Parliament. Each reader on admission had to take an oath that he would not injure any book maliciously by erasing or by detaching sections and leaves; theft of a whole volume was unlikely as the books were chained. The library was to be open from 9 till 11 and from 1 till 4, except on Sundays and the greater festivals, when it was entirely closed. In the long vacation the librarian was allowed one month's holiday. All books used during the day were to be closed at night, and all the windows fastened.

A few years later the university received large gifts of books and money from Humphrey, duke of Gloucester and about 1485 Cobham's library was moved 'to the room, now called

Duke Humfrey', which had been built above the Divinity School. In 1550 the books were dispersed by the Commissioners of Edward VI, and in 1556 the fittings were sold as being no longer needed. The room was restored to its original use by Sir Thomas Bodley, and in 1602 again became the public library of the university.

WORKS FOR REFERENCE

BENNETT, H. S. *English Books and Readers, 1475–1557* (Camb. Univ. Press, 1952).

CLARK, J. W. *The Care of Books*, 2nd ed., 1909.

DARLOW, T. H., and MOULE, H. F. *Historical Catalogue of the Printed Editions of Holy Scripture in the Library of the Bible Society*, i (1903).

DUFF, E. G. *The Printers, Stationers, and Bookbinders of Westminster and London* (1906); *The English Provincial Printers, Stationers, and Bookbinders* (1912); *A Century of the English Book Trade, 1457–1557* (1905).

JAMES, M. R. *The Ancient Libraries of Canterbury and Dover* (1903).

MACRAY, W. D. *Annals of the Bodleian Library*, 2nd ed. (1890).

MADAN, F. *Oxford Books*, 2 vols. (1912).

POWICKE, F. M. *The Medieval Books of Merton College* (1931).

SAVAGE, E. A. *Old English Libraries* (1911).

SAYLE, C. *Annals of Cambridge University Library* (1916).

SHADWELL, C. L. *A Catalogue of the Library of Oriel College in 1375* (Oxf. Hist. Soc., *Collectanea*, i, 1885).

Statuta Antiqua Universitatis Oxoniensis, ed. S. Gibson (1931).

STREETER, B. H. *The Chained Library* (1931).

XVIII. SCIENCE

I

THE history of science in medieval England, as in the medieval west generally, followed much the same course as the history of learning as a whole. It is the history of an intellectual tradition beginning with the literary recovery of classical science, first from Latin and later from Greek and Arabic sources, and leading to thoughts and investigations which gradually took on an independent life of their own. Most of the basic problems of medieval science and the methods of solving them came from classical sources, and to a large extent science remained to the end of the medieval period under ancient tutelage; but from their first contacts with classical learning the barbarian invaders of the old Roman provinces showed so marked and vigorous an originality of mind and intention that they recovered nothing they did not in some degree transform. During the early medieval centuries this is especially true of their approach to practical problems; and where these came within the scope of contemporary formal education, as did the calendar, with its dependence on astronomy, and medicine, their influence upon the development of a theoretical science based on experiment was profound. The connexion is less obvious between theoretical science and the technological problems found in mining and metallurgy, the construction of machinery, architecture, and agriculture, activities in which marked advances were made during the middle ages but which lay outside the scope of formal education. Some interest in these subjects men of learning certainly took. The medieval achievements in technology show the same originality and strongly empirical attitude of mind as is so characteristic of the achievements in theoretical science. In both, not only by her own accomplishments, but also by her external influence, no country in Christendom contributed more than England.

The earliest English science worthy of the name is found in the Anglo-Saxon kingdom of Northumbria in the eighth century; its outstanding representative, Bede, was a figure of more than merely insular significance and has been called 'the schoolmaster of the middle ages'. In Bede's time, western scholars had to guide them only some remnants in Latin of the great tradition of Greek science, and, meagre as these Latin remnants were, the most considerable collection, the translations and commentaries of Boethius, was not yet known in England. The main sources of Bede's scientific ideas were the fathers, especially St. Ambrose, St. Augustine of Hippo, St. Basil the Great, and St. Gregory the Great; the Visigothic encyclopaedist Isidore of Seville, who lived a century before Bede; most important of all, the Roman encyclopaedist Pliny; and lastly, some Latin writings on the calendar. Based on these sources, Bede's writings on scientific subjects fall into two main classes: a largely derivative account of general cosmology, and a more independent treatment of some specific practical problems, in particular those connected with the calendar.

Bede's cosmology is interesting for showing how an educated person of the eighth century pictured the universe. He set out his views in *De Rerum Natura*, based largely on Isidore's book of the same title but also on Pliny's *Natural History*, which Isidore had not known. Because of his more critical exposition as well as his use of Pliny, Bede's book shows a marked improvement over Isidore's. Bede's universe is one ordered by ascertainable cause and effect. Whereas Isidore had thought the earth shaped like a wheel, Bede held that it was a static sphere, with five zones, of which only the two temperate were habitable and only the northern one actually inhabited. Surrounding the earth were seven heavens: air, ether, Olympus, fiery space, the firmament with the heavenly bodies, the heaven of angels, and the heaven of the Trinity. The waters on the firmament separated the corporeal from the spiritual creation. The corporeal world was composed of the four elements, earth, water, air, and fire, arranged in order of heaviness and lightness. At the Creation these four elements, together with light and man's soul, were made by God *ex nihilo*; all other phenomena in the corporeal world were combinations. From Pliny Bede got a much more detailed knowledge of the Greek understanding of the diurnal and annual movements of the heavenly bodies than had been available to Isidore. He held that the firmament of stars revolved round the earth, and that within the firmament the planets circled in a system of epicycles. He gave clear accounts of the phases of the moon and of eclipses.

The problem of the calendar had been brought to Northumbria along with Christianity by the monks of Iona, but long before that time methods of computing the date of Easter had formed part of the school science of *computus*, which provided the finger exercises of early medieval science. The main problem connected with the Christian calendar arose from the fact that it was a combination of the Roman Julian calendar, based on the annual movement of the earth relative to the sun, and the Hebrew calendar, based on the monthly phases of the moon. The year and its divisions into months, weeks, and days belonged to the Julian solar calendar; but Easter was determined in the same way as the Hebrew Passover by the phases of the moon, and its date in the Julian year varied, within definite limits, from one year to the next. In order to calculate the date of Easter it was necessary to combine the length of the solar year with that of the lunar month. The basic difficulty in these calculations was that the lengths of the solar year, the lunar month, and the day are incommensurable. No number of days can make an exact number of lunar months or solar years, and no number of lunar months can make an exact number of solar years. So, in order to relate the phases of the moon accurately to the solar year in terms of whole days, it is necessary in constructing a calendar to make use of a system of *ad hoc* adjustments, following some definite cycle.

From as early as the second century different dates of Easter, resulting from different methods of making the calculations, had given rise to controversy and become a chronic problem for successive Councils. Various cycles relating the lunar month to the solar year were tried at different times and places, until in the fourth century a nineteen-year cycle, according to which 19 solar years were considered equal to 235 lunar months, came into general use. But there was still the possibility of differences in the manner in which this same cycle was used to determine the date of Easter, and, even when there was uniformity at the centre, sheer difficulty of communication could and did result in such outlying provinces as Africa, Spain, and Ireland celebrating Easter at different dates from Rome and Alexandria.

Shortly before Bede's birth Northumbria had, at the synod of Whitby, given up many practices, including the date of celebrating Easter, introduced by the Irish-trained monks of Iona, and had come into uniformity with Rome. But there was still much confusion, by no means confined to Britain, as to how the date of Easter was to be calculated. Bede's main contribution, expounded in several treatises, beginning with De Temporibus written in 703 for his pupils at Jarrow, was to reduce the whole subject to order. Using largely Irish sources, themselves based upon a good knowledge of earlier continental writings, he not only showed how to use the nineteen-year cycle to calculate Easter tables for the future, but also discussed general problems of time-measurement, arithmetical computation, cosmological and historical chronology, and astronomical and related phenomena. Though often relying on literary sources when he could have observed with his own eyes—as, for example, in his account of the Roman Wall not ten miles from his cell—Bede never copied without understanding. He tried to reduce all observed occurrences to general laws, and, within the limits of his knowledge, to build up a consistent picture of the universe, tested against the evidence. His account of the tides in De Temporum Ratione (chap. xxix), completed in 725 and the most important of his scientific writings, not only shows the practical curiosity shared by him and his Northumbrian compatriots, but also contains the basic elements of natural science.

From his sources Bede learned the fact that the tides follow the phases of the moon and the theory that tides are caused by the moon's attraction. He discussed spring and neap tides, and, turning to things which 'we know, who live on the shore of the sea divided by Britain', he described how the wind could ad-vance or retard a tide, and enunciated for the first time the im-portant principle now known as 'the establishment of a port'. This states that the tides lag behind the moon by definite inter-vals which may be different at different points on the same shore, so that tides must be tabulated for each port separately. Bede wrote: 'Those who live on the same shore as we, but to the north, see the ebb and flow of the tides well before us, whereas those to the south see it well after us. In every region the moon always keeps the rule of association which she has accepted once and for all.' On the basis of this, Bede suggested that the tides at any port could be predicted by means of the nineteen-year cycle, which he substituted for Pliny's less accur-ate eight-year cycle. Tidal tables were frequently attached to *computi* written after Bede's time.

Compared with the science of the twentieth century, and even with that of the thirteenth century, Bede's was humble enough, but against the background of its time it was a remark-able achievement. It contributed substantially to the Carolin-gian renaissance on the Continent, and found its way into the educational tradition dating from the cathedral schools estab-lished for Charlemagne by Alcuin of York. Bede's treatises on the calendar remained standard textbooks for five centuries, and were used even after the Gregorian reform of 1582; *De Temporum Ratione* is still one of the clearest expositions of the principles of the Christian calendar.

Besides Northumbria, Anglo-Saxon England saw some scientific developments in Wessex. In the seventh century astronomy and medicine were taught in Kent, there is evidence that surgery was practised, and Aldhelm, abbot of Malmes-bury, wrote metrical riddles about animals and plants; but the most notable contribution came in the first half of the tenth century in the *Leech Book* of Bald, who was evidently a physician living during or shortly after the reign of King Alfred, to whom the book contains allusions. The *Leech Book* gives a good picture of the state of medicine at the time. The first part is mainly therapeutical, containing herbal prescriptions, based on a wide knowledge of native plants and garden herbs, for a large number of diseases, working downwards from those of the head. Tertian, quartan, and quotidian fevers are dis-tinguished, and reference is made to 'flying venom' or 'air-borne contagion', that is epidemic diseases generally, small-pox, elephantiasis, probably bubonic plague, various mental ailments, and the use of the vapour bath for colds. The second part of the *Leech Book* is different in character, dealing mainly with internal diseases and going into symptoms and pathology. It seems to be a compilation of Greek medicine, perhaps mainly derived from the Latin translation of the writings of Alexander of Tralles, together with some direct observation. A good example is the account of 'sore in the side', or pleurisy, of which many of the 'tokens' or symptoms are described by Greek writers, but some are original; the Anglo-Saxon leech recognized the occurrence of traumatic pleurisy, and the possi-bility of confusing it with the idiopathic disease, which the ancient writers did not. Treatment began with a mild vegetable laxative administered by mouth or enema, followed by a poul-tice applied to the painful spot, a cupping glass on the shoul-ders, and various herbs taken internally. Many other diseases were described, for example pulmonary consumption and abscesses on the liver, treatment here culminating in a surgical operation; but on the whole there is little evidence of clinical observation: no use was made of the pulse and little of the appearances of the urine, which were standard 'signs' for the Greeks and Romans. Anglo-Saxon surgery presents the same combination of empiricism with literary tradition as the medi-cine; treatment of broken limbs and dislocations, plastic surgery for hare-lip, and amputations for gangrene are de-scribed.

A remarkable work, showing the intelligent interest of the Anglo-Saxon scholars in improving their knowledge of natural history in relation to medicine, is the translation into Old English of the Latin *Herbarium* of Apuleius Platonicus, probably made about 1000–1050. As in most early herbals, the text is confined to the name, locality found, and medical uses of each herb; there are no descriptions for identification, which was to be done by means of diagrammatic paintings, copied from the manuscript source and not from nature. About 500 English names are used in this herbal, showing an extensive knowledge of plants, many of them native plants which could not have been known from the Latin sources.

2

Some time before the Norman Conquest Canute and the Earl Harold introduced into England astronomers and mathe‑maticians from Lotharingia, the scene of a scientific revival in the eleventh century, and after the Conquest William con‑tinued the same policy. The schools of Lotharingia had been the first to benefit from scientific writings translated from Arabic, especially those dealing with astronomy and the astro‑labe (see Pl. 125 a). In 1091 Walcher, the Lotharingian abbot of Malvern, observed an eclipse of the moon while travelling in Italy, and noted the considerably different hour at which the same eclipse was observed by a brother monk in England. The following year he was able to fix a second eclipse accurately by means of an astrolabe. Some years later he worked out a set of lunar tables based on this observation, using, in a first treatise, the clumsy method of Roman fractions, but in a second, written in 1120, using the Arabic method of degrees, minutes, and seconds derived from translations made by a converted Spanish Jew named Petrus Alphonsi, who seems to have spent some time in England. In the twelfth century, England was to play a leading part in the revival of science brought about by this great movement of translating, which, by the third quarter of the thirteenth century, had put nearly all the known works of Greek science and many Arabic commentaries into Latin.

   From the end of classical times Greek scientific writings had passed through a number of different languages. In the sixth and seventh centuries many of these were translated in Syria and Mesopotamia into Syriac; in the eighth, ninth, and tenth centuries they were translated, both from the Syriac and the Greek, into Arabic. Though some Arabic scientific influence is detectable in the west as early as the end of the tenth century, the new translations into Latin did not begin effectively until the end of the eleventh century, when the Norman conquest of Sicily and the reconquest of New Castile brought many Arabic-speaking subjects under Christian rule. For over a century and a half scholars journeyed from all over the west to these frontiers of Christendom and Islam, and made Sicily and Toledo the chief centres of translating into Latin from the Arabic. About the same time translating began also from the original Greek, Sicily again being an active centre, and some scholars travelling to Byzantium.

The first English scholar to take part in this movement was Adelard of Bath. Little is known of Adelard except from his own writings, but the evidence shows that he was born at Bath, of English stock, went early to France to study at the cathedral school at Tours, and later taught at Laon. He travelled widely, visiting Greece and probably Sicily some time before 1116. He refers to a seven-years' absence in search of Arabic learning, specifically mentioning things heard in Tarsus and an earth-quake witnessed from a bridge at Antioch, then under a Crusader prince; at this time he possibly visited the Latin king-dom of Jerusalem. He may also have been in Spain. By 1126 he was back at Bath, making the geometry and astronomy of the Arabs available to the Latin world. After this the evidence connects him with the Anglo-Norman court of Henry I, possibly with a post in the exchequer, and suggests that he was tutor to the future Henry II; he wore a green cloak and was almost certainly not a monk.

Educated in the old Latin tradition of the cathedral schools, Adelard belonged to the generation of scholars who brought about the first stages of the intellectual revolution coming with the new learning from the old Byzantine regions of southern Italy and from the Arabic east. Adelard himself was the first known Latin scholar to assimilate Arabic science in the revival

of the twelfth century, and he did so, not merely passively, but
with an intellectual independence that matched his vigour as a
traveller. This is evident in two original treatises, *De Eodem et
Diverso* and *Questiones Naturales*, both belonging to an early
period in his Arabic studies and written as dialogues in which
he explains the purpose of his journeys to a nephew presented
as having been his pupil at Laon. The second treatise is especially lively. The nephew taunts his uncle: 'I am sure you praise
[the Saracens] shamelessly and are too keen to point out our
ignorance.' Adelard rejoins: 'It is hard to discuss with you, for
I have learned one thing from the Arabs under the guidance of
reason; you follow another halter, caught by the appearance of
authority, for what is authority but a halter! . . . If reason is not
to be the universal judge, it is given to each to no purpose.
Those who are now called authorities reached that position by
the exercise of their reason. . . . Wherefore, if you want to hear
anything more from me, give and take reason.' Later he says: 'I
call myself a man of Bath, not a Stoic, wherefore I teach my
own opinions, not the errors of the Stoics.'

Down to the end of the twelfth century the predominantly
theological interests of scholars had led them generally to treat
the natural world as a kind of shadow, and a symbol, of divine
power and providence. The context of Adelard's use of reason
marks the first explicit assertion in the middle ages that recognition of divine omnipotence did not preclude the existence of
proximate natural causes, and that these could be known only
by independent, scientific inquiry. Though relying mainly on
a priori reasoning, Adelard had some recourse to observation
and experiment. Discussing the question why plants sprung up
from earth collected and put in a pot, the nephew asks: 'To
what else do you attribute this but to the marvellous effect of the
wonderful Divine will?' Adelard agrees, but asserts that it
also has a natural reason. Nature 'is not confused and without
system, and so far as human knowledge has progressed it should
be given a hearing. Only when it fails utterly should then be
recourse to God.'

Of Adelard's translations from the Arabic, by far the most

influential was that of Euclid's *Elements*. It is scarcely possible to exaggerate the importance of this work. Before it became available to them, the Latin mathematicians and natural philosophers had known only the conclusions of some of Euclid's theorems and perhaps the proofs of one or two; Adelard's translation introduced them to the full conception of the Greek axiomatic method and provided a model for their scientific thinking. It remained the standard translation, the thirteenth-century revision becoming the first printed edition of 1482. Other translations by Adelard were of the astronomical tables, including an account of trigonometry, and (in all probability) the *Liber Alchorismi*, a work on the principles of arithmetic, geometry, music, and astronomy, by the ninth-century Persian mathematician, Al-Khwarizmi. These translations were the first serious introduction of the Latins to the Arabic treatment of their subjects. Adelard also wrote, early in life, a work on the abacus and the first known Latin treatise on falconry, based largely on English usage; and among his later works was a treatise on the *Astrolabe*, apparently written at Bath, which is taken as the meridian for purposes of illustration, and dedicated to a young Henry, doubtless Henry Plantagenet, the future Henry II. In that case this admirably succinct and clear account, based on Arabic sources, of elementary astronomy and the various uses of the astrolabe would have been written for his royal pupil probably between 1142 and 1143. Another work attributed to him, which would show still further the wide range of his interests, is an expanded version of the *Mappe Clavicula*, which goes back to Greek sources and deals with the preparation of pigments and other chemical products.

Following the lead given by Adelard, a succession of Englishmen throughout the twelfth century joined in the work both of translating and of introducing Arabic and Greek scientific thought into England. About the middle of the century the problematical figure Robert Ketene, or Robert of Chester (if the two names refer to the same person), working in Spain, translated from the Arabic one of the earliest treatises on alchemy to appear in Latin, by a certain Morienus; he also translated Al-Khwarizmi's fundamental treatise on *Algebra*, a work by Alkindi on astrology, and some important astronomical tables, recalculated for the meridian of London. Another English astronomer, Roger of Hereford, wrote in 1176 a *Compotus* and later some astronomical treatises, including an adaptation of some Arabic tables for the meridian of Hereford. A contemporary, Daniel of Morley, describes how he abandoned his studies in Paris, finding it dominated by law and pretentious ignorance, and went to Toledo to learn of Arabic science at the most famous Christian centre. There he was taught by Gerard of Cremona, distinguished translator of Ptolemy's *Almagest* and of several of Aristotle's works; from the number of translations attributed to Gerard, he was undoubtedly the head of a school of translators. Daniel expounded his Toledan knowledge in a work written for Bishop John of Norwich. Also probably connected with Hereford and with Spain was Alfred of Sareshel, who, sometime before 1200, translated from the Arabic the pseudo-Aristotelian *De Plantis*, a Greek work written in the first century B.C. which provided the middle ages with most of its botanical theory. Alfred's commentary on *De Plantis* and still more his *De Motu Cordis*, written early in the thirteenth century for the medical profession, are among the earliest Latin works showing some detailed knowledge of Aristotle's natural science, as they do also of Hippocrates, Galen, and Arabic medicine.

The turn of the twelfth century in fact marked an important change in the content of Latin science. Ever since contemporaries of Adelard of Bath had made a renewed study of Plato's *Timaeus* (of which the first 53 chapters were available in Chalcidius's Latin translation) an essential part of the revival of learning at Chartres, giving to this cathedral school the intellectual leadership of the west until the rise of Paris and the universities, this work of Plato's had provided the main framework for a conception of the physical world. Adelard himself shows its influence, citing, for example, in *Questiones Naturales*, a long extract from the *Timaeus* on the physiology of vision and, in answer to the nephew's inquiry, expounding Plato's theory that a stone dropped through a hole bored through a diameter of the earth would fall only as far as the centre and then come to a stop.

As the new translations, at the end of the twelfth century, revealed more and more of Aristotle's physical conceptions, these came to replace Plato's as a guide for scientific thinking, though the *Timaeus* was certainly not forgotten, but joined with the new translations of Ptolemy's astronomy, of the medicine, anatomy, and physiology of Hippocrates and Galen, of the numerous Arabic writings on these subjects, especially the commentaries of Avicenna and the Spanish Arab, Averroës, and of various important works on mathematics, mechanics, and optics, to enrich with variety and to change in many details a predominantly Aristotelian scene.

The first important influence of Aristotle came, about the middle of the twelfth century, with the so-called 'new logic', especially the translations of the *Prior* and *Posterior Analytics*, Aristotle's main treatises on formal logic and scientific method. John of Salisbury, who became bishop of Chartres, shows a good knowledge of these in his *Metalogicon*, written in 1159. Aristotle's writings on natural science came to be studied seriously in the first decade of the thirteenth century. Alexander Neckham, who taught at a school at Oxford and died in 1217 as abbot of Cirencester, cited many of Aristotle's opinions about animals, cosmology, and other matters in his *De Rerum Natura*. Though written rather for moral than for scientific instruction, this work shows Neckham to have been a keen student of science. Alfred of Sareshel dedicated his *De Motu Cordis* to him. Neckham recalls the happy past when 'the greatest princes were diligent and industrious in aiding investigation of nature', but he is not dissatisfied with the schools of his own day, which he believed had surpassed those of contemporary Greece and Egypt. Of special interest are Neckham's accounts of the mariner's compass (the first in Latin) and of glass mirrors; like many medieval writers he had an optimistic expectation of the practical results of science, in peace and in war. 'What craftiness of the foe is there', he asked, 'that does not yield to the precise knowledge of those who have tracked down the elusive subtleties of things hidden in the very bosom of nature!' His book is mainly a compilation, but it was made with some discrimination. He knew something of vacuums and siphoning, and asserted that the antipodes were no more under his feet than he was under theirs. He rejected certain popular stories about animals, but accepted others, for example the story of the barnacle goose growing on trees. The story that the lynx had such keen sight that it could see through nine walls was supposed to have been experimentally verified by showing that a lynx, with nine walls between it and a person carrying a piece of meat, always stopped, when the person stopped, at a point exactly opposite the meat; Neckham accepted the experi⁄ ment but attributed the result rather to the sense of smell. In keeping with a tradition dating from the fathers and revived with especial vigour at Chartres, he tried to show how physical phenomena described in the Bible, particularly in Genesis, could be rationally understood in terms of contemporary physics. Here again he was discriminating, and several times questioned the literal truth of biblical statements. For example, he said that Adam's body was made of all four elements, not only of earth, as stated in Genesis; and that in making the state⁄ ment, 'God made two great lights', the sun and the moon, 'The historical narrative follows the judgement of the eye and the popular notion', for the moon was not one of the largest planets. Neckham's frankly didactic purpose comes out in his assertion that the Fall had physical effects on nature, causing the spots on the moon, the wildness of animals, insects to become pests and other animals venomous, and the existence of disease.

Before Neckham died several other scholars began to lecture on the 'new Aristotle' at Oxford, among them the great Robert Grosseteste, first chancellor of the young university in 1214 and chief ornament and guide of its early years. Grosseteste recognized clearly that, at that stage of the western revival, natural philosophers needed not only to think and observe with independence, but also to continue the work of recovering the past. He gave to Oxford scholars their characteristic interest not only in mathematics and physical science, but also in languages, especially in Greek. His own translations from the Greek, though mainly of non-scientific works, included the pseudo-Aristotelian *De Lineis Indivisibilibus* and a substantial part of Simplicius's commentary on Aristotle's *De Caelo*, a late Greek treatise containing a fundamental analysis of astronomical theories, with a profound influence on astronomy from Grosseteste himself to Galileo. With the appearance of Grosseteste upon the scene, science in England took on an entirely new life and became, for a century and a half, for all practical purposes synonymous with science in Oxford. Grosseteste's influence was especially strong among the Franciscans, in whose house at Oxford he had taught, and who provided the most original scientific thinking of the period.

3

The achievements of English science in the thirteenth and fourteenth centuries can only be briefly indicated. The revolution introduced by Grosseteste was primarily one of method, and this made Oxford for a time the leading scientific centre in the west; the study of mathematics, of physics, and of the logic of science came to be as characteristic of Oxford as were metaphysics and theology of Paris, and law and medicine of Bologna. Only in astronomy, dynamics, and magnetics could the Parisian science of the period match that of Oxford, though some of the best work was to be done neither in England nor in France, but in Germany, for example Jordanus Nemorarius's mechanics, Albertus Magnus's zoology and botany, and Theodoric of Freiberg's optics, and in Italy, for example Rufinus's botany, and medical studies at Bologna and Padua, whose medical schools were equalled in the west only by Montpellier.

By personality and position Grosseteste was well placed to exploit for their own good the historical circumstances in which he found the Oxford schools. In the twelfth century philosophers had learnt from Euclid's *Elements* and Aristotle's

two *Analytics* the basic Greek conception of scientific explanation, according to which a phenomenon was explained
when it could be deduced from general principles or a theory
connecting it with other phenomena, just as the conclusions
of Euclid's theorems were deduced from his axioms, postulates,
and definitions, and the conclusions of previous theorems.
Aristotle had given a generalized account of the method, and
shown that there were definite rules for selecting premisses and
for distinguishing between valid and invalid arguments. The
first subjects to benefit from this new rational thinking were
theology and law; its application to science at the end of the
twelfth century was simply the last stage of a general intellectual
movement, and by that time the formal structure of the new
method had been filled in with material examples from the
many specialized scientific writings translated from the Greek
and the Arabic. Of these Grosseteste had a wide knowledge,
and he saw that if science was to progress in his time, the primary
problems to be investigated were those of method. His own
scientific work, begun before 1209 and continuing even after
he became bishop of Lincoln in 1235, made two major contributions.

First, in commentaries on Aristotle's *Posterior Analytics*
and *Physics* he made a systematic application of logical
methods of analysis, verification, and falsification to the problems of constructing and testing scientific theories by observation and experiment. His methods can best be described by
means of a concrete example, the attempts made by himself and
his chief disciple, Roger Bacon, to explain the rainbow.
Grosseteste wrote several short treatises on optics, leading up to
one on the rainbow; Roger Bacon's account of the problem
appears in his *Opus Majus*, and follows the lines laid down by
Grosseteste. Bacon in fact gave it as an example of the experimental method; his *Opus Majus*, *Opus Minus*, and *Opus
Tertium*, all written in 1266–7, contain the chief thirteenth-
century development of Grosseteste's conceptions of experimental and mathematical methods in science.

The basic problem in searching for an explanation of a

phenomenon was, according to Grosseteste, to find the conditions necessary and sufficient to produce it. The inquiry began
with a 'resolution' of the phenomenon into its elements, and of
this process Bacon gave an excellent example in describing how
he collected instances of colours similar to those seen in the
rainbow, so that the rainbow could be related to the general
phenomenon of spectral colours. He examined the colours seen
in rainbows, in spray made by mill-wheels and by squirting
water from the mouth, in sunlight passed through a glass flask
full of water or through a glass prism or hexagonal crystal on
to a screen, and in different kinds of iridescent feathers. He
concluded that an essential condition for the production of a
rainbow was the presence of spherical water-drops in the atmosphere; he showed also, by means of an astrolabe, that the rainbow was always seen at an angle of about 42° from the incident
light going from the sun to the drops.

The next stage was to find out how these conditions operated
to produce a rainbow, and for this Grosseteste, Bacon, and
their successors used the fruitful device of constructing a theoretical model. Grosseteste's model supposed that a cloud as a
whole acted as a huge refracting lens, Bacon's that the effect
was produced by the reflection of sunlight from the outer surfaces of individual raindrops. Neither will stand detailed examination, but, though they did not grasp their faults, both
investigators did test the models they considered by subjecting
consequences deduced from them to experiment. Later continental investigators, Albertus Magnus, Witelo, and Theodoric
of Freiberg, all directly or indirectly influenced by the work
of Grosseteste and Bacon, continued their work of searching
for an adequate theoretical model; Theodoric, shortly before
1311, finally constructed a successful theory, based on the
fundamental discovery that the sunlight entering each raindrop
was not only refracted, and thus broken up into colours, but
also reflected internally by the concave surface, which returned
the colours to the eye of the observer. This same model was to
be used by Descartes and Newton.

In using this process of experimental verification and falsification, Grosseteste assumed the principle of the uniformity of nature, and was guided in his choice of possible theories by the principle of economy. An important philosophical consequence of his logical analysis was his conclusion that scientific theories are at best probable, and not necessarily true. His understanding of these matters established the methods and interpretations of science developed by his successors both in Oxford and abroad.

Grosseteste's interest in optics was directly related to his second contribution to the scientific methods of his time. For two reasons, one methodological and the other metaphysical, he held that methematics was essential for a scientific understanding of the physical world. The method by which he used mathematics for this purpose was Aristotle's principle of 'subordination', according to which some physical sciences, for example optics and astronomy, were logically subordinate to a mathematical science, for example geometry, in the sense that they used particular cases of general mathematical laws. Grosseteste held that mathematics could be used to describe what happened, for example the reflection and refraction of light and the movements of the planets, but that the mathematical expressions did not reveal the physical cause of these optical and astronomical laws, which was to be sought in the nature of the substances involved. This distinction between mathematical and physical laws, analogous to the modern distinction between kinematics and dynamics, had been developed by Simplicius, from whom Grosseteste undoubtedly learnt it.

Grosseteste's conception of the nature of fundamental physical substance was a peculiar one which provided his second reason for holding that mathematics was essential for physical inquiry; he maintained that the fundamental physical substance was a fundamental 'light' (*lux*), not identical with, but manifesting itself in, visible light. In a short treatise, *De Luce*, he described how in the beginning God created formless matter and a point of this fundamental light; this propagated itself in a sphere and produced the dimensions of space, and then, by a complicated series of changes and interactions, the heavenly spheres, the earth, and all the substances and creatures on it. This 'cosmogony of light' was of Neoplatonic origin. Its importance in the history of science is, first, that it convinced Grosseteste himself that optics was the fundamental physical science; and secondly, because optics could not be studied without mathematics, that Grosseteste's influence committed a growing body of natural philosophers, both in Oxford and on the Continent, to the use of mathematical theories, not only in optics but also in all possible branches of science.

Grosseteste's own contributions to optics, apart from the study of the rainbow, consisted of a partially-correct explanation of the spherical lens and the suggestion that lenses could be used to aid weak sight, an unsuccessful attempt to formulate the law of refraction, and a most suggestive theory that light propagates itself in a series of pulses or waves. Other contributions were made by Grosseteste's followers. Roger Bacon, writing about 1266-7, developed his theory of propagation in the theory known as the 'multiplication of species', designed to explain action at a distance, whether by light, heat, magnetism, or gravity, extended his work on the rainbow and tried to explain the halo, gave a systematic classification of convex and concave lenses (see Fig. 107) and discussed their use as aids to sight, and used his knowledge both of optics and of anatomy to try, with partial success, to understand the formation of an image in the eye. Bacon also discussed the reflecting properties of surfaces produced by rotating various conic sections about their axes, stimulated perhaps by the man whom, next to Grosseteste, he most admired, Petrus Peregrinus de Maricourt, a Frenchman who made a fundamental experimental study of the elementary properties of magnets; Bacon described experiments which he probably made himself with a floating magnet.

A follower of both Grosseteste and Bacon, the unknown author of the *Summa Philosophiae* formerly attributed to Grosseteste himself, seems to have been the first writer to point out that the colours produced by passing sunlight through a prism were refracted through different angles. The whole *Summa* is an excellent review of science about 1270, ranging from astronomy and cosmology through discussions of meteorology, optics, the magnet, chemistry, fossils, zoology, botany, and physiology. Later in the century, John Pecham wrote an ad⁄mirable short textbook on optics, and in the first half of the fourteenth century John of Dumbleton, at different times a fellow of Merton and of Queen's Colleges at Oxford, tried to formulate the mathematical law relating intensity of light to distance from the source.

Throughout the middle ages meteorology formed a single, if heterogeneous, subject with optics, mainly because both were discussed in Aristotle's *Meteorology* and medieval scientists habitually published their original results in the form of com⁄mentaries on Aristotle and other authorities. Moreover, comets were regarded as meteorological phenomena, belonging to the region below the moon. Grosseteste seems to have observed 'Halley's comet' in 1228, and he used his method of falsification in an interesting discussion of theories of comets. Roger Bacon also described a comet seen in July 1264, and attributed to its influence various distressing political consequences. Another meteorological phenomenon studied with interest in medieval as in modern England was the weather. A most remarkable series of records were kept during 1337–44 for the Oxford dis⁄trict by William Merlee, with a view of making predictions for farmers. He based forecasts partly on the state of the heavenly bodies, and partly on inferior signs of humidity: the moisten⁄ing of salt, the carrying of sound from distant bells, and the increased activity of fleas.

Other physical problems discussed by Grosseteste in various special tracts were heat, which he regarded as a mode of motion of particles of matter, falling bodies, and astronomy; a mathe⁄matical problem that extended into his cosmogony was the summation of infinite aggregates; and a practical problem on which he wrote several treatises was the reform of the calendar. By the beginning of the thirteenth century the cumulative in⁄accuracy of the accepted Julian calendar had produced gross errors in the date of Easter, and, as Roger Bacon put it in his development, in the *Opus Majus*, of Grosseteste's proposals for

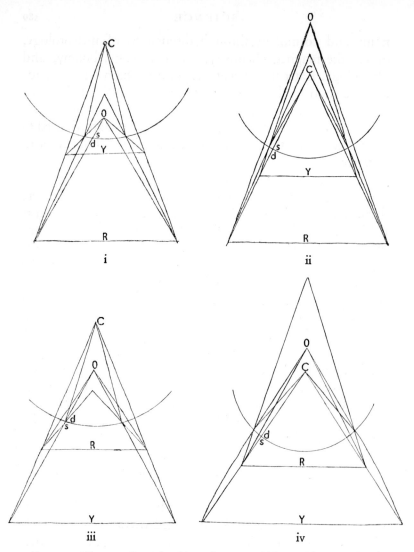

FIG. 107. Diagrams from the thirteenth-century MS., Royal 7. F. viii, the British Museum, illustrating Roger Bacon's classification of the properties of curved refracting surfaces, in the *Opus Majus*, v. Rays go from each end of the object (*res, r*), are bent at the curved surface separating the optically rarer (*subtilior, s*) and denser (*densior, d*) media, for example air and glass, and meet at the eye (*oculus, o*). The image (*ymago, y*) is seen on a projection of these bent rays entering the eye, and is magnified or diminished according to whether the concave (i–iv) or convex (v–viii) surface is towards the eye, whether the eye is on the rarer (i, ii, v, vi) or denser (iii, iv, vii, viii) side of the curvature, and whether the eye is on the side of the centre of

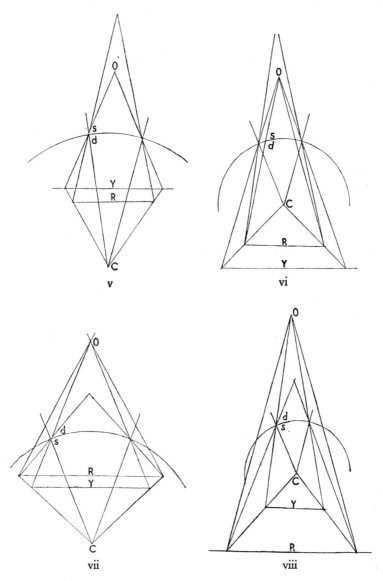

v

vi

vii

viii

curvature (*centrum, c*) towards (i, iii) or away from (ii, iv) the object, or the centre of curvature on the side of the object towards (vi, viii) or away from (v, vii) the eye. A confusion between the appearance of size and of nearness, which led Bacon incorrectly to draw a diminished image in i and a magnified image in iii, is corrected in a later section of the *Opus Majus*, where Bacon points out that 'the size of the (visual) angle is the prevailing factor in these appearances'; that is, the angle subtended by the object or the image at the eye. He recommended a convex lens forming a hemisphere (vi) or less than a hemisphere (v) to aid weak sight.

reform, 'every computer knows that the beginning of lunation is in error 3 or 4 days in these times, and every rustic is able to see this error in the sky'. The recommendations made by Grosseteste and Bacon, based on determining accurately, from astronomical evidence, the exact length of the year and the relation between this and the mean lunar month, were used in attempts made to revise the calendar in the fourteenth and fifteenth centuries, but such is institutional and popular conservatism that nothing was achieved until the Gregorian reform of 1582, and this was not accepted in England until 1752.

In astronomy itself there was little advance in England during the fifteenth century. An English contemporary of Grosseteste, John Holywood or Sacrobosco, as he was called, working mainly in Paris, gave an account of the Ptolemaic system in his *De Sphaera*, an elementary textbook based on Arabic sources which remained standard for three centuries; an English translation was made for Prince Henry, son of King James I, and reading it as a schoolboy is said to have decided John Flamsteed (1646–1719), first astronomer royal, to devote himself to astronomy. Sacrobosco also wrote a treatise on the quadrant, an instrument for measuring angular altitudes. Roger Bacon observed the heavens with instruments and discussed astronomical theories at length in various writings; his emphasis on measurement seems to have helped to build up both the Parisian school of astronomy at the end of the thirteenth century and the school associated with Merton College, Oxford, in the fourteenth century.

Walter de Merton made his foundation, towards the end of the thirteenth century, expressly for the training of secular clergy, so that the learned professions and the civil service would be adequately supplied with men of sound education. The success of the college was immediate, and in science, especially in astronomy, mathematics, and medicine, it rapidly took over in England the leadership that had formerly belonged to the Franciscans. Practically every important English scientist of the fourteenth century was at some time in his career associated with Merton College, many of them as fellows.

PLATE 125

a. An astrolabe in use, from a twelfth-century English MS.,
Bodleian, MS. Bodley 614

b. Richard of Wallingford measuring a circular instrument
with a pair of compasses. Note his abbot's crook and the
mitre on the floor, and the spots of his face, perhaps from
the leprosy he contracted in early life and of which he died at
the age of 43. From a fourteenth-century British Museum
MS. Cotton Claud, E. iv

PLATE 126

The Merton Astrolabe, *c.* 1350 (face)

The main achievements of the Merton school in astronomy were in the field of measurement and calculation. Basing them-selves in the first place on the so-called Alfonsine Tables made at Toledo for King Alfonso X of Léon and Castile about 1272, men like John Maudith, William Rede, and Simon Bredon constructed astronomical almanacs for Oxford which gave this city something like the modern position of Green-wich. They have left manuscripts describing the construction of a variety of instruments, mainly for measuring and com-paring altitudes and for representing planetary motions. Most striking are the instructions for making two such instruments, invented by himself, left by Richard of Wallingford (Pl. 125 b), son of a blacksmith and eventually abbot of St. Albans; and at St. Albans he constructed, about 1320, an elaborate astro-nomical clock, showing the motions of the sun, moon, planets, and stars, and the ebb and flow of the tides. The excellent treatise on the astrolabe, a standard work on the subject in English, written later in the century by Chaucer, poet and busy administrator, is a product of this Oxford school (Pl. 126). No less important than the work on measuring instruments were the improvements made by the Merton astronomers in mathe-matical technique, especially in trigonometry, of which John Maudith, Richard of Wallingford, and the contemporary Pro-vençal Jew, Levi Ben Gerson may be considered the founders in its rigorous modern form. So important did astronomy be-come that William of Wykeham made special provision for two fellowships in the subject in the statutes of New College.

Another set of problems to which Merton mathematicians and other Oxford philosophers made fundamental contribu-tions in the fourteenth century were those of dynamics and kinematics. In many respects these were the central problems of medieval physics, and in them can be seen most clearly that process of reformulation, leading to replacement, of originally Aristotelian conceptions and methods, which was the chief and essential medieval contribution to the revolution in physics completed in the seventeenth century.

Aristotle had conceived of the motion of a body from one

place to another as a process requiring the continuous action o
a motive agent, a conception precisely opposite to the seven-
teenth-century conception of inertia. So long as the external
motive agent continued to operate, the Aristotelian theory held
that velocity would be directly proportional to the motive
power and inversely proportional to the resistance of the
medium; remove the external agent, and the motion would
stop. Many everyday phenomena supported these judgements,
but three did not. First, according to this Aristotelian 'law',
there should be a finite velocity with any finite values of power
and resistance, yet in fact if the power is smaller than the resistance it may fail to move the body at all. To escape this difficulty, Bradwardine used a modification of the 'law' according
to which velocity was proportional to the *excess* of power over
resistance, and he tried to express by means of an algebraic
function how *change* in velocity was related, as a dependent
variable, to the independent variables, power and resistance.

Bradwardine's use of mathematical functions seems to have
inspired the attempt made by the French physicist, Jean
Buridan, to deal with the other two phenomena that provided
difficulties for Aristotle's conception of motion, the motion of
a projectile after leaving the projector, and the acceleration of a
freely falling body. What was the motive power that kept the
projectile going? This question had worried physicists since
Aristotle himself. Buridan introduced a quantitative notion
of *impetus*, analogous to Newton's *momentum*, imparted by the
projector; this *impetus* maintained the projectile's velocity and
enabled it to impart velocity to other bodies with which it col-
lided. The acceleration of freely falling bodies Buridan attributed to successive increments of *impetus* added by gravity.

Work relevant to both problems was taken up again in Oxford. William of Ockham, in accordance with his general
principles of inquiry, reduced motion to the fact that from instant to instant a body is observed to change its spatial relations
with other bodies. He rejected Buridan's *impetus* as an un-
necessary complication. Science, he declared in effect, should,
in the interests of economy, confine itself to the description of

changing relations between observable entities; 'a plurality should not be postulated without necessity', as he expressed what came to be called Ockham's Razor; it was 'futile' to postulate causes like *impetus*. Ockham's parsimony in hypotheses was here in some respects misplaced, for Buridan's *impetus* became the ancestor of Galileo's *impeto* or *momento*; but Ockham's general approach to scientific problems encouraged the view, to be used by Galileo and Newton in their negative criticism of contemporary physics, that the function of a scientific theory is in the first instance to correlate the observed data and not to reveal the essences of things.

In keeping with this view some contemporaries of Ockham developed some fruitful mathematical methods of describing changing relations between phenomena and rates of change. Bradwardine developed a kind of algebra in which letters of the alphabet were used for variable quantities while the operations of adding, dividing, &c., were described in words. John of Dumbleton described how to express relationship between two quantities by means of graphs, in which the lengths of vertical lines drawn at intervals perpendicular to a horizontal line represented, for example, velocity at successive intervals of time. Dumbleton and two other Mertonian mathematicians, William of Heytesbury and Richard Swineshead (the famous 'Calculator'), proved algebraically, some time before 1335, the important rule, which may be called the Mertonian Rule, that the space traversed in a given time by a body moving with uniformly accelerated velocity was equal to the product of the total time of moving multiplied by the mean of the initial and final velocities. The French mathematician Nicole Oresme, later in the fourteenth century, proved this geometrically, and it gave Galileo the kinematic law of falling bodies, which he himself regarded as his profoundest discovery.

4

In none of the other sciences cultivated in the west in the middle ages did England achieve such profound and influential results as in the methodological and mathematical inquiries just considered, but some mention of them must be made to give a true picture of the scope of the medieval English interest in the problems of nature. Many of these problems were practical.

The long-characteristic English love of plants and animals is seen in the illustrations from nature in a bestiary and a herbal dating from the twelfth century, those in the latter, executed at Bury St. Edmunds, being especially good (Pls. 127 and 128 *a*). A number of thirteenth-century English manuscripts contain excellent illustrations of animals of various kinds, especially of birds; Matthew Paris about 1250 described an immigration of crossbills, and illustrated the bird. Keen observation of nature by sculptors and carvers is shown in the capitals, bosses, and misericords of churches such as York, Ely, and Southwell. Books on falconry and fishing, especially the fifteenth-century *Treatyse of Fysshynge with an Angle* and *Boke of St. Albans*, and Walter of Henley's *Hosebondrie*, a standard treatise on agriculture from the thirteenth to the sixteenth century, are also the work of naturalists. Bartholomew the Englishman's popular work, *On the Properties of Things*, said to have been a source of Shakespeare's natural history, contains some good observation, for example his famous description of the domestic cat. The descriptions of plants in herbals improved generally in the fourteenth century, an English example being the herbal of the surgeon, John Arderne. At the same time commentaries on Aristotle's zoology, for instance those of Walter Burley and John Dymsdale, show an interest in theoretical biology.

The field of biology in which it was possible most easily to obtain some both practical and theoretical training was medicine. The *Anatomia Ricardi* probably the work of an Englishman written in the late twelfth century, asserts that 'a knowledge of anatomy is necessary to physicians in order that they may understand how the human body is constructed to perform different movements and operations'. Some practical instruction in anatomy was probably required of the medical student at Oxford, as in continental medical schools, by the end of the thirteenth century; a manuscript of about that

PLATE 127

Bramble (*Rubus fructicosus*) from the twelfth-century *Herbal of Apuleius Barbarus*,
Bodleian, MS. Bodley 130, executed at Bury St. Edmunds

PLATE 128

a. Bees, from a twelfth-century bestiary, British Museum, MS. Royal 12. c. xix

b. Dissection, or *post mortem*, from Bodleian, MS. Ashmole 399 (*c.* 1298). Above the corpse are the kidneys and below it are the heart and lungs, stomach, and intestines; the dissector holds the liver in his right hand

date illustrates a dissection, or post-mortem (Pl. 128 *b*); but certainly the opportunities for dissection were necessarily meagre and there is no evidence of research. The structure of the body was seen through the eyes of Galen and Avicenna, just as a modern medical student follows his textbook. But on going into practice the surgeon had perforce to rely on his own knowledge and skill, and the thirteenth and fourteenth centuries saw considerable improvements both in this art and in medicine in general, in which Englishmen played their part. In the mid-thirteenth century Gilbert the Englishman, who became chancellor of Montpellier, wrote a comprehensive work on medicine in which he described a number of diseases, including the local anaesthesia of the skin as a diagnostic symptom for leprosy, recognized for the first time that smallpox is contagious, advised operating for cancer, and recommended travellers to drink distilled water and sea-travellers to eat fruit. Early in the fourteenth century John of Gaddesden, the Oxford physician mentioned by Chaucer, gave, among much nonsense, good clinical descriptions of cases of ascites with obstructive jaundice, phthisis, leprosy, variola, small pox, and other diseases; of operations for the stone and for hernia; of the reduction of dislocations; and described a new instrument for extracting teeth. Later in the century John Arderne served as army surgeon to two dukes of Lancaster, and saw the use of gunpowder; afterwards he practised at Newark-upon-Trent and London. He was a surgeon of genius, describing his practice of cutting boldly, keeping the instruments clean, and using light dressings. He made a special study of fistula, describing and illustrating a new type of syringe and other instruments used in treatment; and he gave a good account of the Black Death in England. A medical encyclopaedia written at the end of the fourteenth century by John Mirfeld, who seems to have been connected with the priory and hospital of St. Bartholomew, gives a good picture of medical knowledge and practice in London: at that time the number of hospitals, large and small, in the city ran into hundreds.

Another science to which both men of learning and un-

lettered craftsmen contributed in medieval England was chemistry. The learned were interested mainly in alchemy which, as
Roger Bacon described in his *Opus Tertium*, both included a
theory of matter and chemical change based on Aristotle's
conception of elements and qualities, and as a practical subject
'teaches how to make the noble metals and colours ... not only
can it yield wealth and very many other things for the public
welfare, but it also teaches how to discover such things as are
capable of prolonging human life ...'.

Bacon regarded science as a whole as a means of obtaining
power over nature, power that would not only increase wealth
and health, but would also enable the military forces of Christendom to overcome the Tarters and Antichrist, whose advent
he expected 'from beyond the Caspian gates'. Though no base
metal was ever transformed into gold, no elixir found to pro-
long life, no powerful weapon invented to repel at a blow any
possible invasion from the east, the pursuit of the objectives described by Bacon did achieve some valuable results for chemistry and for science in general. Alchemists learnt to use the
balance, and discovered the properties of some metals, acids,
and other substances. Bacon himself referred, without giving
the recipe, to an explosive powder, and pointed out that its force
would be increased by enclosing it in an instrument of solid
material. Early in the fourteenth century Walter of Odington,
a versatile mathematician who made astronomical observations
at Oxford and wrote on optics and musical theory, composed
a most interesting treatise on alchemy in which he attacked contemporary alchemists, with their gold-making, as humbugs,
and tried to give mathematical precision to the whole subject.
He described various chemical processes, calcination, solution,
sublimation, congelation, and proposed a method of measuring
the qualities of dryness, heat, and so on in degrees represented
graphically by an adaptation of the procedures being worked
out by his contemporaries at Merton.

The most striking results in industrial chemistry pursued in
the middle ages in almost complete independence of learned
interests, were achieved in metallurgy, and this, even more than

PLATE 129

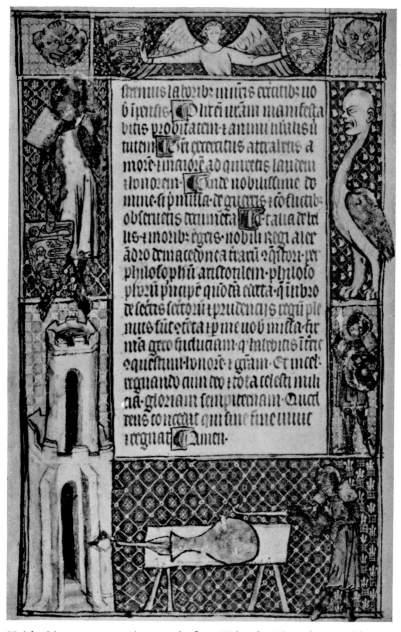

Knight firing a cannon against a castle, from Walter de Milemete's *De Nobilitativus Sapientiis et Prudentiis Regum*, Christ Church, Oxford, MS. 92

PLATE 130

Matthew Paris's map of Great Britain, from British Museum MS. Cotton Claudius D. vi
(c. 1250), Note the compression of Scotland, the two Roman walls, and that the whole of
south-east England is shifted round to the west, putting the mouth of the Thames on the
south coast

alchemy, laid the foundations of quantitative chemistry, mainly through the processes used in assaying, which involved the use of the balance. Throughout the whole period the main advances, especially with the introduction of the blast furnace, were made in central Europe, but English metallurgy, centred mainly in the Weald of Kent and Sussex, was also active. The empirical control of processes to produce an accurate result is especially evident in the founding of bells of different pitch that would ring in tune. When firearms, apparently invented in China about the beginning of the thirteenth century, began to be made in the west in the fourteenth century, it was the bellfounders who turned out the guns. Cannon were introduced into England by Edward III, and the earliest-known illustration of a cannon occurs in an English work, by Walter de Milemete, dedicated to that monarch in 1327 (Pl. 129).

Cannons may have been used by the English at the siege of Berwick in 1319, and at Crécy in 1346; they were certainly used by them at Calais in 1347 and, according to Froissart, the English used 100 cannons, probably small mortars, at St. Malo in 1378. These were probably manufactured in Flanders or Germany, but by the end of the fourteenth century cannons were being made in England.

The same empirical control of processes and materials is found also in the arts of building and of constructing machinery. The overcoming of the many mechanical problems that culminated in the building of the great churches lies beyond the scope of this chapter; but achievements no less interesting were made in the medieval west in machinery: the water-mill, the windmill, the use of geared wheels, the spinning wheel, the loom, the gigmill, the brace-and-bit, the lathe, the printing press, the mechanical clock all show the same restless inventiveness; nor must we forget the improvements in construction and rig, and the invention of the rudder, by means of which, at the end of the medieval period, western ships began to carry western arms, science, and manners to conquer the whole world.

In England, the use of machinery in the cloth industry, the

staple of English trade from the twelfth century, is especially interesting. The number of water-mills had steadily increased in the west, regardless of political disturbances, since the fourth century, and, in the eleventh century, Domesday Book records some five thousand mills in England. In the twelfth century the undershot wheel on a horizontal axle was the common type; evidence for overshot wheels comes in the fourteenth century. Such mills were used for grinding corn and other purposes, but their most dramatic effect came at the end of the twelfth century with the introduction of the fulling-mill, in which trip-hammers were operated by a waterwheel. The cloth industry shifted wholesale from the cities of the plain like York, Lincoln, Winchester, and Oxford, into the hills of the West Riding, Cumberland, and the Cotswolds, where fast streams were available to drive the mills.

The first medieval machines were made of wood; this, in Mumford's phrase, 'provided the finger exercises for the new industrialism'. But machines of greater precision needed a material susceptible of more accurate shaping, and this was provided by the development of metallurgy. From the metallurgical, as well as the mathematical skill, first of Byzantium and the Arabic east and eventually, from the twelfth century, of the Latin west, came the earliest scientific instruments, the astrolabes and other devices requiring an accurate arrangement of parts, for measuring the movements of the heavenly bodies; refinements of metallurgy gave the surgeon the instruments to develop his art; and, at the end of the thirteenth or the beginning of the fourteenth centuries, the west produced, in the mechanical clock, the prototype of modern automatic machinery, with parts designed to produce a precisely controlled result.

The mechanical clock, driven by a falling weight which set in motion a train of geared wheels, was the latest of a series of time-keeping machines going back to the simple water-clocks of antiquity; its originality consisted in the complete mastery it showed of geared wheels and in the use of an oscillatory escapement mechanism which controlled the rate of motion. There are references to what may have been clocks of this kind in

London, Canterbury, Paris, and other places at the end of the thirteenth century, and in Milan, St. Albans, Glastonbury, Avignon, and elsewhere in the early fourteenth century. But the earliest true clocks of which the mechanism is definitely known are the Dover castle clock, which is now in the Science Museum in London and used to be dated 1348 but is almost certainly later, and Henri de Vick's clock set up on the Palais Royal in Paris in 1370.

Clocks may be said to have introduced the ordinary man to the notion of mathematical time, divided into equal and indifferent intervals; mathematical space, extended into three dimensions in equal units of length, was made the measure of his world by the cartographer. As the natural and liturgical seasons gave way in the organization of time to a mechanical measure, so, alongside the hieratic maps, like the Hereford *Mappa mundi* of 1314, depicting the world divided into regions according to their spiritual relation with the holy city of Jerusalem, there were made maps by which travellers and mariners could find their way over the surface of the visible globe. Of the most accurate of these medieval maps, the *portolani* or compass-charts, made and used by mariners in conjunction with a compass, there are no known English examples; but two maps of England are pioneer ventures in mapping on land and show that progress was made. The first was drawn by Matthew Paris about 1250 (Pl. 130), and the second, the so-called 'Gough map', was drawn by an unknown cartographer somewhat less than a century later (Pl. 21 in Chap. VI). Both show roads and towns, but the second is much more accurate, and also indicates mileages, probably as estimated by travellers. Roger Bacon belongs also to the history of English cartography, not only for his recognition of the need for accurate astronomical measures of latitude and longitude, but also for a pregnant mistake. His belief that there was no great width of ocean between Europe and China became known to Columbus through the writings of Pierre D'Ailly and Aeneas Sylvius; it is said to have encouraged him to make the voyage by which he discovered the New World.

After the great advances of the thirteenth and fourteenth centuries, English science, and indeed that of almost the whole west outside Italy, showed little or no originality for over a hundred years. There were still astronomers at Oxford, and at Cambridge, but their writings mostly copied the work of their great predecessors; medicine was scarcely more alive. Thus it came about that when, in the sixteenth century, English scholars began once more to inquire vigorously into the prob׳ lems of nature, they saw their work as a revival, and especially as a revival of the great days of Grosseteste, Roger Bacon, and Merton College. One of the most interesting figures in that revival, the mathematician Dr. John Dee, took pains to collect manuscripts of the mathematical and physical writings espe׳ cially of Grosseteste, Roger Bacon, Pecham, and Bradwardine. Thomas Digges of University College, Oxford, describes how the pioneer work with telescopes done by his father, Leonard, 'grew by the aide he had by one old written booke of the same *Bakons Experiments* . . .'. The astronomer Robert Recorde, with Dee and the Diggeses among the first English׳ men to support the Copernican theory, wrote in recommending astronomical books: 'Dyuers Englyshe menne haue written right well in that argument: as Grostehed, Michell Scotte, Batecombe, Baconthorpe, and other dyuers . . .'. Later Sir Henry Savile, Warden of Merton, linked the great past with the greater future of English science by founding at Oxford the chairs in Geometry and Astronomy that bear his name.

From the science of Bede to that of such a Savilian Professor as Sir Christopher Wren, to say nothing of Newton, is as great a distance in achievement as it is in time. Far more than was realized by the iconoclastic enthusiasts of the seventeenth cen׳ tury, that achievement was the measure of the scientific vigour and originality of the medieval west; and, of the western peoples, none entered with more enthusiasm than the medieval English upon those inquiries that have made the outlook of the modern world scientific, its arts industrial, and its hopes material. But it has also been from early times a virtue in the

English to throw up, besides great and original scientists, philo-sophers who have made the methods and implications of science their special study and have measured these, with generosity and perception, against the whole ambit of human knowledge and expectations. Many of the problems of modern philosophers of science may be read in the works of their medieval English predecessors. And if the theme of con-tinuity, which has been stressed in this chapter, is true, we might expect to find in the habits of medieval scientists some-thing to remind us of the modern laboratory student. Chaucer's description in the *Miller's Tale* of 'hende' Nicholas, a free-lance at Oxford, may perhaps be not unfamiliar.

> A chambre hadde he in that hostelrye
> Allone, with-outen any companye,
> Ful fetisly y-dight with herbes swote;
> And he him-self as swete as is the rote
> Of licorys, or any cetewale.
> His Almageste and bokes grete and smale,
> His astrelabie, longinge for his art,
> His augrim-stones layen faire a-part
> On shelves couched at his beddes heed.

WORKS FOR REFERENCE

The list includes only works in English. For a general history of medieval science see A. C. Crombie, *Augustine to Galileo. The History of Science A.D. 400–1650* (London, 1952), and for a more specialized study, *Robert Grosseteste and the Origins of Experimental Science 1100–1700* (Oxford, 1953); both have extensive bibliographies. Basic works in this subject are C. H. Haskins, *Studies in the History of Mediaeval Science* (Cambridge, Mass., 1928), which deals with the translators; G. Sarton, *Introduction to the History of Science*, 3 vols. (Baltimore, 1927–47), a fundamental bibliographical study; and Lynn Thorndike, *A History of Magic and Experimental Science*, 6 vols. (New York, 1923–43).

Special studies of English medieval science and technology are:

Roger Bacon, Essays contributed by various Writers on the Occasion of the Commemoration of his Birth, ed. A. G. LITTLE (Oxford, 1914).

Bede: His Life, Times, and Writings, ed. A. HAMILTON THOMPSON (Oxford, 1935).

CROWLEY, T. *Roger Bacon, the Problem of the Soul in his philosophical Commentaries* (Louvain and Dublin, 1950).

EASTON, S. C. *Roger Bacon and his Search for a Universal Science* (Oxford, 1952).

GUNTHER, R. T. *Early Science in Oxford*, ii (Oxford, 1923).

JOHNSON, F. R. *Astronomical Thought in Renaissance England* (Baltimore, 1937).

McKEON, C. K. *A Study of the Summa Philosophiae of the Pseudo-Grosseteste* (New York, 1948).

MOODY, E. A. *The Logic of William of Ockham* (New York, 1935).

PAYNE, J. F. *English Medicine in the Anglo-Saxon Times* (Oxford, 1904).

Works containing studies of particular aspects of English science and techno-logy are:

ALLBUTT, SIR T. C. *The Historical Relations of Medicine and Surgery to the End of the Sixteenth Century* (London, 1905).

SHERWOOD TAYLOR, F. *The Alchemists: Founders of Modern Chemistry* (London, 1952).

USHER, A. P. *A History of Mechanical Inventions*, 2nd edn. (New York, 1954).

WALSH, J. J. *Medieval Medicine* (London, 1920).

A basic reasoned bibliography is Lynn White's article, 'Technology and Invention in the Middle Ages', *Speculum*, xv (1940), pp. 141 seqq.

XIX. RECREATIONS

1. *Minstrelsy*

THROUGHOUT the middle ages the monotony of the life of the people both great and small was relieved by listening to professional entertainers. These strolling minstrels or *joculatores* might be found in any castle or tavern, at any festivity, wedding, or celebration. The official attitude of the Church towards them was one of disapproval. Thus at the council of Clovesho in 747 it was decreed that monasteries must not be *ludicrarum artium receptacula*, and these arts are defined as those of versifyers, harpers, minstrels, or buf foons (canon 20). The canon law sternly forbade the clergy from having anything to do with mimes, jesters, or play actors (Dec. Greg. III. i. 15). This attitude is not unnatural, for their songs and turns, their jesting and buffoonery were often coarse and obscene and anyhow far from becoming. It is, however, necessary to draw a distinction. In its wildest sense the word minstrel was applied to all these variety performers. It was applied to those who recited epics, romances, or *chansons de geste*, and to the travelling players with their bawdy songs and comic acts (*more ribaldorum*). These two classes inherited differ ent traditions, the one those of the respectable Teutonic glee men (who correspond to the Celtic bards), the other those of the disreputable mimes of decadent Rome. The former were tolerated if not approved by the ecclesiastical authorities, for it would be difficult to find anything seriously objectionable in the recitation of *Beowulf* or of the Arthurian romance; and even Robert Grosseteste, a severe critic who directed the attention of the clergy of his diocese to the canonical prohibition of min strelsy, is said to have kept a harper. It was the latter class to which they, or the majority of them, were so bitterly hostile. The distinction is clearly brought out in a penitential written early in the fourteenth century by Thomas de Chabham, sub-dean of Salisbury.[1] He describes three kinds of *histriones*: some, he says, distort their bodies by lewd dance and gesture, or strip themselves and put on horrible masks; all such are damnable. Then there are those of no fixed abode (*non habentes certum domicilium*) who follow the courts of the great and talk scandal; such are called wandering buffoons (*scurrae vagi*) because they are good for nothing except gluttony and scandal-mongering. These, too, are damnable. Then there is a third class, those who have musical instruments for the amusement of men; they are of two kinds. Those who frequent drinking-parties and lascivious gatherings where they sing indecent songs. These also are damnable. But there are others called *joculatores* who sing of the deeds of heroes and of the lives of saints. These alone are capable of salvation. This class of entertainment was generally regarded, as we have said, as respectable. Books of romantic literature were highly prized. Even those who could not read the books themselves could enjoy looking at the pictures in such a volume, for example, as the splendidly illuminated manuscript of the *Romance of Alexander* (MS. Bodley 264) brought to England in 1466 by Richard Woodville, earl Rivers, father-in-law of Edward IV. King Edward III bought a 'book of romance' from a nun of Amesbury for 100 marks and kept it in his own chamber; Richard II had a copy of the *Romance of the Rose* and *Romances of Percevall and Gawayn* and many monastic and cathedral libraries contained volumes of this class of literature. At St. Swithun's at Winchester a *joculator* recited the romance of Guy of Warwick and the apocryphal legend of Queen Emma (about the ordeal of the hot ploughshares).

Some minstrels were maintained in the households of the great and were held in much higher esteem than the vagrant entertainers who moved from tavern to tavern living on the road or where they could; they are designated as 'minstrels of honour' in the fourteenth century. At the head of the court minstrels was a *rex* or *marescallus ministrallorum*; and just as the king had his

[1] The relevant passage is printed by E. K. Chambers, *The Medieval Stage*, ii, pp. 262-3.

establishment of minstrels, so the aristocracy, municipal cor⁄
porations, and even some ecclesiastical foundations had their
own troupe. We hear not only of the *histriones* of the earls of
Stafford or Derby or the *ministralli* of the countess of Westmore⁄
land or the duke of Gloucester; of the *histriones* of the town of
Shrewsbury or the *mimi* of the city of Coventry, but also of the
minstrels and mimes of the lord cardinal (Bishop Beaufort). It
is evident from the accounts of Durham priory that in the first
years of the fourteenth century a troupe of *histriones* were accus⁄
tomed to perform there at Christmas or on the feast of St.
Cuthbert, and that a fool, *stultus* or *fatuus*, whose appropriate
garments were paid for, was kept on the establishment for the
delectation of the monks (Pl. 131 *a*). In the fifteenth century
the players (*lusores*) of the city or the minstrels of the bishop of
Winchester paid visits to Winchester College, whither also the
minstrels of the king or nobility were sent to provide entertain⁄
ment for the young scholars. In France there were *scholae minis⁄
trallorum* to which English minstrels occasionally resorted to
improve their art. At the end of the period there was a guild or
fraternity of minstrels at London and at one or two other places
formed with the object, if possible, of controlling the profession.

But in the long run it was all but impossible to keep the
classes, the reputable and the disreputable, the household and
the vagrant entertainers entirely apart. The Church had not only
relaxed its stern attitude, but was actively participating in min⁄
strelsy. The great men kept buffoons and respectable gleemen
might be found in the taverns. Berdic, the *joculator regis*, who
held lands in Gloucestershire recorded in Domesday Book,
may, like the *histrio* who rushed to death at the battle of Hastings
singing of Charlemagne and Roland, have recited epics; but
the *joculator regis* of the twelfth century, who held a considerable
property in the county of Suffolk, performed as his service any⁄
thing but an edifying act at the Christmas festivities. It is at least
understandable that the great men found the recital of long
heroic epics a trifle tedious and would encourage their versatile
entertainers to turn to the lighter side of their art, to songs, even
if a little coarse, to juggling and tumbling, to dancing on ropes,

on swords, or upside-down (Pl. 131 *b*), and to music. Music, till the fourteenth century, was chiefly used to accompany the voice and the dance; it then became an entertainment in itself (Pl. 132 *a*). It was a normal practice in the great houses to have music during meals or on festive occasions. No less than eighty named instrumentalists, including players of tabors, kettle-drums, harps, gitterns, citoles, trumpets, flutes, pipes, psalter-ies, organs, and various forms of fiddle, were gathered together at the court of Edward I to celebrate the knighting of his son in 1306.[1] Edward III had a band attached to his household (which served as a military band in time of war) composed of five trumpeters, one citoler, five pipers, one tabouretter, two clarion players, one nekerer (kettle-drummer), one fiddler, and three waits. It was not uncommon for noblemen to have a musician or two on their staff; at the close of the middle ages the earl of Northumberland had a little orchestra consisting of a tabouret, a lute, a rebeck, and six trumpets.

Pet animals provided amusement in the middle ages as they do today. King Henry I kept a menagerie at Woodstock which included lions, leopards, lynxes, camels, and a porcupine; Henry III had three leopards and a camel presented to him by his brother-in-law, the Emperor Frederick II, and an elephant, the gift of Louis IX of France, which he kept in a house spe-cially built for it in the Tower of London; and Henry II had a bear which sometimes travelled with him as he moved about the country. Animals also play a part in the repertoire of the pro-fessional entertainer. Some dressed up as animals, some led live animals on to the stage. Bulls and bears were baited (Pl. 132 *b*). In the honour of Tutbury, where the minstrels were organ-ized in the time of John of Gaunt under *le roy des ministraulx*, it was customary for the prior of Tutbury to provide the bull for the *histriones* after they had attended matins on the feast of the Assumption of the Blessed Virgin.[2] Performing dogs and

[1] The payments made to these musicians are printed by E. K. Chambers, op. cit. ii, pp. 234-8.
[2] This obligation survived the reformation and became vested in the family of Cavendish (later earls of Devonshire) as bailiffs of Tutbury castle. An interesting

PLATE 131

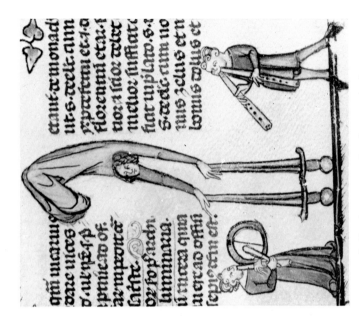

b. Juggler: woman dancing on swords

a. Costume of a fool

PLATE 132

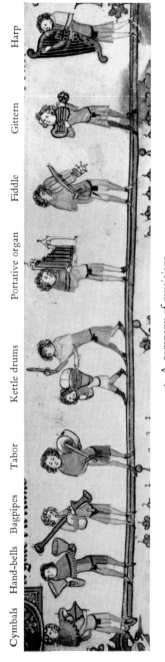

Cymbals Hand-bells Bagpipes Tabor Kettle drums Portative organ Fiddle Gittern Harp

a. A company of musicians

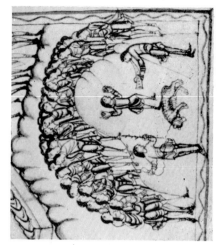

c. Performing bear

b. Bear-baiting

monkeys and bears were common shows (Pl. 132 c). A bear-
ward (*ursinarius*) was a not unusual appendage to a nobleman's
household in the later middle ages and doubtless earlier; and
he appears to have been a person of some social position, for
when in 1485 Lord Stanley's bears were staying at Magdalen
College, Oxford, the *ursarii* dined with the fellows at the high
table. A few years later this college had a bear of its own, the gift
of the king. A strange entry in the Magdalen accounts of about
this time records a payment to a college servant for looking
after *quandam bestiam vocatam ly merumsytt* (marmoset).

We have seen that the Church had been obliged to modify
its opposition to the prevalent forms of entertainment. However
much the Church reformers might dislike these pastimes, they
found themselves in an embarrassing position, for the lower
clergy had their own occasions for jollity which provided an
outlet from the normal restraints of ecclesiastical discipline.
They had their feast of fools, *festum stultorum, fatuorum*, or *folo-
rum*, generally centred on a cathedral and held on one of the
feasts following Christmas, usually the day of the Circumcision (1 January) or the Epiphany (6 January). Bishop Grosseteste in 1236 tried to suppress it at Lincoln on the ground that
it was 'replete with vanity and foul with voluptuosity', and two
years later the prohibition was repeated lest 'the house of
prayer should become a house of wantonness'. But these attempts were not apparently altogether successful for at the end
of the fourteenth century when Archbishop Courtenay made
a visitation to Lincoln he was told that the vicars and other
clergy on the day of Circumcision dressed in secular garments
disturbed the divine office by their din, buffoonery, chattering,
and games, which they commonly call the Feast of Fools.
Details of the English celebrations are lacking; but if it was
anything like the similar feast in France, where it was firmly
entrenched, with its annual election of a *dominus festi*, a 'king' or
'bishop' from among the canons or vicars (sometimes baptized
with three buckets of water), its procession to the church, its

account of the ceremony is given by Robert Plot, who witnessed it in 1680, in his
Natural History of Staffordshire.

ribald office, its riot of song and dance, of eating and drinking, and dicing on the altar, it was hardly an edifying example to the laymen. Somewhat similar to the celebration of the Feast of Fools were the *ludi theatrales* or masked shows (*spectacula lar-varum*) which are found in the fourteenth century at Wells and Exeter and the custom prevalent in many cathedrals from quite early times when in the days following Christmas, especially on the feast of the Innocents (28 December) a choir boy was appointed bishop for the *festum puerorum*. These 'boy bishops' both preached and sang the mass; and on these occasions ac-cording to the royal ordinance which abolished them in 1541 'children be strangelye decked and apparelid to counterfaite priestes, bysshopps, and women' and there is much singing and dancing 'to the derision of the glory of God'.[1] If the Church countenanced foolery within their own circle, they could scarcely adopt a very stern attitude towards the amuse-ments of laymen.

By the close of the middle ages society had wearied of the recitation of long romances. Those who could appreciate these romances could now read at least some of them in print. This form of entertainment died a natural death with the invention of printing and the development of the theatre. With the buf-foonery it was otherwise. There were fools at the court of Henry VII, and payments are also made from the Privy Purse to 'one that joculed before the king' and 'to a Spaynyard that tumb-led'. These amusements, in spite of the renaissance, in spite of Tudor legislation which classed wandering minstrels and the like with rogues and vagabonds, in spite of the strictures of the Puritans, survived. Thomas More kept a fool in his household and Erasmus wrote *In Praise of Folly*. It is the stock-in-trade of the sideshows at fairs and of the music halls of today.

2. Board Games

When books were scarce and reading the accomplishment of the few it was customary to pass the long winter evenings by playing indoor games. At once the most ancient and the most

[1] Wilkins, *Concilia*, iii, p. 860, quoted by Chambers, op. cit. i, p. 366, n.

prevalent was the game of dice. It required no skill; it was purely a gambling game of throwing the dice and betting on the result of the throw. A great variety of games played with pieces on boards of different design were known in the middle ages. The game of merels (tokens, counters) figures under many names—morris, merrypeg, miracles, &c.—and was played with three, five, nine, or even twelve pieces; boards for these games were often scratched on the stone seats in the cloisters of monasteries and elsewhere. The object was to get the 'men' in a row. In its simpler form this was done by merely entering them on the board, somewhat as in the modern game of 'noughts and crosses'. But in the more elaborate form the pieces, when entered on the board, were moved in turn to attain the align-ment. Draughts, derived in part from chess, was invented in the twelfth century, probably in the south of France; but, though played in England, it never attained to much popu-larity until the seventeenth century. Backgammon, on the other hand, or 'tables' as the medieval game (which did not differ essentially from the game of today) was called, was much in vogue. It was an ancient game, a race game, developed from the Roman game of *alea* or *tabula* and the Persian *nard*, and played with 'tablemen' resembling draughts but larger, and three or two dice. It was known in Anglo-Saxon times for it is mentioned in old English glossaries of the eighth and ninth centuries. Like chess it was a favourite game of the upper classes throughout the middle ages. King John was fond of playing with his court favourites *ad tabulas* for modest stakes which, if he lost, were faithfully recorded on the roll of his daily expenses; and the knights in Robert of Gloucester's metrical chronicle composed at the end of the thirteenth century played 'atte tables oþer atte chekere (chess)'.

Among the aristocracy, however, by far the most popular and universal of indoor recreations was the game of chess. Originating in India, it came to the west by way of Persia (where it was known in the seventh century) and the Muslim world. The word 'chess' (Latin, *scaci, scacci,* meaning chess-men) is derived from the chess king, the Persian shah. It was a war game, a contest between two armies on the field of battle, and in the eastern game the pieces have a military character. It is the king with his army composed of a counsellor or vizier (the queen of the European game), horses (knights), chariots or rooks, elephants (later bishops), and infantry (pawns or *pedites*). Through Islam before the year 1000 the game had passed into Spain and Italy, and thence northward by way of France and Germany into England. Apart from one or two texts of late date and doubtful authority which connect King Canute with the game, there is little to suggest that it had reached England before the Norman Conquest. But shortly after that event it was certainly known. By 1110 at latest *scaccarium*, the chessboard, had been adopted as the name of the financial department, the exchequer; a poem composed at Winchester in the first half of the twelfth century describes the game, the pieces, and the moves; and the *de Naturis Rerum* of Alexander Neckham, probably written about the turn of the century, contains a chapter *de Scaccis*. Henceforth the historical and romantic literature of the middle ages abounds in allusions to chess. The wardrobe accounts of Edward I show that monarch possessed of two 'families' of chessmen, one of jasper and crystal and another of ivory, and inventories of the chattels of the nobility would sometimes make mention of a set. In Europe some of the pieces changed their form and movement; the counsellor changed sex and became the queen (as did the promoted pawn) and the elephant became the bishop. But at this stage in the development of the game neither of these pieces was held to be of great value; the queen's movement was very restricted and the bishop, who is referred to as a bald head (*calvus*) or an old man (*senex*) or even as a thief or a spy, was held in some contempt. The powerful pieces in this early game, the pieces on which the player relied in making his attack, were the knight and the rook. The game was generally played for a stake, and often violent quarrels broke out in which the heavy board of wood or metal was effectively used as a weapon. The continued popularity of the game throughout the middle ages is shown by the fact that the second book which Caxton printed

(Bruges 1476?) was his translation of the thirteenth-century treatise by the Italian Cessolis, *The Game and Playe of the Chesse*, and he printed it again at Westminster a few years later. But the book was already almost out of date, for a significant change in the last years of the fifteenth century revolutionized the game. This change is marked by the freedom of movement given to the queen and the bishop: now, as in the modern game, the former could move in any direction, and the latter in a diagonal direction as far as the way was clear; it enormously enhanced their strength, and the queen became the dominating piece on the board. The new game, more scientific and elaborate, originated in southern Europe, spread rapidly, and quickly superseded the old game of which we hear no more in England after 1529. But by this time it had lost its unrivalled supremacy among the indoor recreations of the aristocracy. Other forms of gambling, and especially card-playing which came into vogue in the fifteenth century, were introduced to relieve the boredom of the leisured classes during the long winter evenings.

The game of cards, which probably originated in Asia, is not known to have reached Europe till the fourteenth century. In 1393 an artist was paid for painting 'in gold and diverse colours ornamented with many devices' packs for King Charles VI of France; seventeen of these cards are still preserved in the Bibliothèque Nationale. The earliest clear reference to the game in England is in 1461 when it was prohibited except during the Christmas festivities. The next notice of it comes in a statute two years later (3 Edw. IV, c. 4) forbidding the importation of *cardes a juer*; the object here, however, was not to stop this form of amusement, but to reduce unemployment by encouraging the home manufacture of this and other commodities. Henceforward it was a popular pastime. Though no English cards earlier than the seventeenth century have survived, the traditional costumes of the court cards appear to be of the early Tudor period. The first two Tudor kings were evidently much addicted to this form of amusement; and it has been reckoned that Henry VIII lost £3,243. 5s. 10d. in three years at cards and other forms of gambling.

3. *London Games*

William FitzStephen writing in the twelfth century ends his well-known description of the city of London, which he prefixed to his life of Thomas Becket, with an account of the sports and amusements of the citizens.[1] London he tells us 'instead of theatrical shows and stage plays has more holy plays, representations of miracles, and the sufferings of martyrs'. Indeed miracle and liturgical plays were everywhere the essence of the medieval drama, a subject too involved to develop in the space of a brief chapter. FitzStephen then proceeds to speak of boys' games, for, he says, 'we were all boys once'. On a carnival day they bring fighting-cocks to school, and all the morning is given up to the sport of watching their cocks doing battle; after lunch they go to the fields for a game of ball; the scholars of each school have their own ball, and most of the tradesmen too. The city fathers and rich men ride out to watch the sport of the young men, and by so doing revive their own youth. Every Sunday in Lent the youths would ride out with lance and shield and engage in jousting in the meadows, while during the Easter holidays they would occupy themselves with aquatic sports on the river (tilting at a quintain, Pl. 133 *a*), the bridge and the houses on the banks being thronged with spectators who came to laugh at the fun of seeing boys tumbling into the water and being hauled out by their companions in boats alongside. On feast days in the summer they exercised themselves with archery or in running, jumping, wrestling, putting the stone, or in practising with javelins and shields; and while the boys were engaged in these vigorous and manly pursuits the girls of course danced. 'Cytherea', writes our author imitating Horace, 'leads the dance of maidens, the bright moon overhead, and the earth is struck with free foot.' On winter mornings boars are set to fight each other and bulls and bears are baited by dogs. When the great marsh north of the city (Moorfields) was frozen over the young men would disport themselves on the ice, sliding, tobog-

[1] It is printed in *Materials for the History of Thomas Becket,* ed. J. C. Robertson (Rolls Series), iii, pp. 2–13.

PLATE 133

a. Quintain from a boat

b. Quintain from a wooden horse

c. Quintain with a tub of water

d. Wrestling pick-a-back

e. Swinging

PLATE 134

a. Blind man's buff

b. Punch and Judy show

c. Catching butterflies

ganing on large blocks of ice, and even skating with shinbones of animals bound to their feet, and in this way moving as swiftly as a bird in flight or a shaft from a cross-bow. These evolutions, it may be added, were not performed without many accidents and broken limbs. The London citizens also engaged in the more aristocratic sports, hunting and hawking, for they had a special privilege of pursuing game in the Chiltern Hills and the woodlands of the home counties. In another place Fitz-Stephen gives a lively picture of horse-racing which took place at the weekly horse fair at Smithfield. He describes the impatience of the horses for the contest and the eagerness of the jockeys urging them on with spur, whip, and shout. References to this sport are rare in medieval literature, but there is an interesting description of it in the early fourteenth-century metrical romance *Sir Beves of Hamtoun* (E.E.T.S., 1886, ll. 3261–8):

> In Somer about wytsontyde,
> Whan Knyghtes most on hors ryde,
> A cours they cryed on a day,
> Stedes and palfrayes to assay,
> What hors that best myght ren;
> Thre myle the cours was then,
> Who fyrst came to the ende, sholde
> Have twenty pounde of redy golde.

FitzStephen's account is the earliest comprehensive description of the recreations of Englishmen in the middle ages. But John Stow, who quotes the passage in his *Survey of London* written in the closing years of the sixteenth century, tells us that these or like exercises have been continued till his own time; and the pastimes of the metropolis, we may safely assume, were common to the country as a whole. There were of course changes in fashion; the dangerous and warlike jousting gave place to riding at the quintain. Matthew Paris[1] relates how in 1253 the citizens of London tried their prowess and the speed of their horses at a game 'quod quintena vulgariter dicitur'. They were challenged by some members of the king's household who contemptuously call them scurvy fellows and 'soapy'

[1] *Chron. Maj.* v. p. 367.

(*saponarios*). Yet the despised citizens hit the king's men about with broken spears, making them 'black and blue', knocked them off their horses, and won the prize—a peacock. This game, which consisted of riding at a target—a sand bag or some such thing—hung on a cross-bar fixed to a pole, became a favourite sport in fashionable society.

The quintain was also a game for children. Children's games are seldom described; they are, however, frequently depicted in the borders of manuscripts. Many of the best appear in the well-known fourteenth-century manuscript of the *Romance of Alexander* (MS. Bodley 264) which is illuminated by a Flemish artist. Nevertheless the proximity of England and Flanders and the close relations which existed between them render it unlikely that the amusements of youth in the two countries differed materially. This manuscript has therefore been used for the purpose of illustration. Boys are shown playing at the quintain in a variety of ways: they are drawn towards the target seated on a wooden horse (Pl. 133 *b*), or running naked (doubtless to avoid drenching their clothes) towards a tub of water set on a post (Pl. 133 *c*), or again rowed in a boat, the performer standing with a levelled pole (Pl. 133 *a*). In other respects children amused themselves much as they do today. They engaged in sham fights and wrestled, sometimes pick-a-back (Pl. 133 *d*), and in gymnastics on a horizontal bar; they swung on swings (Pl. 133 *e*), they whipped tops, they played cup and ball, and they discharged pellets through tubes (trunks) like pea-shooters; they played blind-man's-buff (Pl. 134 *a*) and prisoners' base, which by a proclamation of 6 Edward III (1331–2) was not allowed to be played near the Palace of Westminster while Parliament was sitting. They took pleasure in looking at puppet shows which bear a close resemblance to the Punch and Judy of later times (Pl. 134 *b*); there are also pictures of children catching birds and butterflies (Pl. 134 *c*).

4. *Hunting and Falconry*

The favourite sport of kings and the aristocracy throughout the middle ages was the chase. Asser in his life of King Alfred mentions hunting as a suitable occupation of the nobility and Edward the Confessor, according to his biographer, spent much time among the forests and woodlands in the pleasures of the chase. With the Norman kings it became almost a passion.

The forest [wrote Richard Fitz Neal in the *Dialogue of the Exchequer* (*c.* 1179)] is the sanctuary and special delight of kings where, laying aside their cares, they withdraw to refresh themselves with a little hunting; there, away from the turmoils inherent in a court, they breathe the pleasure of natural freedom.

Some two centuries later hunting is described as 'to every gentle heart most disportful of all games' (Pl. 135 *a*). It was conducted under prescribed and elaborate rules. A literature of the sport soon grew up in which the habits of the different kinds of game, how each should be hunted, and the breeding and training of hounds, is carefully described. The earliest treatise, *Le art de Venerie*, was written in French by Twici or Twety, huntsman to Edward II, and published a century later in English; but a more detailed one, *The Master of Game*, was produced about 1406 by Edward, second duke of York, who held the office of Master of Game under Henry IV and was killed at the battle of Agincourt. Though the greater part of this is merely an English translation, with some interpolations, of the famous book of Gaston de Foix (or Gaston Phoebus as he is generally called) the friend of Froissart, the concluding chapters are original and no doubt drawn from the author's personal knowledge. Here he describes the tracking down and starting the quarry with the hound on a leash (the limer), the uncoupling of the hounds of the pack (*de mota*), the pursuit with the appropriate hunting cries and blowing of horns, the death, the distribution of game, and finally the hunt supper where the hunters

drink not ale, and nothing but wine that night for the good and great labour they have had for the lord's game and disport . . . and that they may the more merrily and gladly tell what each of them has done all the day and which hounds have best run and boldest.

Two varieties of hounds were commonly used in the chase, greyhounds (*leporarii*) which hunted by sight and running hounds (*canes currentes* or raches) which followed the scent. We hear also of harriers, for, says our author, 'the hare is a good little beast and much good sport', and of foxhounds, 'for a fox is fair for the good cry of the hounds'; and Edward IV kept a pack of otterhounds. Particular attention is given in the hunting literature to horn-blowing and hunting cries. Thus Twici tells us

Then ye shall begin to blow a long mote and afterwards two short motes in this manner, *Trout, trout,* and then *trout, tro ro rot,* beginning with a long mote, for every man that is about you, and can skill of venery may know in what point ye be in your game by your horn.

The cries of the huntsmen, a curious mixture of languages, seem to be traditional, for they appear with slight variation in most of the manuals of hunting, thus to encourage the hounds to go forward 'Sa, sa, cy, avaunt, sohow' or 'how amy, swef, mon amy, swef' (gently, my friend, gently) or 'illoeques, illo-eques' (*illo loco*, there there), possibly, as has been suggested, the origin of the familiar cry 'Yoicks'.

Vast tracts of land embracing numberless farms and villages were set aside for the enjoyment of this sport and were protected by harsh and irksome forest laws imposed to make them 'a safe dwelling place of beasts'. An army of men were engaged in managing this enormous game preserve: huntsmen and keepers of hounds, foresters and warreners, and officers of the forest courts over which the chief forester had supreme control. The beasts of the forest thus protected were the red and the fallow deer, the roe and the wild boar. The roe, however, ceased to be a pro-tected 'beast of the forest' in the fourteenth century on the ground that it chased away the other deer; henceforth it was classed as a 'beast of the warren'. Sometimes great men also had their pri-vate forests or 'chases', and many more had enclosed parks in which to preserve deer and to exercise the pleasure of hunting. The king also claimed, at least over his demesne lands, the right to take the smaller game, the fox and the hare, the rabbit and the wild cat, the pheasants and partridges; but the right to hunt these beasts and fowl of the warren, as they were called, was often granted away to privileged subjects. Indeed, these

PLATE 135

a. Hunting scene

b. Ferreting

PLATE 136

a. King Harold riding with a hawk on his wrist

b. Hawking
(Two women, with a perch in the centre, and a hawk seizing its prey)

grants of 'free warren', which gave to the tenant an exclusive sporting licence to hunt and shoot over his estates outside the bounds of the forest anything except the protected beasts, became more and more frequent until by the middle of the fourteenth century the majority of manorial lords seem to have enjoyed this right. Further, in the later middle ages sporting licences were more freely given and more generous. Thus in 1384 Richard II gave to the dean of St. Martin le Grand 'on account of the affection we bear to him', a very comprehensive permit for life

to hunt and kill with greyhounds and other hounds and with weapons (*cum artillariis*) harts, hinds, bucks, hares, and all other wild beasts capable of being hunted with dogs and bows, and rabbits with ferrets and otherwise, also to catch and kill as he knows best pheasants, partridges, plovers, quails, larks, and all other birds of the warren in our forests, chases, parks, woods, and warrens; and also to catch all kinds of fish throughout England, Wales, and the county of Chester, on condition that he does so in measure and season and by view of foresters, parkers, and other the king's ministers, who are to permit him to hunt, hawk, and fish and carry the same away at pleasure (Pat. Roll 1381–5, p. 408).

Hunting, as we have said, was essentially an aristocratic sport. Nevertheless, poaching at all times, despite the severity of the penalties imposed by the forest law, was a popular pastime of the masses not merely for the purpose of stocking the larder, but for the sport of the thing. This is evident from numberless cases brought before the forest courts and from the tales of Robin Hood and similar romances. Moreover it was increasing (free hunting and fishing were among the demands of the rebels of 1381) to the alarm of the privileged classes. So action was taken in the parliament of 1389–90.

Forasmuch as divers artificers, labourers, and servants, and grooms [the preamble declares] keep greyhounds and other dogs, and on the Holydays, when good Christian people be at church, hearing Divine Service, they go hunting in parks, warrens and connigries of lords and others, to the very great destruction of the same.

A property qualification was therefore required to keep hounds, to use ferrets, nets, or 'other engines for to take or destroy deer, hares, or coneys, or other gentlemen's game' (Pl. 135 *b*). The qualification for a layman was lands worth 40s. a year, for a clergyman a benefice worth £10 a year. The penalty which the justices of the peace were authorized to impose was one year's imprisonment (Statute 13 Ric. II, c. 13).

The forest law in the course of time had been considerably relaxed. Indeed, when towards the end of the sixteenth century John Manwood published his classic treatise, the forest system was already in a state of confusion and decay. It had been gradually superseded by the game laws of which the Act of 13 Richard II may be regarded as the first. The harshness of the forest law has often and rightly been condemned; but it is doubtful whether the system to which it gave way was more considerate to the peasant and the poacher. It is little remembered that by an Act of 1828 (9 Geo. IV, c. 69), which remained unrepealed for a great part of Queen Victoria's reign, a poacher who took even a rabbit at night was liable in certain circumstances to transportation for seven years.

Like hunting, falconry was a favourite sport of kings and gentry. The birds in general use were the gerfalcon ('the noblest of birds'), the peregrine, the goshawk, the sparrowhawk, the lanner, and the saker; and all are mentioned in English records. The last two species came from the countries bordering on the Mediterranean; the chief source of supply of the others, which were much more commonly used in England, was Norway, and they were generally obtained at the great fair of St. Botolph at Boston (Lincs.), though they sometimes came as gifts from the Norwegian kings. They were flown to cranes, herons, partridges, and to small ground game, such as hares and rabbits. Falconry was a highly technical and scientific art, and much was written on the subject. The earliest treatise known in western Europe was written by an Englishman, the well known Arabic scholar, Adelard of Bath. The book itself is disappointing, for it chiefly deals with the ailments of the birds and the methods of curing them according to the prescriptions of early medical lore; but he tells us that he derives information from King Harold's books. Harold son of Godwin was evidently a keen falconer, for more than once he is represented on the Bayeux Tapestry with a hawk on his wrist (Pl. 136 *a*). The Normans and Angevins were no less interested in falconry than the last pre-Conquest king. It was indeed a universal sport, and the literature of one country was applicable to another. The most famous, interesting, and comprehensive book was the treatise written between 1244 and 1250 by the Emperor Frederick II, who married the sister of the English king Henry III. Though in the *De Arte Venandi cum Avibus*, the emperor drew chiefly on his own personal experience and observations, he was at pains to discover developments and particular practices of other countries; thus he claims to have introduced the practice of hooding the falcons from the Arabs, and he is aware of a custom peculiar to England of not shouting when they lure, that is when they entice the bird back after its flight (*non vociferant in loyratione*).

Hawks had to be trained and fed with infinite care and patience for they were liable to 'bate', that is to say, become restless in the hands of an inexperienced falconer; they needed regular exercise (Pl. 136 *b*) and good and substantial food, meals of meat and poultry. King John, for instance, gave instructions that his gerfalcons were to be given doves and pork, and chicken once a week. They required specially careful treatment in the moulting or 'mewing' season if they were to be good for flying after the moult. The falconer's was a highly-skilled profession and tended to run in families; no less than ten members of the family of Hauville were engaged in the business during the first half of the thirteenth century. With the extravagant diet of the birds, with the expense of maintaining so large an establishment, with the relatively small return of game, it can never have been, like hunting, a contribution to the economy of the country. It was indulged in purely as a sport, and its popularity persisted until the advent of the shot-gun.

5. *The Tournament*

The tournament was a sport of knights, and, like everything characteristic of chivalry, it seems to have originated and developed in France; it was the *ludus* or *conflictus Gallicus*. Despite repeated papal prohibitions from the time of Innocent II (1130) till that of John XXII (1316), it flourished, and many reputa, tions and fortunes were made by young landless knights by prowess on the tournament ground and by ransoms and prizes won. The outstanding example of a man who made his fortune in this way is William Marshal, earl of Pembroke, in the twelfth century. In the reign of Henry II, if not earlier, the tournament was introduced into England; in 1194 it was legalized by Richard I in order to improve the skill in fighting of English knights who were reputed inferior to the French, but under certain conditions: the tournament must be licensed by the king, the combatants must pay (in advance) entrance fees according to their rank, ranging from twenty marks for an earl to two marks for a landless knight, and it must be held on one of five recognized grounds distributed about the country. It was a battle game, indeed in its early days more battle than game; it was a dangerous and bloody affair in which the opposing teams of knights armed with swords charged about in a general mêlée on the open plain without rules, goals, or boundaries (Pl. 137). Fatal casualties were a frequent occur, rence. Moreover, as it was often the prelude and the training for baronial uprisings, it was prohibited by the government during most of the reign of Henry III, though the penalties for dis, obedience were often little more than nominal. These violent and disorderly mêlées continued long into the later middle ages. But often, it should be said, the most turbulent element was not the combatants, but the squires on foot who attended upon them. Incentive was given to the tournament by Edward I, himself a keen and skilful performer, both before and after he ascended the throne, and he became the moving spirit in its development. Under his direction rules were drawn up in 1267 (which about 1292 became statutory) and a committee ap, pointed to enforce them. Tourneying was also much affected by changes of fashion in arms and armour; blunted (or re, bated) instead of sharp weapons came into use, and plate armour superseded mail in the fourteenth century and gradually

PLATE 137

Tournament (*mêlée*)

PLATE 138

Tournament (joust) showing the tilt

became heavier until at the end of the period the combatants were completely encased in metal.[1]

It was, however, the penetration of the ideas of chivalry, and particularly Arthurian romance that exerted the most remark able influence on this form of sport. As early as 1232 a 'Round Table' is officially prohibited; in 1252 Matthew Paris draws the distinction between this and the ordinary tournament:

in this year [he writes] the knights in order to prove their skill and prowess in knightly exercise decided to try their strength not in a *hastiludium*, which is commonly called a tournament, but in that knightly game called a Round Table.[2]

The difference is that instead of the team game or mêlée, two combatants 'jousted' or charged each other with levelled lance over a course; in the fifteenth century a barrier or 'tilt' was pro vided, on each side of which the riders charged, to prevent the horses from colliding (Pl. 138). It was no longer necessary to tourney over wide open spaces; it was done in clearly defined enclosures, even in streets and city squares. The Round Table was now attended by all the pageantry and display of chivalry; it was proclaimed by heralds, who acted as masters of the ceremonies; the 'lists' or enclosures were surrounded by gaily coloured tents and stands crowded with spectators. It was now a great social occasion which often lasted several days, and was followed by feasting and dancing. In 1279 'an innumer able concourse of knights and ladies' attended a *convivium* and a Round Table at Kenilworth which Roger Mortimer orga nized 'at enormous expense'. Henceforth ladies figure promi nently at tournaments. They might give away the prizes or even be the prizes themselves. This at least is a common theme of the romances; knights tourneyed for the love of a lady, and her favours were the reward of success. Thus in the semi historical thirteenth century *Legend of Fulk Fitz Warin* a pro clamation invited 'all valiant knights who wished to tourney

[1] Above, Chap. X.
[2] *Chron. Maj.* (Rolls Series), v, p. 318. Despite the use of the words *hastiludium* or *behourd* to indicate the team game, it seems clear that blunted swords rather than lances were the weapons usually employed. See Plate 137, and Denholm Young, *The Tournament in the Thirteenth Century*, p. 260.

pur amurs' to present themselves and the prize was to be the land
and the love of a lady. The tournament opened with the sound
of trumpets and horns; there is much hitting about with swords,
knights were thrown from their chargers, the ladies watch from
a tower. This continued till nightfall. The next morning a joust
was proclaimed and the hero entered the lists. After unhorsing
three knights with his lance, the lady 'sent him her glove and
begged him to defend it'; this he did clad in scarlet armour and
successfully, and 'the great lords, the heralds, and the arbiters'
awarded him the prize 'and with great joy he took her and the
damsel him. So they sent for the bishop who married them.'[1]
This savours more of romance than history, of troubadours
and courtly love, but the picture of the tourneying and jousting
may well be realistic.

By the end of the thirteenth century the tournament had
assumed the form it was to retain till the end. There is, however, an increasing emphasis on the pageantry and the social
aspect and perhaps less on the skilled action of the combatants.
The climax is reached with the fantastic display exhibited on
the occasion of the meeting of the kings of England and France
in 1520 at the Field of the Cloth of Gold. This sumptuous
parade of magnificent folly with its prefabricated palace, its
towers and battlements, its decorative statuary representing
classical antiquity, and its rich hangings of crimson and gold;
with its feasting and dancing and fountains spouting malmsey
and claret into silver cups; and with its jousting according to an
elaborate code of rules drawn up for the event at which the two
monarchs entered the lists against all comers, marks the approaching end of long-decaying chivalry. Changes in the art
of war, among other things, had made the tournament an
anachronism.

6. *Athletic Games*

Authorities on folk-lore see the origin of some modern games
in very remote antiquity, in primitive pagan cults and seasonal

[1] Printed with the *Chronicon Anglicanum* of Ralph of Coggeshall, ed. J. Stevenson
(Rolls Series), pp. 289–93.

festivals. Thus the children's game of 'Gathering Nuts in May' may be a reminiscence of marriage by capture, the 'nuts' being more probably 'knots' or 'posies';[1] the chopping-off-the-head action in 'Oranges and Lemons' may represent the selection of the victim for human sacrifice. Or again football may have originated in a fertility cult, in a scramble, a scrimmage, for the possession of the head, the most prized portion of the sacrificial beast. Such games formed part of the celebrations at village festivals on May Day, Midsummer Day, and other feasts which survived from pre-Christian times. However that may be, games of ball are certainly of great antiquity. Nennius, who compiled his *Historia Brittonum* in the ninth century, speaks of boys playing *pilae ludum* (ch. 43). We have seen that ball-games were played by the London citizens in the twelfth century in the fields; but they were not confined to the fields. In 1303 a student was attacked and killed while playing at ball with others in Oxford High Street;[2] and Robert Braybrooke, bishop of London, complained in 1385 that people played at ball both within and without St. Paul's, breaking windows and damaging the sculpture.[3] The game known as handball may have been some form of fives which was commonly played between the buttresses of buildings (as at Eton). We do not, however, hear how games were played, but rather that they ought not to be played at all. Thus in 1365 the sheriffs throughout England were required to issue a proclamation forbidding all able-bodied men under pain of imprisonment 'to meddle in hurling of stones, loggats and quoits, handball, football, club ball, cambuc, cock fighting or other vain games of no value'. Instead, on Sundays and holidays they must practise with bows and arrows, for thus 'by God's help came forth honour to the kingdom and advantage to the king in his actions of war'. The government no doubt had in mind the decline in the fortunes of war since the glorious victories of Crécy and Poitiers won by the British archers. In 1388 the gist of the

[1] E. K. Chambers, *Medieval Stage*, i, p. 189.
[2] *Records of Medieval Oxford*, ed. H. E. Salter (1912), p. 11.
[3] Wilkins, *Concilia*, iii, p. 194.

proclamation of 1365 was made statutory, and tennis and dice are added to the list of prohibited games. This statute with slight variations was re-enacted from time to time till the six-teenth century.

University legislators also discouraged games and sport of any kind. In the fifteenth century the chancellor of Oxford for-bade scholars to play at dice, tables, handball, or any other dishonest game. The statutes of several colleges contain similar prohibitions; they must not go hunting or hawking, play at chess, dice, or ball. The austerity of life imposed by the statutes of Queen's College, Oxford, drawn up in 1340, was almost unrelieved: all they may do *causa recreationis* is occasionally to play (*jocari*) among themselves, honestly and peaceably.

Notwithstanding these stern prohibitions, it is evident that all sorts and conditions of men, not excepting ecclesiastics, played these games. Thus in 1321 Pope John XXII granted a dispensation to William of Spalding, a canon of Shouldham of the order of Sempringham, who accidentally killed another player in a game of football.[1] At a conference held near Calais in July 1439 to discuss peace terms, the archbishop of Rheims, the French Chancellor and one of the commissioners, was injured while playing football and was unable to attend one of the meetings.[2] Even kings played the game. In 1497 a sum is charged on the accounts of the Lord High Treasurer of Scot-land 'to buy fut ballis' for the king. In Elizabeth's reign strong measures were taken to suppress football at Oxford:

> If anie Master of Artes, Bachelor of Law, Bachelor of Artes, or Scholler being above the age of eighteene yeares shall use anie plaieing at Footeball in New parke or elsewhere within the precinctes of the universitie . . . for the first offence he shall paie 20s. and suffer imprisonment.

The punishments were increased if the offence was repeated; for the second it was 40*s.*, for the third banishment out of the university. Those who were under the age of eighteen suffered

---

[1] *Cal. of Papal Letters*, ed. Bliss, ii, p. 214; for another early example of a football casualty (1280) see *Cal. of Inquisitions, Misc.* i, no. 2241.

[2] Thomas Beckington's Journal, printed by Sir Harris Nicolas in *Proc. and Ord. of the Privy Council*, v, p. 363.

open imprisonment in St. Mary's church. No mercy was allowed to ministers of religion or deacons who committed this
indiscretion; they were sent down forthwith.[1]

It was an unruly, rough game. Accidents were frequent and
sometimes fatal. It was played with an inflated pig's bladder
which was usually covered with leather, but might be bare and
filled with peas and beans; and this, it seems, could be pro-
pelled either by hand or foot. So Alexander Barclay (1475?–
1552) in the Fifth Eclogue:

> Eche one contendeth and hath a great delite
> With foote and with hande the bladder for to smite.

In the sixteenth century it was rather a game for rustics than for
gentlemen and not held in high repute. Sir Thomas Elyot in
his book called *The Governour* written in 1531 says 'Foote balle,
wherein is nothinge but beastly furie and exstreme violence'.
This would hardly seem to be an understatement, for the
Register of Burials at North Moreton in Berkshire contains
under the year 1598 the following entry:

> 1598 John Gregorie the son of William Gregorie was buried the 20th of Mai.
> 1598 Richard Gregorie was buried upon Ascension Day.
> These two men were killed by ould Gunter. Gunter's sonnes and the
> Gregories fell by the years at football. Old Gunter drew his dagger and broke
> their heads and they died within a fortnight after.

The story of the tennis-balls sent by the Dauphin to Henry V,
made familiar by Shakespeare, rests on good contemporary
authority; the incident may probably be dated 27 February
1414. This, however, is not the earliest mention of the game.
It was very likely the game to which Chaucer alludes in *Troilus
and Criseyde* (c. 1374):

> But canstow pleyen raket, to and fro,
> Netle in, dokke out, now this, now that, Pandere?

It was, as we have seen, added to the list of prohibited games in
the statute of 1388. It seems to have come to England from
France where it was certainly known in the thirteenth century.
In the later middle ages and after it enjoyed a great popularity
in this country. Sir Thomas Elyot, who disapproved so

[1] Strickland Gibson, *Statuta Antiqua Universitatis Oxoniensis*, pp. 431–2.

strongly of football, regards tennis as 'a good exercise for young men'. It was played, Stow remarks, by gentlemen in courts and by people of the meaner sort in open fields and streets. The Privy Purse expenses of the first two Tudor monarchs bear witness to their fondness for the game, which, like most other games, was played for stakes. Thus, for example, in 1530 there is an entry 'for betting at tennes' 45*s*., and two years later at a game with Monsieur de Guise and the cardinal of Lorraine the king lost £46. 13*s*. 4*d*. Henry VIII was a good all-round athlete and a keen tennis player. 'It was the prettiest thing in the world to see him play', the Venetian ambassador reported to his senate in 1519, 'his fair skin glowing through a shirt of the finest texture.'[1]

Ball-games played with a bat or stick present a very puzzling problem. In the proclamation of 1365, already quoted, mention is made of a game called *cambuc*. The word is used for a pastoral staff and is equivalent to *cammock* which means, according to the *Oxford English Dictionary*, a stick with a crooked head used in games to drive a ball. Hockey is suggested. A drawing in an English manuscript of the fourteenth century depicts two players with crooked sticks and a ball between, as if in the act of bullying (Pl. 139, *a*).[2] The word *cambuc* does not recur in the other statutes which deal with games; but hockey *eo nomine* was known in Ireland, for a local statute of the city of Galway dated 1527 forbids 'the horlinge of the litill balle with hockie stickes or staves'.[3] This too is an isolated notice of a game of which we know nothing more before the eighteenth century when the poet Cowper remarks in one of his letters that 'the boys at Olney have a very entertaining sport; they call it hockey'. Nevertheless, we cannot be sure that by *cambuc* hockey is meant, for it is known that the earliest form of cricket was also played with a crooked stick. The confusion is illus-

[1] *Cal. State Papers, Venetian*, ii, p. 559.
[2] The antiquity of this opening of a kind of hockey game is illustrated by a relief on marble at Athens of the sixth century B.C. See Pl. vii of the *Journal of Hellenic Studies*, xlii (1922). My attention was drawn to this by the Rev. R. L. P. Milburn of Worcester College.
[3] *Hist. MSS. Com.* 10th Rep., App. Pt. v, p. 402.

PLATE 139

a. Hockey

b. Club ball

PLATE 140

a. Game of ball

b. Putting at golf

trated by the French word for a crosier, *crosse*, which today is
used to mean a hockey-stick; but the word is explained by
Randle Cotgrave in his French–English dictionary, published
in 1611, as 'the crooked staffe wherewith boyes play at cricket'.
The word 'cricket' is first mentioned in 1598 by a Surrey
coroner, aged 59, who asserted on oath that he, being a scholar
in the free school at Guildford, 'did runne and play' on a
certain field at 'Creckett'.[1] This would carry the game back to
the middle years of the sixteenth century. There is, however,
yet another game which may have contributed to the evolution
of cricket. In the same proclamation of 1365 mention is made
of club-ball. This game is referred to in a case which came before the Husting Court at Oxford in 1292; complaints were
brought against two men who were playing in the street with
a club and a great ball, and while doing so damaged the goods
displayed in a neighbouring shop.[2] A fourteenth-century picture shows a man holding a ball and a second figure ready to
hit out with a club-shaped bat (Pl. 139, *b*). It may be that both
the disciplined games of modern times—cricket and hockey—
have developed from the confused rough-and-tumble game
depicted in a twelfth-century manuscript of Bede's *Life of
St. Cuthbert* (Pl. 140, *a*)[3] which illustrates the prowess of the
youthful saint who boasted that he could surpass his contemporaries and sometimes even his seniors in leaping or running
or wrestling or anything else which required agility of limb.

The game of golf originated in the Low Countries and a
famous illumination in an early sixteenth-century Flemish
Book of Hours depicts a game in progress (three players are
engaged in putting (Pl. 140, *b*)). The Scottish like the English
government made a series of statutes prohibiting games in order
to encourage archery. In the Act of 1424 there is no mention of
golf; but in that of 1457 golf, like football, is to 'be utterly cryt
down and not usyt'. From this we may infer that it was between these dates that the game became popular. Though the

---

[1] See under 'cricket' in the *Oxford English Dictionary*.
[2] *Records of Medieval Oxford*, ed. H. E. Salter, p. 11.
[3] I am indebted to Dr. Otto Pächt for drawing my attention to this picture.

statute was re-enacted in much the same terms in 1491, it was without effect, and did not deter James IV himself (1488–1513) from playing the royal and ancient game. We find him, for example, playing a round with the earl of Bothwell and buying clubs and balls at the public expense. Golf, however, was never played south of the Tweed in this period. A few Scottish residents in London were accustomed to resort to Blackheath for a game from the early seventeenth century. But it was not till the mid-Victorian era that golf was generally taken up in England.

By a statute of Edward IV (1477) the game of closh is added to the already long list of prohibited games. Though little is known of this game, which appears to be of Dutch origin, it seems to have consisted in driving a ball with a spade-like implement through hoops, somewhat in the manner of croquet. But a more direct ancestor of this sedate Victorian game is pall mall which probably came to England from Italy via France in the late sixteenth century. Already in Charles I's reign the citizens of London were taking air and exercise with mallet and ball over the ground to the north of St. James's Park which still bears the name of this pastime.

7. Early Tudor Festivity

The close of the fifteenth century is marked by an atmosphere of gaiety hitherto not to be observed. In this the court took the lead. Henry VII is often represented as a sombre character; yet his household was by no means devoid of amusements. We have noticed that he had fools and other comic entertainers at his court; that he gambled at cards and dice; he also played tennis and engaged in archery. His household accounts included payments to musicians and singers, to dancing girls and morris dancers. The primitive jollifications of the folk had also penetrated to high places. The folk festival of Midsummer Eve was celebrated in 1493 by a bonfire at the public expense; both Henry VII and Henry VIII kept the May-Day festival, the latter at enormous cost in 1515 when the king and his courtiers dressed up (a 'disguising' it was called) as Robin Hood, Little

John, Friar Tuck, Maid Marian, a Queen of the May, or
'Lady May', as she is named, and the rest for a pageant at
Greenwich. Christmas too had always been not only a religious
feast but also a season of secular merriment. It was Yuletide
(mid-November to Candlemas) associated with logs, mistle-
toe, and boars' heads; and never perhaps was it celebrated more
elaborately than in the time of the first two Tudors when a
'Lord of Misrule' or as Stow calls him 'Master of merry dis-
ports' was annually appointed to supervise the revels. This
practice was not confined to the royal household; a Lord of
Misrule was commonly elected in the houses of great men, in
the Inns of Court, and in the colleges of Oxford and Cambridge. It was at the universities that it survived longest; the
Christmas Prince, an account of the revels held at St. John's
College, Oxford, which lasted from the Feast of St. Andrew
1607 to Shrove Tuesday 1608, contains perhaps the most detailed account of this form of entertainment.[1] Where the court
gave the lead, the people followed. Hitherto the simple enjoy-
ments of life had been impeded by government legislation and
decrees of the Church. After the battle of Bosworth a relaxation
is discernible. Though in 1495 a statute was again enacted
forbidding artificers and labourers from playing games, little
notice seems to have been taken of it. Outdoor games were becoming more general, more varied, and more orderly; bowling-
greens, skittle-alleys, and shovel-boards were everywhere to be
found. The cruder forms of amusement were giving place to
more civilized recreations. Above all the printed book, music,
and drama were fast developing to relieve the boredom of the
hours of leisure. Yet the problem of the long dreary winter
nights was not entirely overcome, and perhaps the most satisfying pastime was love-making. So Thomas Campion, who
wrote at the end of the sixteenth century, after recounting
various forms of amusement concludes his poem:

> Though love and all his pleasures are but toys,
> They shorten tedious nights.

[1] Printed by the Malone Society, 1922. Cf. F. S. Boas, *Stuart Drama* (Oxford,
1946), pp. 401–12.

BOOKS FOR REFERENCE

The standard and most comprehensive work is Joseph Strutt, *The Sports and Pastimes of the People of England*, first published in 1801; new edition by J. C. Cox (London, 1903), but it is much in need of revision. E. K. Chambers, *The Medieval Stage*, 2 vols. (Oxford, 1903) is invaluable. The two volumes by H. J. R. Murray, *A History of Chess* (Oxford, 1913) and *A History of Board-Games other than Chess* (Oxford, 1952), are the authoritative works on these subjects. Catherine P. Hargrave has written a careful *History of Playing Cards and a Bibliography of Cards and Gaming* (Boston, 1930). John Stow has incorporated in his *Survey of London*, ed. C. L. Kingsford (Oxford, 1908), with other material William FitzStephen's famous account of London games in the twelfth century. The English medieval literature on hunting is contained in *The Master of Game* by Edward, second duke of York, ed. W. A. and F. Baillie-Grohman (London, 1904). Much useful information on Falconry may be found in the elaborate edition of Frederick II's treatise on the *Art of Falconry*, ed. C. A. Wood and F. Marjorie Fife (Stamford Univ. Press, 1943). The excellent essay by N. Denholm-Young on 'The Tournament in the Thirteenth Century' in *Studies in Medieval History presented to F. M. Powicke* (Oxford, 1948) should be consulted for the early history of this martial exercise in England. See also F. H. Cripps-Day, *The Tournament* (1918). The laws forbidding games are mostly contained in the *Statutes of the Realm* (Record Commission), i–ii (1810). Useful information on sports of various kinds can be found from the accounts of the Privy Purse. See particularly the *Privy Purse Expenses of Elizabeth of York and Wardrobe Accounts of Edward IV* (London, 1830), *Privy Purse Expenses of Henry VIII 1529-32* (London, 1827), all edited by Sir N. Harris Nicolas; and extracts from the *Privy Purse Expenses 1491-1505* contained in *Excerpta Historica*, ed. S. Bentley (London, 1831). The most recent *History of Football* is by Morris Marples (London, 1954).

INDEX

Abbeville (Somme), 153; coins struck at, 287.

Aberystwyth (Cards.) castle, 114, 116.

Abingdon (Berks.), 200; bridge, 207; printing at, 560.

— abbot of, 207.

Abinger (Surrey), motte at, 101, 102, 104.

Acre, siege of, 142.

'Ada' group (carvings), 489.

Adelard of Bath, 578–81, 620.

Admiralty, Admiral, 178–80, 190–1.

Ælflæd, w. of Edward the Elder, 488.

Ælfric, 518.

Ælfric's *Colloquy*, 220.

Ælla, k. of Northumbria, 272.

Æthandune, Guthrum defeated at, 273.

Æthelberht, abp. of York, 517.

Æthelberht, k. of East Anglia, 269.

Æthelberht, k. of Kent, 269.

Æltheldreda, St., 212; her chapel, 75.

Æthelflæd, Lady of Mercia, 132.

Æthelheard, abp. of Canterbury, 269.

Æthelred, abp. of Canterbury, 271, 274.

Æthelred I, king, 131.

Æthelred II, king, coinage of, 277, 278, 279, 291.

Æthelweald, coin attributed to, 274.

Æthelwold, St., bp. of Winchester, monastic reform of, 400, 442, 489, 518.

Æthelwold, St., Benedictional of, 301, 489–90.

Æthelwulf, k. of Wessex, 271, 272.

Aeneas Sylvius, 601.

Agincourt, battle of, 158–60, 290, 327, 550, 617.

Aigues Mortes, 114.

alabaster effigies, 503–4.

Albertus Magnus, 584.

Alchred, k. of Northumbria, 266.

Alcock, John, bp. of Ely, 537.

Alcuin, 517, 546.

Aldfrith, k. of Northumbria, 266.

Aldhelm, St., 516, 575.

Aleppo, miners of, 143.

Alexander, bp. of Winchester, 494.

Alexander II, pope, 390.

Alexander III, pope, 396, 417.

Alfonso X, k. of Léon and Castile, 593.

Alfred, king, 383; boroughs built by, 216–17; builds a fleet, 173; church reform under, 383, 400; coinage of, 271–2, 273, 274, 278; Danes, wars against the, 130–2, 272; educational work, 517–18; jewel, 488.

Alfred of Sareshel, 581, 582.

Al-Khwarizmi, Persian mathematician, 580–1.

Alkindi, astrologer, 581.

Almeric of Winchester (moneyer), 278.

Alnwick (Northumb.), 200, 204.

Alresford (Hants), 198, 202.

Als (Denmark), 171.

Alton (Hants), 198, 202, 204.

Ambrose, St., 572.

Amesbury nunnery, 406.

— psalter, 500.

Amiens (Somme): treaty of, 286; woad imported from, 233, 234, 237.

— cathedral: sculpture at, 494; choir of, 497.

Anderida, *see* Pevensey.

Anderne, John, herbalist and surgeon, 596–7.

animals, 596, 608–9, 614.

Anlaf Guthrithsson, k. at York, 275.

Anlaf Sihtricsson, k. at York, 275.

Anne of Bohemia, w. of King Richard II, 304; effigy of, 504.

Anselm, abp. of Canterbury, 519.

Apocalypses, illustrated, 501, 508.

Appleby (Westm.), 202.

Appledore (Kent), *see* Horne's Place.

— Marsh, 31.

Apuleius Platonicus, his *Herbarium*, 576.

Aquinas, Thomas, St., 533.
Aquitaine, duchy of, 157; coins of, 286–7, 288, 290.
Arab coins, 267.
Arabic, translations of scientific works from, 577–82.
archdeacon, 395, 414.
archery, archers, 133, 134, 140, 142–3, 147–63, 326–7, 625.
architecture: domestic, 37–96; ecclesiastical, 439–84; Gothic, 23, 447, 448, 451, 462; military, 98–125; Norman or Anglo-Norman Romanesque, 440–53; Tudor, 480.
Arden (Warws.), forest of, 12, 16, 32.
Aristotle: study of at Oxford, 531–3; study of, banned at Paris, 531; natural science, 581–94, 596, 598, 600.
armigers, 373–7.
Armingford hundred (Cambs.), 197.
Arms, Assizes of, 139, 164, 317.
Arsuf, battle of, 317.
art, influences on English: Bohemian, 506; Burgundian, 506; Byzantine, 485, 493; Carolingian, 487–90; Flemish, 507–10; Italian 505; Northumbrian, 486–7; Norman, 492; Romano-Celtic, 485; St. Denis, 494; Scandinavian, 491.
— Gothic, 499–512.
artillery, 161–6, 189.
Arundel (Sussex), 203; castle, 102, 108.
Arundel, Richard, earl of, 76, 153.
Arundel, Thomas, abp. of Canterbury, 534.
Arnside (Westm.) castle, 120.
Ascot d'Oilli, castle, 106.
Ashby-de-la-Zouche (Leics.), 50; castle, 124; hall, 43.
Ashdown (Berks.), battle of, 272.
Asser, 616.
astrolabe, 577, 580, 600.
astronomy, 589–93.
Athelney (Som.), 78–79, 131.
— abbey of, 15.
Athelstan, king: church policy, 383;

coins of, 273, 276, 277, 278; fleet, 174; sub-king of Kent, 271.
Atton, John, canonist, 535.
Auckland, West (Durham), 80.
Audley, John Touchet, Lord, 376.
Augsburg, armour made at, 325.
Augustine, St., abp. of Canterbury, 382, 383, 384, 415, 546; his life by Goscelin, 547.
Augustine, St., of Hippo, Rule of, 405–6, 409, 572.
Austen, William, of London, his effigy of Richard Beauchamp, 511.
Austin canons, 401, 405, 407, 521; architecture of the houses of, 454; at Oxford, 529.
— hermits, 410.
Averroës, 582.
Avicenna, 582, 597.
Avon (Bristol) river, 237–9.
Axholme, Isle of, 82.
Aylesbury (Bucks.), 80.
Aymery of Tours (moneyer), 282.

Bacon, Robert, 532.
Bacon, Roger, 531, 532, 585, 588–92, 598, 601, 602.
Bado Aureo, Johannes de, his treatise on heraldry, 361, 362.
Baguley Hall (Ches.), 44.
Baker, William, artist, 508.
Bakewell, Robert, 20 n.
Bakewell (Derbys.), Lady Foljambe's tomb at, 309.
Baldred, k. of Kent, 269.
Baldwin, abp. of Canterbury, 408.
Baldwin, count of Flanders, seal of, 352, 353.
Balliol, Edward, 151.
Balliol, Hugh de, arms of, 368.
Balsham, Hugh, bp. of Ely, 528.
Baltonborough (Som.), 14.
Bamborough (Northumb.), 200.
Banbury (Oxon.), 204.
Bannockburn (Stirling), battle of, 147, 149–51.
Barclay, Alexander, quoted on football, 627.

London, coins minted at, 264, 265,
270, 271, 280, 282, 285, 293.
— Danish invasions, effect of, 214, 216.
— Dowgate, see Cold Harbour.
— FitzStephen's description of, 225–6,
614–15.
— gilds: armourers, 330; goldsmiths,
241; minstrels, 607; weavers, 228.
— Hanse, 234.
— Harold's march to, 133.
— Holborn, bp. of Ely's house in, 75.
— houses in, 75–77.
— Ironmonger Lane, 71.
— Livery companies at, 260.
— mayor of, 261.
— Mercers' Company, 260.
— Pall Mall, 630.
— population of, 1, 261.
— printing at, 559–60.
— roads from, 196–7, 202.
— Roman survival at, 53.
— St. Martin le Grand, dean of, 619.
— St. Paul's cathedral, 211, 225, 474–
5, 625; canons of, 88.
— schools at, 521, 538.
— shipping at, 177, 192.
— Smithfield, horse fair at, 615.
— Temple church in, 319, 408.
— Tower of, 106, 113, 225; armouries
of, 330.
— trading centre, 209.
— University, 76.
— Willysdon, tallow chandler, his
house in Thames str., 76.
— mentioned, 206, 214, 237, 291.
Longleat (Wilts.), 34.
Long Sutton (Lincs.), church at, 481,
482.
Longthorpe (Northants.), 46, 47.
Longtown (Herefs.) castle, 110.
Lotharingia, scientists from, 577.
Lothbroc, Ragnar, banner woven by
his daughters, 338.
Loughborough (Lughborow) (Leics.),
69.
Louis IX, k. of France, coinage of, 288.
Louis XII, k. of France, his marriage,
311.

Louth (Lincs.), 200, 229.
Lovel, Lord John, 124.
Lovell lectionary, 507.
Lübeck, 235.
Lucca, 235, 304.
Lucy, arms of family of, 369.
Luddesdown Court (Kent), 46, 47.
Ludgershall (Wilts.), 200.
Ludican, k. of Mercia, 269.
Ludlow: castle, 105; planning of, 58–
59, 64–65.
Ludlow, Laurence of, merchant, 234.
Lumley (Durham) castle, 120.
Luttrell psalter, 304, 307.
Lydford (Devon) castle, 107.
Lyndwood, William, bp. of St.
David's, canonist, 535.
Lynn: merchants of, 227, 235–7; port
of, 227, 230; St. Margaret's, brasses
in, 505.
Lyons, Richard, 76.

machinery, 599–601.
Machlinia, William de, printer, 560,
564, 565.
Macworth, John and Thomas, arms of,
376.
Maes-Celyn (nr. Crickhowell, Brecon)
castle, 110.
Maes Maydog, battle of, 148.
Magna Carta sealed by King John,
556.
Magnus Maximus, emperor, coins of,
264, 265, 273.
Maidenhead (Berks.), 202.
Maldon (Essex), 132; battle of, 301.
Malmesbury (Wilts.), 248, 460; sculp-
ture at, 494–5.
Malvern, Great, priory, glass at, 510.
Man, Isle of, 4.
Manchester, 216.
Mandeville, Geoffrey de, earl of Essex,
family connexions of, 352.
manor-houses, 37–52.
Mansel, John, 426.
Mansion, Colard, 559.
manuscript abbreviations, 547–8.
Manwood, John, 620.

Spalding (Lincs.), 205.
Sparke, Sir John, 187.
Stafford: earthworks at, 217; houses of bp. of Lichfield at, 219; knot, 357; plan of, 218.
Stafford, Lord, arms granted by, 376.
Staffordshire, exemption of the royal free chapels of, 417.
Staines (Middx.), 13; bridge, 198.
Stainforth (Yorks.), 19.
Stamford (Lincs.), 202, 206, 237, 242, 257; castle at, 53; cloth, 228, 257; fair at, 242; migration of students to, 524, 525; Queen Edith's hall at, 74; roads through, 202, 206; trade in woad, 237.
Stamfordbridge, battle of, 133.
Standard, battle of the, 140.
Stanley, Sir John, arms of, 366.
stannaries, see tin mines.
Stansfield (Suff.), 41.
Stanton Harcourt (Oxon.), 45.
staples, 258–60.
Steelyard, see Hanse.
Steeple Barton (Oxon.), 28.
Stephen, king: captured, 140; coinage of, 281–2.
Stirling castle, 149, 150.
Stockland (Devon), 204.
Stockton (Durham), 200.
Stokesay (Salop) castle, 47, 234.
Stone (Bucks.), 202.
Stonor family, 258.
Stony Stratford (Bucks.), 202.
Stourton, Lord, of Stourton (Wilts.), 50.
Stow (Lincs.), 200.
Stow, John, his Survey of London, 615, 628, 631.
Stow-on-the-Wold (Glos.), 204.
Strange, barony of, 373.
Strangways, Richard, 375.
Strasbourg cathedral, 474.
Stratford-on-Avon (Warws.), 245–6, 538.
Stretton Baskerville (Warws.), 33.
Stretton, Great (Leics.), 8.
Stukeley, William, 477.

Stuteville, Robert de, coins of, 282.
Suffolk, Alice, duchess of, her tomb at Ewelme, 511–12.
Suffolk: churches in, 386; industrial towns in, 257; population of, 1, 24; mentioned, 13.
Surigone, Milanese humanist, 539.
Surrey, John earl of, 145.
Surrey, Thomas earl of, 165.
Surrey, Warennes earls of, 342.
Sussex, 229; marshes, 15; population, 25; villages in, 3; weald, 14, 32.
Sutton Coldfield (Warws.), 92.
Sutton Courtenay (Berks.), 48, 78.
Sutton Hoo (Suff.), 173, 316, 485.
Swineshead, Richard, 595.
Symonds, Richard, 81.
Syon (Middx.), Bridgettine abbey, 432.

Tacitus, quoted, 78.
Talbot, John, see Shrewsbury, earl of.
Tamworth (Staffs.) castle, 108.
Tandridge (Surrey), 26.
Tattershall (Lincs.), tower house at, 50, 122–3, 124.
Taverner, John, merchant of Hull, 187.
Tavistock (Devon), 231; printing at, 560.
'Teapot Hall', see Scrivelsby.
Teffont (Wilts.), 21.
Temple, Templars, order of, 408.
Tetsworth (Oxon.), 202.
Tewkesbury (Glos.) abbey, 441, 446–7, 452, 476–7.
— battle of, 162, 165.
Thame (Oxon.), 45.
Thames, river, 205, 206, 207 et passim.
Thanet, Viking settlement in, 272.
Theobald, abp. of Canterbury, 412, 522.
Theobald of Étampes, 520, 523.
Theodore of Tarsus, abp. of Canterbury, 383, 398, 516.
Theodoric of Freiburg, 584.
Thetford (Norf.), 1, 68, 270.
— bishopric of, 391.
— priory, 405.
Thomas, William ap, 124.
Thorlak of Iceland, 522.

PRINTED IN
GREAT BRITAIN
AT THE
UNIVERSITY PRESS
OXFORD
BY
CHARLES BATEY
PRINTER
TO THE
UNIVERSITY